AN AMERICAN
BATTLESHIP

AT PEACE
AND WAR

**THE U.S.S.
TENNESSEE**

MODERN WAR STUDIES

Theodore A. Wilson
General Editor

Raymond A. Callahan
J. Garry Clifford
Jacob W. Kipp
Jay Luvaas
Series Editors

AN AMERICAN BATTLESHIP
AT PEACE AND WAR
THE U.S.S. *TENNESSEE*

Jonathan G. Utley

UNIVERSITY PRESS
OF KANSAS

Published by the University Press of Kansas (Lawrence, Kansas
66045), which was organized by the Kansas Board of Regents and is
operated and funded by Emporia State University, Fort Hays State
University, Kansas State University, Pittsburg State University, the
University of Kansas, and Wichita State University

Library of Congress Cataloging-in-Publication Data
Utley, Jonathan G., 1942–
An American battleship at peace and war: the U.S.S. Tennessee
Jonathan G. Utley.
p. cm. — (Modern war studies)
Includes bibliographical references and index.
ISBN 0-7006-0492-8 (alk. paper)
1. Tennessee (Battleship) I. Title II. Series.
VA65.T4U84 1991
359.3'252'0973—dc20
90-23002
CIP

British Library Cataloging in Publication Data is available.

Printed in the United States of America
10 9 8 7 6 5 4 3 2 1

The paper used in this publication
meets the minimum requirements of the
American National Standard for Permanence of
Paper for Printed Library Materials
Z39.48-1984

Design: John Baxter

**FOR JOSHUA
AND GIDEON**

CONTENTS

PREFACE

Shortly after 2:00 P.M. on April 12, 1945, a Japanese pilot turned his plane toward the battleship *Tennessee* and headed for her bridge. In the confusion of battle, no one aboard ship noticed the single plane until it was only 2,500 yards away. Eight seconds later it ripped into the ship's starboard side, twisting steel and dismembering bodies. The big ship shuddered under the impact. Twenty-two men died and another ninety-nine were injured, some very seriously. But *Tennessee* stayed at her post. She did not even stop to bury her dead until 6:30 that evening and spent the night maneuvering to avoid another air attack even as the ship's crew patched the damaged areas. The next day she was back firing support for the American troops ashore on Okinawa, and she did that again day after day for another three weeks before retiring to make repairs. Of such stories is the battleship mystique made.

Today, when the day of the battleship has long since passed, the few remaining battleships in service capture the popular imagination. Whether it is *Wisconsin* firing shells into Kuwait in 1991 or *Iowa* suffering a massive explosion in one of her turrets in 1989, the sheer power of these ships holds our attention. Their massive steel armor, often a foot and a half thick, makes them appear impregnable. When their huge guns fire a shell the weight of a small car beyond the horizon, there is flame, smoke, and a concussion that emphasizes the fragility of human flesh. In their golden age before World War II, battleships were perceived as the ultimate weapon and were widely called dreadnoughts, after the British battleship HMS *Dreadnought,* a ship so fast, so heavily armored, and so powerfully gunned as to fear no conventional warship.

This is the story of one of these dreadnoughts. Touted as the most powerful ship in the world when put into service, *Tennessee* was a battleship that grew old, fought a war in her later years, and was eventually scrapped. She was not the best, or the biggest, or the fastest battleship the United States ever built. Still, when the test of war came she did what was asked of her and did it well at places that are legendary: Tarawa, Kwajalein, Eniwetok, Saipan, Surigao Strait, Iwo Jima, and Okinawa. As a consequence of her service, she was one of only two battleships to earn a naval unit citation for action during World War II.

Tennessee's war experience amounted to less than four of her twenty-five years of active duty; she was in combat only 339 days over those nearly four years. So her story is far more than guts and glory. For

most of her life she was a ship of war in a time of peace. She filled her days preparing for the war that would surely come; she drilled, maneuvered, replaced what was worn out, and repaired what was broken in an endless struggle to keep operating efficiently. By regularly updating her weapons of war, she fought the obsolescence that newer battleships and aircraft threatened to impose on her.

A handful of men came aboard and stayed, but for the most part there was an endless exodus of shipmates to new assignments or out of the service. The new men coming aboard had to be taught the time-honored lessons of their predecessors so they too could be welded into a cohesive fighting unit.

The ship was conceived during World War I, put into service during the anti-militarism of the 1920s, and lived most of her life during the age of isolationism that dominated the interwar years. On December 7, 1941, at the venerable age of twenty-one years, she went to war.

I have told her story in a way that is somewhat different from that of many other books generally classified as naval history. Some of those are technological analyses that explain in detail how machinery operated and what guns or equipment were added or removed. Some are chronicles of a ship's movements that describe where the ship went and what it did but do not seek to put the ship in a larger context. Some are more general histories that take as their focus the policy- and strategy makers in Washington, the officers who com-

manded the ships, the social history of the sailors, or the international negotiations affecting the navy. Each study has its place and its value. In writing this book, I have borrowed from many of these approaches but have embraced none of them.

Tennessee's story is, in part, technological — how a state of the art warship grew old and outmoded. It is, in part, social — how the sixteen thousand or so men who served aboard her at one time or another during a quarter century lived and worked together. Her story is diplomatic as well, since ultimately where she went and what she did were determined by the people in Washington, who had a vision of the kind of world they wanted and an idea of how to achieve it. And, of course, her story is also operational — how she received a new mission during World War II and went about fulfilling it.

In exploring each of these aspects I have a wider focus than this single ship. I see the USS *Tennessee* as part of history; she was part of what was going on in the navy, in the United States, and even in the world during the years from 1915 when she was authorized, to 1946, when she went into storage. To understand her we must see her as part of that larger historical context. By understanding her, we also learn something about the navy, nation, and world of which she was a part.

This broad focus has led me to exclude certain aspects of the ship's history. For example, in chapter 3, in which I examine how the ship operated, I deal with gunnery and engineering rather than navigation, the deck force, or the cooks, tailors, cobblers, launderers, and storekeepers, each of whom had a hand in the operation of the ship. In part this focus is a choice made because of space limitations. I did not want this book to be so long that only a handful of buffs and researchers would read it. In part it is because the navy considered gunnery and engineering performance the key elements in the ship's operation and kept extensive records on these areas but virtually nothing on the other aspects of the ship's operation. The historian, unlike the novelist, is at the mercy of the surviving records; I cannot write what I cannot document, and there are aspects of *Tennessee*'s history for which the navy either did not keep or did not preserve records. Oral history can plug some of these gaps, but memories of events a half century or more before are best used in conjunction with written records. Inevitably some readers will wish I had written more on their favorite topic; I wish I had been able to write more on some topics as well. But as the nineteenth-century British historian Lord Bryce put it, "The secret to historical composition is to know what to neglect." Choices have to be made.

A word about words. I have avoided using naval jargon as much as possible when writing about the ship or the navy. During her career, *Tennessee* was assigned to a fleet. (Actually she was usually part of a battleship division, within a battle force, within a battle fleet, within a fleet.) During most of her peacetime years, the fleet in question was the United States Fleet. In the early 1920s and again just before World War II, that same group of ships was called the Pacific Fleet. All along I simply refer to it as the Fleet.

After studying a ship for a good while, one is tempted to attribute to it human characteristics. Yet we know that *Tennessee* was an inanimate mass of steel and machinery; she was not alive, did not come with a gender, and did not have a personality. Over the years the type of men who served aboard her changed and in doing so changed what we call the tone or character of the ship — by which we really mean the tone and character of the officers and men aboard her. Contrary to all logic, however, I have retained the naval tradition of calling a ship "she" and written of her as if it were the ship, rather than the men aboard her, that acted. Perhaps even a historian engaged in an analytical dissection of a ship's life is permitted that small poetic license.

The historian David Healy once said that it is very difficult to write a bad book. To write a good one is almost impossible. Whichever book this is, it owes its existence to a variety of people. Most important are the veterans of *Tennessee*. In lengthy interviews and brief conversations, they helped me make sense of the records I was finding elsewhere and explained how things really operated aboard ship. Dozens of them have shared their time, photographs, and copies of the ship's newspaper as well as other memorabilia that the navy never bothered to save. Helping me find my way through the maze of naval records are the archivists

at the National Archives (Tim Nenninger, Richard VonDernhoff, and Elaine Everly) and those in Dean Allard's Naval Historical Center (Greg Walker and Martha Crawley).

At various stages of the writing, Ken Hagan of the Naval Academy, Clark Reynolds of the College of Charleston, Ted Wilson of the University of Kansas, and Charles Johnson of the University of Tennessee read all or parts of the manuscript and provided invaluable insights and suggestions. I am also indebted to four graduate students at the University of Tennessee, Knoxville. Nancy Carden, Ben Gates, and Margaret Ellen Crawford helped me uncover valuable information. Beth Vanlandingham oversaw the drafting of the map and pointed out how some chapters simply could not be published the way I had initially drafted them.

Writing a book requires more than readers and researchers, it requires people who will encourage and support the effort. The people at the University Press of Kansas encouraged me to write this book the way I envisioned it. My colleagues in the Department of History at the University of Tennessee, Knoxville, provided the personal support and intellectual stimulation that made being a historian fun. And there are nonhistorian friends in Knoxville and Chicago who took an interest in my work and always had an encouraging word for me.

Finally, there is my family. Carol Marin, my wife, provided the faith and support (in addition to the merciless reading she gave the manuscript) essential to the completion of this project. Had it not been for our two young children, Joshua and Gideon, this book would have been completed at least two years earlier. But they reminded me, even during the most intense writing periods, that there are things more important than one more book.

J.G.U.
Chicago, Illinois
March 1, 1991

AN AMERICAN BATTLESHIP AT PEACE AND WAR

THE U.S.S. *TENNESSEE*

CHAPTER ONE
MEN FIGHT, NOT SHIPS:
CREATING
TENNESSEE

It was a good launch. In the pit beneath the warship, John Niedemair saw to the greasing of the ways and removed the blocks that had held battleship number 43 in place for two years. On his signal, sixteen-year-old Helen Roberts declared in a firm, clear voice, "I name thee *Tennessee*," and smashed a bottle of champagne against the ship's red painted prow. The last restraints were knocked away at precisely 9:44 A.M., April 30, 1919, and 16,500 tons of warship hummed down the ways into New York's East River. Bands played, 50,000 people cheered, and sirens on the recently launched battleships *New Mexico* and *Arizona* rose above the din.

The only casualty was Albert H. Roberts, who, standing opposite his daughter as she smashed the champagne bottle, caught the full force of the liberated wine, an unseemly position for the governor of bone-dry, prohibitionist Tennessee. Roberts had suggested substituting spring water from the Hermitage, Andrew Jackson's home. Though prohibition was sweeping the country, the navy was not about to launch the world's greatest battleship with spring water. In fact, officers planning the launch were determined to make this a festive occasion. Though the Great War was over, Britain and France were expanding their navies at the same time that the United States Navy was sending men home. With the outlook for congressional appropriations bleak, the navy needed all the good publicity it could get. The launch also was a good opportunity to tout the enormous power of the modern battleship before the public began paying too much attention to those aviators who bragged that their planes had made battleships obsolete. So the men planning the launch issued 75,000 tickets and invited a dozen bands to play.

Half a year later, Captain Richard H. ("Reddy") Leigh, *Tennessee*'s first commanding officer, watched workmen slowly transform his ship from so many pieces of steel and machinery into "a mass of inanimate efficiency." But "men fight, not ships," as the saying went, and to make *Tennessee* "a living efficiency of the highest order" required a good crew. In 1919, a good crew, or any crew, was hard to find. Even as *Tennessee* was launched, nearly half the men in the wartime navy had returned to civilian life. In July, the Navy Department yielded to congressional pressure and issued a general demobilization order that let just about everyone who had volunteered during the war go home. By the fall, the navy had discharged four out of five sailors, leaving fully one-third fewer sailors than Congress authorized.[1]

Tennessee passed beneath the Brooklyn Bridge on her maiden voyage in October 1920, more than five years after Congress authorized her construction. It would be another six months before she was ready to join the Fleet, however. Building a state of the art warship and training a crew to sail her proved to be a long and difficult task.[2]

In this gloomy situation, navy recruiters began searching for the 1,000 to 1,200 enlisted men needed to man *Tennessee*. Ideally, 40 percent of the crew would be experienced men drawn from other ships. But where were there six hundred young men who wanted to leave home and serve in the peacetime navy? Lieutenant Lon H. Robb of the naval recruiting station in New York had an idea. He suggested recruiting Tennesseans to serve aboard *Tennessee*. The idea of focused geographic recruiting had been broached in 1904 and again in 1916, but naval officials had not approved it. Occasionally a city had "adopted" a ship, resulting in a large number of recruits from that city, but nothing as sweeping as Robb's suggestion had been tried in the modern navy. There was little for the navy to lose, and it detailed ten chief petty officers under Robb's command to tour the state and enlist the sons of Tennessee. After a week of training, the team began recruiting after Thanksgiving Day, 1919.

Recruiting tactics were straightforward. Two-man teams settled into a hotel in a centrally located town for about a week and toured each of the surrounding counties. Before they arrived, the navy provided and local newspapers usually published lengthy reports on *Tennessee* and the need for young men to serve on her. Posters adorned public buildings and smaller signs were distributed for homes and small businesses. As volunteers came forward, they were sent to the nearest recruiting substation for preliminary processing and then to Nashville for medical examination and enlistment. When a particularly presentable young man was found, usually one with previous naval service, he was sworn in, given a uniform, and returned to a substation near his home, where the navy paid him $4 a day to convert his friends and neighbors. This tactic worked brilliantly. The chiefs were good at their job, but no one could recruit the way a local man could, especially in a new uniform.[3]

The campaign soon became more elaborate. Commander W. E. Cheadle, the naval officer supposedly in charge of recruiting in Tennessee, chafed at being left out of this recruiting program and decided to invite Captain Leigh to visit the leading cities of Tennessee and address the people of the state. Leigh's tour was a smashing success; he spoke to large crowds in Knoxville, Chattanooga, Nashville, and Memphis. Governor Roberts, like any good politician, sought to capitalize on *Tennessee*'s favorable image and urged the navy to send a band and charter a train to carry on a whistle-stop campaign across the state. The train alone would cost $24,000 (about two months' pay for the men who would be recruited). To the Navy Department, that was money well spent, so it sent the same twenty-four-piece band that accompanied President Woodrow Wilson on his triumphal tour of Europe a year earlier. Naturally Governor Roberts volunteered to ride the train and make some of the speeches.[4]

The band was a great draw. In smaller towns where the train stopped for only a few hours, schools were let out and huge crowds gathered at the railroad station to escort the band and accompanying dignitaries to a school, church, or courthouse where politicians spoke, the band played, and everyone enjoyed the potluck dinners that were always served. In larger cities, the concert and speeches were held at night or on a Sunday afternoon. In either case, the band always began with the "Star-Spangled Banner," quickly followed by "Dixie." The navy recruiters were not taking any chances.

Young Tennesseans who flocked to the band concert heard civic leaders praise naval service as a great educational opportunity and a great adventure. They heard nothing about duty or national defense. The war that had ended all wars and made the world safe for democracy made such patriotic appeals useless. But the speakers were not above exploiting the xenophobia that was reaching epidemic proportions in the United States during 1920. The men of *Tennessee* will be a "homogeneous mass," they proclaimed. "They will be all-American. They will speak a common language. They will understand one another, as men can not understand their fellows when picked from every state and from the four quarters of the globe."

Fanning regional pride, they stressed that the ship's captain was from Mississippi and her executive officer another southerner from North Carolina. Local pride was fostered when the navy promised to name the captain's cabin after the county with the most recruits. Even small towns were encouraged to turn out the men so there would be "a gun crew from every town." Though the navy only wanted about half the men aboard ship to be from Tennessee, recruiters and local politicians brazenly proclaimed that every man aboard *Tennessee* would be a Tennessean. Rather than leaving home, these young men would be taking home with them. They would also be carrying with them the honor of their state and hometown.

Navy pitchmen painted a wonderful picture of life aboard ship. She was the newest ship of the new navy. Her larger crew meant less work for each man. Crew quarters were more spacious. Food had improved. There would be ample time for sports and other recreation. Chief petty officers were more like big brothers than taskmasters. And in this comfortable if not luxurious setting, the men would visit exotic ports in the Caribbean, pass through the Panama Canal, and journey into the Pacific Ocean to visit parts of the world few Tennesseans could have dreamed of seeing. They would get all that and learn a trade too.

The navy needed skilled workers: carpenters, blacksmiths, painters, stenographers, bookkeepers, wireless operators, engineers, pharmacists, musicians, coppersmiths, cooks, plumbers, and electricians. Recruiters assured the young men of Tennessee that every man with talent and willing to learn would be given a trade "which will secure him rapid promotion in the navy, or an excellent position in civil life." This claim was made easier by the reforms Secretary of the Navy Josephus Daniels had implemented. Chief among these were self-improvement courses sailors could take in their spare time to add to their skills. Less impressive was the pay scale, which was considerably lower than the private sector. Emphasizing the positive, recruiters noted that there would be a pay raise in spring 1920 and that in addition to pay, the navy supplied all medical care, a place to sleep, and three square meals a day. As a result, a sailor might be able to save enough cash while in the service, as one politician suggested, to buy a farm and start raising potatoes and Democrats.[5]

If the opportunities aboard *Tennessee* excited young men of Tennessee, the navy had to worry about their parents, who

Go to Sea On the Tennessee

THIS FAIR DAUGHTER OF TENNESSEE CHRISTENED THIS GREAT SHIP NAMED IN HONOR OF THE STATE

TENNESSEE WANTS TO MAN THIS NEWEST DREADNAUGHT OF AMERICA'S VICTORY NAVY WITH MEN FROM HER OWN TOWNS and COUNTRYSIDE

"I CHRISTEN THEE TENNESSEE!"
SPONSOR—MISS KATHY ROBERTS, DAUGHTER OF GOVERNOR A. H. ROBERTS

If you want to be a Tennessee sailor on the Battleship Tenneesse and cruise the world with home folk boys, have a talk with the Navy Recruiting Officer---Now.

The Navy wants Tennessee men between the ages of 18 and 35 to enlist for a period of 2, 3, or 4 Years. Talk this over with your postmaster

Men who take advantage of this un-equaled opportunity to serve their country with friends, will be sent to the great Naval Training Station at Norfolk, Va.

WHEN THE TENNESSEE TOOK HER MAIDEN DIP
LAUNCHING OF THE SHIP AT NEW YORK NAVY YARD, APRIL 30, 1919

A RECRUITING PARTY DUE HERE

"Cruise the world with home folk boys" was a good promotional idea developed by Lieutenant Lon H. Robb, who was languishing in the naval recruiting station in New York and may have been seeking a way out. His concept worked. It not only got him command of the recruiting mission to Tennessee, it also landed him a post aboard the battleship when she was commissioned. Lieutenant Robb's next idea was not so good. He was charged with embezzling funds from *Tennessee*'s accounts. He escaped from the Brooklyn Navy Yard in September 1921 by changing into civilian clothes and simply walking off the base. He made his way to Europe before being arrested and returned to the United States for trial.[6]

before he was convicted of moonshining and the court was content to allow him to pursue his naval service. But naval regulations prohibited it, so Governor Roberts wrote directly to the secretary of the navy seeking an exception and he got one.[8]

There was also the question of the sexual conduct of sailors. Though contracting a venereal disease was a punishable breach of naval regulations, venereal disease was a fact of life in the United States Navy as it was throughout American society at that time. Of course, no recruiter ever mentioned that sailors on liberty in Panama or Los Angeles might visit prostitutes, and Captain Leigh assured the parents of potential recruits that their sons would not be tarnished by their years aboard *Tennessee*. She would be a clean ship, Leigh proclaimed. "But we are going to be more than physically clean, we are going to be clean in our work, clean in sport, in competitions and morally clean and are going to take care of the splendid young men of Tennessee who join us." He stressed the same parental tone when he announced his eagerness to come to the state where he could "assure the fathers and mothers that I will take care of their sons who serve with me on their great warship, *Tennessee*."[9]

With so many promises ringing in their ears, young Tennesseans poured out of the cities, small towns, farms, and mines of the state to serve on the great ship. Lieutenant Robb was successful beyond his wildest dreams.

Initially *Tennessee* needed 100 firemen third class and 385 seamen plus any experienced or skilled men who could be found. By February 10, when the special campaign ended, 565 Tennesseans had been enlisted, about all that could be absorbed aboard *Tennessee* at one time. But the popularity of the campaign is revealed not in the number chosen but in the number who volunteered, perhaps as many as 2,000. Local recruiting stations screened

might hold old stereotypes of the service as a dumping ground for men with unsavory reputations. Recruiters stressed that they sought only the highest caliber men and rejected out of hand anyone with a criminal record. Recruiters also kept a sharp eye out for men such as the infamous Gordon Ashman, who fraudulently enlisted or attempted to enlist in the navy twenty-six times. The worst of these men who had been thrown out of the navy and were trying to get back in under an assumed name could be identified by the kind of tattoo they had. So navy recruiting officers were specifically instructed to check the fingerprints of every recruit with the bad kind of tattoo, "since these men have invariably been found to have had prior discreditable naval service."[7] Nor did the navy want men who were told by a judge to join the navy or go to jail. Thus naval recruiters could not have been happy with the *Chattanooga Times* headline that declared, "Gov. Roberts Recruits Sailor From The Pen," though that was in fact what the governor had done. Oscar Holt had volunteered for *Tennessee*

U. S. S. TENNESSEE

... FROM STERN

NAVY YARD, NEW YORK,

AUG 2, 1917

3383.

out those would-be recruits who were obviously too young, too small, or lacked the proper moral character. They then sent 1,090 Tennesseans to the receiving station in Nashville. About 6 percent of those young men never appeared at the receiving station, apparently having had a change of heart. Of those who did arrive, eager to join and serve on *Tennessee,* navy examiners rejected nearly one out of two.[11]

Those rejected were either too young or too small. Recruits had to be eighteen years old, at least 5 feet 4 inches tall, 128 pounds, with a mean chest circumference of 33 inches. Medical officers had been free to waive any of these requirements for an otherwise particularly well-suited recruit, but just as the *Tennessee* campaign began, the navy insisted that medical officers strictly enforce the table of physical proportions. Old habits died hard, however. Many examiners signed up the young man who was slightly underweight, believing a few weeks of navy food would bring him up to standards. Eager to enlist young men, examiners asked no questions when a sixteen- or seventeen-year-old listed his age as eighteen years. And recruits with some disability, usually flat feet, but who claimed that it did not affect them adversely were accepted in Nashville. When these underweight or underaged recruits reached boot camp, examiners there sent them home. After a few weeks of training, some men with flat feet decided their handicap was a blessing and reported that in fact their feet would keep them from being good sailors and they should go home. They were given medical discharges. Similarly, mentally retarded recruits were sent home. But those who were simply illiterate were accepted into the service and special classes

NAVY YARD, NEW YORK 4-1-19. VIEW FROM AFT CRANE LOOKING AFT FROM MID-SHIPS. U.S.S. TENNESSEE. -3739-

On March 28, 1919, the navy decided to pay overtime and have riveters and drillers work on Sunday to get *Tennessee* launched on April 30. If they missed that date they would have to wait until May 26, and *Tennessee* was already so heavy that further construction was too dangerous. That would mean laying off yard workers who would find work elsewhere and not be available when the navy wanted to hire them back at the end of May. The sign on the deck announces the launch date as April 30 and counts down the days left to go.[14]

set up to teach them to read and write.[12]

As far as the navy was concerned, if an applicant was black, it made no difference if he had the size, feet, age, clean record, and even experience the navy was looking for — he need not apply. Though blacks had served in the navy before and during World War I, on August 4, 1919, enlistment of blacks, even as lowly mess attendants, was suspended. Exceptions were made for a very few blacks of the highest qualifications with previous military service. By November 1921, the navy had 12,000 "of these exceptionally well qualified men on the waiting list for enlistment" but did not expect to take any of them.[13]

The first 250 men accepted for *Tennessee* left home early in 1920 for sixteen weeks of training in Hampton Roads, Virginia, where the process of transforming civilians into sailors began. They learned to drill, follow orders, handle small boats, fire 3-inch and 5-inch guns, and generally become accustomed to the discipline and regimentation that was characteristic of the battleship navy but had not been mentioned in the recruiting speeches made back home. That the men came from the same area and would stay together after training helped develop a spirit that buoyed most of them through their boot-camp experience. Even so, for many of them it was a difficult time made more frightening by the lethal influenza epidemic that swept across the nation during the winter of 1919–20. The flu killed over 100,000 Americans that winter, four of them recruits at Hampton Roads. Scores of others were forced into the hospital. Beyond that, however, there were few problems. Nine young men who had lied about their age to get into the navy were given "inaptitude" discharges and sent home. Five more men, not finding a legal way out of their commitment, deserted.

A water shortage at Hampton Roads forced the second contingent of Tennessee recruits, about 300 men, to be sent to the naval training station at Newport, Rhode Island. These men were slightly older and better educated than their fellow Tennesseans at Hampton Roads. About a fifth had seen previous military service in either the army or the navy and apparently had been out of the service long enough to conclude that there were better opportunities aboard *Tennessee* than in Tennessee. In contrast to their fellow Tennesseans training in Virginia who went aboard in the lowest grades of apprentice seaman or fireman third class, most of the men training in Rhode Island were promoted before they went aboard and some even jumped to a petty officer rating. None of them deserted from boot camp and only two men had disciplinary reports placed against them during their entire training period, what Captain Leigh called "a remarkable record." Even the influenza epidemic proved less troubling for the recruits in Rhode Island, incapacitating fewer and killing none. The hardest thing they had to cope with was a particularly brutal February that brought frigid temperatures and snows so heavy that one recruit remarked that he had "shovelled more snow in Newport than he had ever seen before."[15]

The recruiting and training moved faster than the construction of the ship. The first volunteers were ready for active duty by April 1920, but *Tennessee* was not. The commandant of the Brooklyn Navy Yard personally inspected *Tennessee* and reported that commissioning the ship on March 31, 1920, as originally planned, would be a detriment to the progress of work aboard and a distinct hardship on anyone who had to live there. Mess rooms, galleys, pantries, and storerooms were not yet ready. He thought it would be at least a month before the ship was ready to receive her crew. So the planned commissioning date was canceled and Captain Leigh had to admit he did not know when *Tennessee* would be ready for the ceremony.

That was just another in a series of delays that had become synonymous with *Tennessee.* Four years earlier, Congress appropriated money for the as yet unnamed battleship number 43 (or BB43 in naval shorthand). But in the first months of the Great War, naval engineers discovered that the conventional design of battleships left them vulnerable to torpedo or mine attack, so they had to redesign their battleships. While they did this, Secretary of the Navy Daniels postponed requesting bids. By fall 1915, the navy had not yet figured out just how BB43 should be built but requested bids while reserving the right to change specifications at a later time. Not surprisingly, when Daniels and Assistant Secretary Franklin D. Roosevelt opened the bids in November 1915, the only shipbuilders that did not exceed the price set by Congress and were willing to make adjustments in design were the government-owned navy yards in Brooklyn and Mare Island, California. *Tennessee* was assigned to the New York yard, and *California*, logically enough, to the California yard. Yard workmen in Brooklyn could not immediately lay *Tennessee*'s keel because the only construction ways big enough to accommodate *Tennessee* were occupied by *New Mexico. Tennessee* finally got her keel in May 1917. By then the United States had just entered World War I, and building ships to send supplies to the Allies in Europe was a higher priority than completing a battleship. Work on *Tennessee* languished. Once the war was over, it could have been full steam ahead on *Tennessee,* but now, naval officers complained, civilian workers slowed down to make the job last and manufacturers failed to deliver equipment when promised. Consequently, *Tennessee* inched her way toward completion.[16]

When she was launched in April 1919, *Tennessee* was not as far along as the navy would have liked, but she was literally getting too big to stay where she was. A month before the launch, she weighed 16,000 tons, 1,000 tons more than any ship to be constructed on those ways. If she got any bigger, she would crush the supports on which she sat. The navy hurried to weld and rivet the mostly uncompleted ship so it would float by April 30, the date of a tide sufficiently high to allow the launching of the massive hull. Because of her low state of completion, the timing of making recruits available for the ship was thrown off and 800 recruits and transfers waited in the Brooklyn Navy Yard to go aboard a ship that was far from ready for them. Because their presence was burdensome to yard officials and demoralizing to the men, the navy decided to put *Tennessee* in commission and move the men aboard.[17] That was a big mistake, one the navy later admitted.

Commissioning was a low-key, brief ceremony. On June 3, 1920, Captain Leigh read his orders and raised the flag while a small group of Tennesseans living in New York looked on. Also present were several hundred workers, who stood quietly by during the ceremony and then turned back to their hammering, riveting, welding, and cutting.

There were 800 sailors aboard at the time of commissioning, but another 300 recruits remained in Newport undergoing rifle training. Though they may have been disappointed at having missed the ceremony, those 300 men were the lucky ones. Duty aboard *Tennessee* was horrible the first months. She was officially attached to the Eighth Battleship Division of the Fourth Battleship Squadron of the United States Pacific Fleet. But in practice she sat at pier D of the Brooklyn Navy Yard while hun-

By the end of August 1920, *Tennessee* was looking like a warship, though she was still trapped in dry dock with scaffolding around her. By this time her crew was sick and tired of New York.[18]

dreds of civilian workmen labored on almost every part of the ship.

Initially Leigh hoped his ship could be outfitted by the end of July or at least early September. But searchlights, bookcases, speaking tubes, food refrigeration units, steering gear linkage, and dozens of other items were yet to be installed, so *Tennessee* spent August in dry dock and September moored to the coaling pier. Captain Leigh blamed the lack of progress on suppliers who paid no attention to navy yard requests to deliver badly needed materials. The Bureau of Construction and Repair concluded that the crew got in the way of the civilian workers and slowed the rate of completion.[19]

Everyone was frustrated. Leigh and his officers were trapped in New York while the battle fleet to which *Tennessee* was nominally attached maneuvered in the Pacific. Enlisted men who had left Tennessee to see the world aboard their ship were seeing more of the bars and brothels of Brooklyn than they had ever bargained for. With compressed air hoses passing through portholes and down passageways, with scaffolding on deck and hundreds of civilian workers constantly underfoot, and with dirt and noise their constant companions, the crew found life aboard ship depressing. It was hard for the sailors to think of themselves as in the navy much less aboard the newest and potentially most powerful warship in the Fleet. To a young, undisciplined sailor required to stand watch on a ship in dry dock, there was a great temptation to sleep. Captain Leigh responded with stern punishment for the guilty, coupled with an increased number of four-to-fourteen-day liberties granted enlisted men. At the same time, he admitted to Governor Roberts that such an environment "is not the kind we want for efficiency and contentment on board."[20]

Stern punishment and generous liberties bought Leigh time, but he could not make much progress training his crew until he could put to sea. At the end of June, he hoped to get to sea by the end of August. By the middle of September, he hoped to be at sea by October, but on October 1 he was still at the coaling pier. Leigh reported that *Tennessee* was ready for combat in regard to construction, navigation, supply, and medical facilities, with minor work and testing to be completed for the critical areas of ordnance and engineering. That was close enough for the increasingly impatient captain, who decided to take his ship to sea.

Leigh picked October 15 to get under way. The Atlantic Fleet was due to arrive at New York that afternoon and perhaps the captain wanted to show off his ship and have *Tennessee* greet *Florida, Utah, Arizona, Oklahoma,* and *Nevada* while under her own power rather than moored to a pier in the navy yard. At 10:50 that morning, Leigh called all hands and sounded quarters for getting under way. At 11:40, tugboats nudged *Tennessee* away from her pier and making a standard 10 knots, she slid out of the New York Navy Yard, firing a thirteen-gun salute to the commandant from the small salute gun she carried aboard. As soon as the tugs left her, an improper valve adjustment caused *Tennessee* to lose control of her steering. But within five minutes it was regained and Leigh gave the order to clean up the ship. Eager sailors set about securing, or in some cases dumping overboard, the scaffolding, tools, and equipment of the workers who had been making their lives so miserable for the past four months.[21] *Tennessee* passed beneath the Brooklyn Bridge and anchored off Staten Island at 1:30 P.M., where two hours later she saluted the Atlantic Fleet as it steamed into the harbor. Though *Tennessee* looked like the formidable and graceful warship she was supposed to be, beneath her sleek exterior was a power plant that was to confound her engineering force and give her grief for several months.

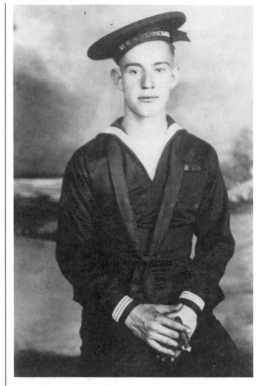

Electric power took *Tennessee* down the East River into New York Harbor. Eight oil-fired boilers produced steam for two 50-ton electric generators, each capable of producing 500 kilowatts. Electricity from those generators powered four motors, one for each of the 14-foot propellers. The system was not exactly experimental. *New Mexico,* commissioned two years before *Tennessee*, was an electric-drive ship. *Tennessee*'s sister ship *California* was also powered by electricity as were *Colorado, Maryland,* and *West Virginia,* which were under construction. But like all innovations, electric-drive ships had their critics. Traditionalists preferred the tried and proven geared drives, which weighed 379 tons less than the electric drives — tons that could be used for added armor protection, for additional fuel to extend the operating range, or to increase speed from 21 to 23 knots.

Champions of electric drives argued

that greater fuel efficiency at cruising speed offset the greater weight of the electric drives. And in every other way, they maintained, electric power was superior to the conventional power systems. It provided greater maneuverability by permitting precise control of propeller speed and much greater power in backing of propellers, thereby permitting improved handling of the giant ships especially when facing a collision. Electric power was more reliable because if one generator was lost, power could be easily diverted from the remaining generator to all four propeller motors, enabling *Tennessee* to maintain a speed of 17 knots with all shafts turning equally. In fact, during sea trials in 1920, one generator did go bad, but the ship carried on with little difficulty. Mechanically geared drives had to pass through bulkheads, reducing the watertight integrity of the area. By contrast, electric power was easily routed from generator to propeller-shaft motors, enhancing the watertight integrity of critical engineering compartments.[23]

That naval engineers should be excited about electric power for battleships is not surprising. Electric power was the fastest growing industry in the nation, and private industry was benefiting profoundly from the substitution of electric motors for cumbersome steam engines. The Navy Department was so convinced electric power was the wave of the future that it was willing to pay a premium in order to have Westinghouse and General Electric build the huge generators and motors rather than giving all the business to General Electric, the low bidder on both *Tennessee* and *California*.[24]

The greatest problem with electric drive was that few people in the navy had any practical experience working with it. As *Tennessee* put to sea on October 15, the only people aboard who understood the entire system were the chief engineer, Commander C. A. Jones, and the engineers from Westinghouse, who had helped install the equipment and had worked closely with Jones. A few men had received training on *New Mexico*'s electric drive, but not enough men and not enough training. During *Tennessee*'s four months in the navy yard, much of the time was spent reading blueprints while Commander Jones tried to teach his engineering officers and crew how everything was supposed to work. It was a task made more difficult because of a shortage of trained electricians. Leigh complained that the navy had sent him sixteen more electricians third class than he needed, while he lacked twelve electricians second class and nineteen first class. Officers in the Bureau of Navigation, which was responsible for personnel, promised to help but they could not supply what the navy did not have. In spring 1921, Leigh complained bitterly that he was supposed to have forty-two first- and second-class electricians but lacked eighteen, protesting that "it is impossible to get the service required of electricians first class or second class from electricians third class, especially when many of the latter are of a caliber which does not justify [even] the lower rating." It has gotten so bad, he told the Bureau of Navigation, that "it is barely possible" to keep the main engines and ship's light, power, and fire-control systems operating. The result was that the response time of the crew was slow when something went wrong, what the navy called a casualty. *Tennessee* would have many casualties.[25]

The first sign of a serious problem came only one day out of the navy yard. As the ship moved toward full power, the magnetic field in one of the huge generators flattened out several curved 4-inch-by-½-inch-thick copper blades, throwing the turbine out of balance. As the power increased, 52 tons of generator began to rock violently back and forth like an unbalanced washing machine. Quick action by the engineering officer on duty shut down the turbine before it could rip itself loose from its mountings. With the second generator functioning properly, *Tennessee* was able to continue operations for another week, but the damage was too severe to repair at sea. On October 29, *Tennessee* headed back to the Brooklyn Navy Yard for repairs classed as emergency and given the highest priority. It took four months to replace the destroyed rotors in the generator. A 25-foot-square opening had to be cut through the deck armor to gain access to the turbine so new parts could be lowered in.[26] No small task.

In February 1921, *Tennessee* began to prepare for her second shakedown cruise. This time she would meet the Atlantic Fleet at Guantánamo Bay, Cuba, and then test her guns near Virginia. The anticipation of seeing Cuba, perhaps seeing any place after a four-month enforced stay at the navy yard, excited the crew. Food, including 9,900 pounds of potatoes, was taken aboard and on February 26, *Tennessee*

started down the East River for the second time. Almost immediately she had problems with her electric drive that put the cruise in doubt. As she approached Staten Island, one of the generators overloaded and stopped. The demand on the other generator was too great and it failed, leaving *Tennessee* without power. Two days later, *Tennessee*'s executive officer, Commander Adolphus A. Staton, wrote his wife: "It is very disconcerting to be depending on the rudder and engines and to have something happen at a critical time."[27]

The "critical time" referred to the liner *Celtic,* which was passing *Tennessee*'s port side at the moment *Tennessee* lost power. Aboard *Celtic* was Rear Admiral Sir Lewis Bayley of the Royal Navy. Admiral Bayley had honored *Tennessee* both by a visit to the ship and by his attendance at the ship's ball held at the Waldorf Astoria Hotel on the Thursday before the Saturday sailing. Leigh was returning the honor by having the crew man the siderails and a band play on deck as the admiral steamed by. But when *Tennessee* lost power, her helm stuck hard over to port, and the battleship veered into *Celtic*'s path. The proper procedure was to warn *Celtic* by raising two black balls on the halyard to signal that *Tennessee* was out of control. But the complete outfitting of signal flags was one of the details not yet seen to, and when Staton shouted in his high-pitched voice "Hoist your balls, Mr. Roby, hoist your balls!" the beleaguered signal officer could only respond, "I haven't any, sir." An alert signalman avoided disaster by hoisting an alternate warning that she was not under control, and *Celtic* backed her engines as fast as she could and narrowly passed beneath *Tennessee*'s stern. Having avoided a collision, *Tennessee* was now at risk of running aground.

One advantage of her electric drive was the ability to generate as much power astern as ahead, thus permitting very quick stops. In fact, during her final trial runs the

There were four 12-foot propellers, each driven by its own electric motor. Keeping these motors running required skilled electricians. Scraping barnacles from the hull so *Tennessee* could make top speed, however, required more courage than skill. Safety precautions consisted of a single line that the men could hold.[28]

ESSEE-RUDDER AND
PROPELLERS-LOOKING TO PORT.
T.316-T, MAY, 1921.
, BOSTON.
21.

next spring, *Tennessee* would set a Navy Department record by pulling her 32,000 tons from 21 knots to a full stop in less than three minutes. Of course, to accomplish this, the generators had to be operating, and at the moment they were not, so *Tennessee* headed for the Brooklyn mud flats. Captain Leigh promptly dropped two anchors, pulling the pride of the United States Navy safely to a stop.[29] Captain Leigh's quick thinking not only saved his ship from a humiliating first cruise but saved his career as well. The navy does not like officers who run their ships aground.

Sitting at anchor off Tompkinsville, Staten Island, that Saturday night, Leigh pondered his options. Engineering prudence dictated turning back rather than inviting another casualty. But four months at the navy yard followed by the promise of a trip to Cuba had left the crew "keyed up." To return to the yard now would destroy the ship's morale. Leigh decided to risk the cruise. On Sunday morning at dawn, *Tennessee* got under way.

Men who had volunteered over a year earlier to see the world with home-folk boys on *Tennessee* would now have their first chance to do so. Morale was high as *Tennessee* left the New York winter behind her. En route to Guantánamo Bay, *Tennessee* sailors had their first exposure to the oceangoing navy. They spent hours scrubbing and painting away the dirt of the navy yard. The engineering force ran through some of the stunts that would be required during the sea trials, and the gun crews practiced loading and aiming. The men also saw whales, flying fish, Portuguese men-of-war (one was hoisted aboard ship), and a waterspout. Meanwhile, boxing, basketball, and rowing teams were organized aboard ship. By the time *Tennessee* anchored at the American base at Guantánamo Bay, almost all vestiges of her New York complexion had been removed.[30] One by one the admirals and battleship captains came aboard to pay their respects to Captain Leigh and the newest ship in the United States Navy. The ultramodern, sleek *Tennessee* looked even more state of the art compared with the older *Utah, Florida, Delaware,* and *North Dakota.* In this case, however, new meant untested.

As *Tennessee* ran a measured mile off Guantánamo, a small piece of debris was sucked into the air vent on electric motor number 4. There was a sharp bang as insulation inside ripped away, catching the motor on fire and pouring dense black smoke through the compartment. The smoke and flames forced back the fire fighters, even the men wearing gas masks. So unexpected was a fire in that compartment that naval designers had not bothered to install steam or freshwater fire-fighting connections. The crew poured foam and seawater on the motor until water in the compartment reached the metal walkways, but still the fire burned in an inaccessible part of the motor. The engineering officer was about to flood the compartment when somebody suggested running full speed on the two interior propellers and allowing the drag on number 4 propeller to turn the motor over, submersing the burning part of it in the water already standing in the compartment. The idea worked and within minutes the fire was out. But once again *Tennessee* faced a long delay for repairs.

To remove the motor, send it to the Westinghouse repair facilities, rebuild it, and reinstall it would take over three months. It was now March 12 and *Tennessee* was scheduled for her final acceptance trials on May 12. The engineering staff and the Westinghouse representative on board believed the repairs could be made aboard ship, cutting the time in half and allowing the final sea trials to begin as scheduled. Captain Leigh, already fed up with delays, sought and received permission from the Bureau of Engineering. He ordered *Tennessee* to Hampton Roads where Westinghouse sent aboard eight men trained in rewiring motors. These men and the ship's engineering company worked around the clock for six weeks to make the repairs.[31] Even as these unprecedented repairs were going on, *Tennessee* entered the Dahlgren Gun Firing Range and calibrated her batteries.

Tennessee's power, perhaps her greatest attraction, sprang from her twelve 14-inch 50 caliber batteries mounted in four turrets of three guns each. Naval officers had been sharply divided over whether this was the right kind of big gun to place aboard the newest battleship. The choice was between 14-inch 50 caliber guns (14/50s) and 16-inch 45 caliber guns (16/45s). Both guns had comparable range and wore out at the same rate, but the 16/45s fired a 2,000-pound shell, while the 14/50s used a 1,500-pound one. Some officers favored the larger explosive charge delivered in the heavier shell. They justified their choice by pointing out that the British were putting 15-inch guns on their battle cruisers and that the *Nagato*-class battleship Japan was constructing carried eight 16-inch guns. But others countered that the 14/50s had a higher muzzle velocity, which meant the shell, though smaller, moved faster and took less time to reach the target. Most important, these people argued, the 14/50s weighed substantially less than the 16/45s — 69 tons versus 94 tons per gun. With a total designed displacement of 32,600 tons, *Tennessee* could carry either twelve 14/50s or nine 16/45s. A broadside of 14/50s, twelve guns firing at the same time, would deliver 21,000 pounds of shells — compared with 18,000 pounds from the larger but less numerous 16/45s. Many defenders of the 14-inch gun were fond of pointing out that a 2,000-pound shell missing its target was no more powerful than a 1,500-pound shell missing its target. More guns meant more hits, and hits were what counted.

Only the experience of combat could resolve this volume-of-fire debate. Mean-

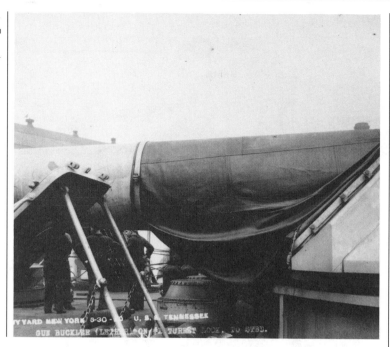

A leather buckler covers the opening where the barrel of the 14-inch 50 caliber gun (14/50) enters the turret. A 14/50 had a muzzle diameter of 14 inches and a barrel length 50 times the diameter. In *Tennessee*'s case, each gun was 700 inches, or just over 68 feet long.[32]

while, a seesaw battle continued between the two sides, and it just so happened that the 14-inch advocates were dominant in spring 1916 when a decision on *Tennessee* was made. By the fall, however, the big-gun advocates were ascendant.[33] As a result, the battleships that followed *(Colorado, Maryland,* and *West Virginia)* were equipped with 16/45s, but those guns proved to be so heavy that the ships could carry only eight of them.

From all this, one should not conclude that *Tennessee* was born a second-rate battleship. As late as 1938 there were those within the navy who still wondered whether the 16/45 was worth the reduction in fire volume.[34] And *Tennessee*'s 14-inch guns were very powerful indeed. Just how powerful was not apparent to her crew until the afternoon of April 17, 1920, when *Tennessee* fired her big guns first singly and then in three-gun salvos. Each salvo sent waves of vibration through the ship, shattering light bulbs and at least one porthole glass. When the number 2 turret fired at zero degrees elevation, the concussion sheered

off bolts holding lockers on deck, buckled a hatch door, shattered twenty-one teak planks, and depressed part of the weather deck, including the stanchions and beams holding it up, so that there was a noticeable, permanent hollow at one point in it.[35]

With her gun trials successfully completed, *Tennessee* headed to Boston for dry docking and a final going-over before her sea trials on May 12. On the way north, a generator malfunctioned once again, causing *Tennessee* to sit dead in the water for almost an hour before repairs could be effected. Back in Washington, naval officials doubted that *Tennessee* would be ready for her tests. But the ship's engineering force was confident it had everything well in hand even though the number 4 motor was still being overhauled and no one knew precisely why the generator had failed. It was not until May 6 that the motor repairs were finished. It took another two days of constant labor to reassemble the motor. Then as it was slowly rotated, there was the clear, sickening sound of a loose piece of metal inside. Somehow a 5⁄8-inch

washer had been overlooked during reassembly. There was nothing to do but take apart the motor and reinspect it for foreign objects. This time the engineering force used streams of air under 100 pounds of pressure to blow away anything that hands could not feel and eyes could not see. Thirty hours later the motor was again ready for testing; again there was the faint sound of metal falling against metal. For a second time the exhausted engineers took apart the motor, removed a tiny piece of loose copper, and cleaned everything with the high-pressure air hoses. It took another thirty hours to reassemble the motor and when tested it sounded perfect. On May 11, the repairs were deemed complete, and on May 12, *Tennessee* set out for her official sea trials.[36]

One can only imagine the pride and elation the engineering force must have felt when they accomplished through hard work what officers in the Bureau of Construction and Repair had thought an impossible task. They did their jobs so well that *Tennessee* passed her trials without mishap. On June 1, 1921, *Tennessee* was ready to take her place in the front ranks of the United States Navy. That was 363 days after she had been commissioned, over two years after she had been launched, four years after her keel had been laid, and more than six years after Congress had appropriated $7 million for her construction. On June 8, she passed through the Panama Canal, and as many men as could be spared went ashore to watch her pulled through the locks. In mid-June she arrived at San Pedro Harbor south of Los Angeles, which would be her home base until war clouds gathered in 1940 and she was sent to Pearl Harbor. Although she was the best warship the United States had ever constructed, the question remained whether *Tennessee* was good enough to carry out her mission. Even as she joined the Fleet, there were those who had doubts.

CHAPTER TWO

UP TO THE CHALLENGE

Tennessee was the most advanced warship the United States Navy had to offer when she joined the Fleet in June 1921. But some people questioned whether that was good enough. Could she defeat the battleships an enemy would send against her? Would the next generation of battleships, either American or foreign, be so advanced as to render her obsolete? And what did the rise of air power portend for *Tennessee?* These questions reflected the reality that obsolescence is the fate of all weapons of war. But there was a special urgency to these questions in 1921 because the weapons of war were changing so rapidly. The United States and other powers were designing bigger, more powerful warships and, most important, the airplane was beginning to challenge the supremacy of the battleship.

That a new generation of weapons would outdate existing weapons did not deter the Woodrow Wilson administration from building more battleships. In fact, it stimulated naval construction so that the United States could keep pace with other powers. In 1914 Congress had appropriated funds for three new battleships and in 1915 enough money to build two more. *Tennessee* was part of the 1915 appropriation. Naval officers had wanted four new battleships that year, but Secretary of the Navy Josephus Daniels cut the request to two ships, a number Congress was more willing to accept. Even then, the House of Representatives approved only one ship, and Daniels worked to have the money for the second ship restored during the conference resolving differences between the House and Senate versions of the appropriation bill.[1] The next year, the mood in Congress had changed and Daniels asked for and received funds to build ten battleships. Here began the idea of having a navy second to none, and at the heart of this navy was the battleship.

Naval officers might disagree with the secretary of the navy over how many battleships were needed, but in Washington there was broad agreement on why they were needed. The United States had developed a major foreign commerce upon which national prosperity rested. To reduce or destroy that foreign commerce would cripple the American economy and lessen national military power, throw large numbers of Americans out of work, and bring great political turmoil. The men who made policy in Washington, both the military officers and the civilians, did not use a cost accounting system of determining whether a war was justified by the amount of trade that came from a particular region. The point was not immediate dollars and cents but a worldwide system upon which U.S.

If necessary, *Tennessee* and her fellow dreadnoughts were supposed to move across the Pacific Ocean, defeat the Japanese navy, and patrol the sea-lanes. Naval strategists believed that if the United States had enough battleships and deployed them properly, their mere existence would deter Japan from attacking vital American interests. Here battleships of the United States Fleet turn in formation during maneuvers in October 1935.[2]

prosperity and power ultimately rested. It was the navy's job to foster that commerce and overseas trade and, above all, to make sure that this "liberal commercial" economic system was not destroyed. The navy continued to be the first line of defense for the American people, "but in the future," naval strategists insisted, "it will also be, far more than ever before, the steward of their prosperity."[3]

This idea that prosperity at home depended on trade abroad was a deeply ingrained concept among people who paid attention to world affairs. In the popular mind, the liberal commercial system meant the open door policy applied to China at the turn of the century in which all countries would have an equal opportunity to buy, sell, and invest in China. Among foreign policy professionals, it took a more general form of a world order in which all nations had access to the markets of the world as opposed to a great power dominating regions for its own exclusive use.

After World War I there were only two countries powerful enough to threaten American access to foreign markets: Britain and Japan. Some naval officers worried about British ambitions now that Germany had been defeated. But few naval strategists could bring themselves to believe that the United States and Britain would actually go to war. The United States Navy's enemy of choice was Japan, but not because of any threat Japan posed to the continental United States. The Japanese navy simply was not powerful enough to operate near the United States. However, Japan did have the ships to cut the commercial sea-lanes on which American prosperity and military power rested.

During the 1920s, Japan had embraced the ideals of a liberal commercial world and sought to expand peacefully within that context. Such a benign policy did not dispel the hostility with which American naval officers viewed Japan. They did not see

Japan as it was — a complex nation pulled in different directions by various political forces. Instead they focused on the military expansionists who sought to conquer and exploit East Asia for Japan's exclusive benefit. Though the military expansionists would not dominate Japan until the 1930s, American naval strategists interpreted Japan's peaceful policy during the 1920s as the tactical accommodation of a nation whose "set and positive maritime purpose" was the conquest of East Asia. It was up to the American navy to prevent this.[4]

War Plan Orange (the code word for Japan) was the navy's plan to stop the Japanese. It called on the Fleet, already stationed in the eastern Pacific, to move across the ocean, seize Japanese-held islands to use as advance bases of operation, and then impose a blockade of Japan and occupy some of its home islands. To do all that, it would be necessary to meet and sink the Japanese fleet.[5] Submarines and cruisers might harass enemy commerce, but they could not secure the sea-lanes for American ships. Battle cruisers, with their high speed and large guns could engage an enemy fleet, but being lightly armored they

might be so damaged after a battle that they could not remain on the scene. To dominate the seas, a ship had to be able to seize and hold the shipping lanes. To do that, it had to absorb punishment as well as dish it out. The conventional wisdom was that only the super battleship could do that.

Tennessee was just such a battleship. Her twelve 14-inch guns could be elevated to 30 degrees, twice the level of the older battleships, and gave her a range of over 35,000 yards, farther than anyone thought she would have to shoot. Spotters perched at the top of a cage mast peered through high-powered glasses to discern the faint splashes where the shells landed. But even from 120 feet above the waterline, spotters were ineffective beyond 27,000 yards during ideal conditions, and conditions were rarely ideal.[7]

In the next war, *Tennessee* would be shooting at Japanese battleships of the *Mutsu* class whose eight 16-inch guns had a range as great as *Tennessee*'s. To protect her from *Mutsu*'s 2,000-pound shells, *Tennessee* had tempered-steel armor plate strategically placed throughout the ship. Along her sides, 14-inch armor plate

What made a battleship different from a battle cruiser was the thick armor plate that shielded her propulsion equipment and big guns. Other parts of the ship were considered expendable and given little protection. Though her superstructure might be mangled and burning after a battle, she would still be able to maneuver and shoot. The large white band along *Tennessee*'s side marks where the thickest armor is being attached. This photograph was taken on April 20, 1920.[6]

shielded the equipment amidships. At the base of the funnel, armor ranging from 9 to 15 inches thick protected her boilers. Around her conning tower, which held the command centers, there was 16-inch armor plate. Her gun turrets were covered with up to 18 inches of hardened steel and below each turret an armored cylinder called a barbette extended several decks down, enclosing the gunpowder and shell handling rooms.

With so much armor of such different thicknesses, how much was enough? It would have been possible to cover every part of *Tennessee* with steel so thick that nothing could have penetrated it. But that would have made her so heavy that she could not have carried guns or been fast enough to catch anything. The theory behind armor was to protect what was vital and leave the rest to chance. The thickness of the armor was determined by the angle at which a shell would hit it. If the shell was going to strike at right angles, very thick steel was required. If it would hit at an oblique angle, the steel could be thinner, since the shell would have a longer distance to travel before it could penetrate.

At the traditional distances of 18,000 yards or so, shells would be fired at a relatively flat trajectory; thus the side armor was very thick. When naval engineers drew up the specifications for *Tennessee*'s deck armor, they assumed only a few shells would hit her deck and then at an oblique angle. So beneath the gleaming teakwood deck, *Tennessee* had one armored deck 3½ inches thick and a second armored deck only 2½ inches thick. Within a few years, however, the addition of spotter aircraft meant that battles would be fought near the maximum gun range. With their guns elevated to the highest point, shells would be lobbed out of sight and when they came down they would be falling as from the sky — what the navy called "plunging fire." At that angle the shells would pass over the

thick belt armor along the ship's side and cut through the armored decks with no difficulty.[8] She would need at least a 6-inch-thick armored deck to deflect a shell strike.

Assuming some shells would penetrate *Tennessee*'s armor, an intricate system of watertight compartments would minimize damage. One compartment flooding would not endanger the ship. In fact, several compartments could flood without seriously hindering the ship's performance. If flooding on one side caused the ship to list, she could be trimmed by pumping fuel oil from bunkers on one side of the ship to the other side and, if necessary, corresponding compartments on the other side could be flooded. She might ride low in the water, but her guns would be above water and her propulsion and maneuvering intact; she would be able to stay on line and in battle. *Tennessee*'s electric drive helped in this respect because if one generator room was flooded, the other generator could distribute its power evenly to all four propellers, causing only minor loss of performance.

As destructive as shell fire could be, torpedoes and mines were a greater menace. When Congress appropriated funds for battleships 43 and 44 (*Tennessee* and *California*) in 1915, the war in Europe was less than a year old and the great naval battle at Jutland was more than a year away. But already "some striking instances of effective torpedo attack" had shown that *Tennessee* would be vulnerable to underwater explosion. Thick belt armor above the waterline would do nothing to stop a torpedo or mine from rupturing the hull beneath the water. So serious was this new threat to the battleship that the navy postponed asking for bids while engineers and architects hurried to design a double bottom, a hull with two steel skins. The first would absorb the explosion and leave the inner hull undamaged. Details of design took time to develop and that put the Navy Department in a predicament. Everyone in the navy

agreed that *Tennessee* had to have the latest design, but if they put off construction much longer, Secretary of the Navy Josephus Daniels would be in the awkward position of asking Congress to fund a major naval building program in 1916 when the administration had not yet let contracts on the battleships authorized in 1915. So Daniels did the only thing he could do — he called for bids on construction while reserving the right to change the specifications after the contract had been let.[9]

That *Tennessee* got her new hull is evidence that the navy could rapidly adapt to a change in warfare. But not all the time. The same naval establishment that saw the need for a double hull to protect her from torpedoes was far less receptive to the complaints of officers that torpedo tubes and a torpedo room aboard a modern battleship such as *Tennessee* were worse than useless — they were an albatross hanging around her neck. The danger came from the size of the torpedo room, which would hold 350 tons of water if flooded, twice that if the compartment below it was also flooded. And it was generally agreed in the navy that an explosion close aboard could easily flood the torpedo room.

Her big guns meant *Tennessee* would engage the enemy well beyond torpedo range. Moreover, in battle conditions when torpedoes might be fired, *Tennessee* should be going near her maximum 21 knots, and torpedoes could not be launched when the ship was going faster than 16 knots. (Torpedoes were launched by compressed air, and the air pressure was not strong enough to overcome the pressure of the water when the ship was pushing through the sea faster than 16 knots.) Battleship commanders argued that the torpedoes and the torpedo rooms served no purpose and should be done away with.

The officers on the Navy Department's General Board who decided this issue did not easily give up the idea that the way

NAVY YARD NEW YORK 11.2.18 U.S.S. TENNESSEE - LOOKING F
FROM CANTELEVER CRANE

The machinery that fed the big guns was protected by barbettes, protective steel cylinders. This view is looking forward from the stern, where the armor for turrets number 3 and number 4 is visible. Number 3 will be the higher turret. This photograph was taken in November 1918.[10]

battleships had fought would be the way they would continue to fight. They argued that technological advancements would eventually enable *Tennessee* to launch torpedoes at top speed. Furthermore, the older battleships could not engage the enemy until they were within 20,000 yards, and since the newer ships would be massed with the older ships, the entire Fleet would be close enough to use the new longer-range torpedoes being developed — including ones that would travel toward the target and then run in figure eights, forcing the enemy to disrupt its maneuvering plans. The more contingencies an enemy commander had to take into consideration, the better for our side, they argued. As they discussed this issue at General Board hearings, it became apparent that a strong motivating force was the idea that since the battleships of other nations had torpedoes on them, American battleships had to as well.

Eventually the anti-torpedo officers won their argument and the newer battleships were designed without torpedoes aboard. But getting the tubes removed from *Tennessee* proved more difficult. She was so well built that the flooding of a torpedo compartment would make little difference in her performance because the bulkheads were strong enough to withstand the pressure generated even during full-speed operations. She would ride 4 feet deep at the bow, but counterflooding of compartments would allow her to ride level and only 5 feet deep. Should the compartment below the torpedo room also be flooded, *Tennessee* would ride 10 feet deep but still stay on the battle line. As the navy slowly moved toward abandoning the underwater torpedo tubes on battleships, it remodeled the older, more vulnerable ships first. *Tennessee* had to wait until 1934 before the antiquated weapons were removed.[11]

With her heavy armor, double hull, watertight integrity, and big guns, *Tennessee*

was probably good enough to challenge the best battleship Japan could send against her. Of course, no one could predict how a battle would come out, because at any given time one ship or the other might have a better-trained crew, be in better material condition, or have a commander who was a superior tactician. There was also the matter of luck. But assuming that all those items were equal, it was possible to calculate what would happen if *Tennessee* met the Japanese battleship *Mutsu.*

The navy carried out its calculations in excruciating detail. The contest boiled down to a formula calculating each ship's "fighting power" as the total hitting power of a ship times its "life," or the number of penetrating shells it could absorb before sinking. *Tennessee*'s life was 16.7, compared with 19.0 for *Mutsu.* In plain terms, *Tennessee* could absorb sixteen enemy shells penetrating her armor and be bloodied but unbowed. A seventeenth would destroy her. *Mutsu,* on the other hand, could shrug off eighteen such hits but the nineteenth would spell her doom. What would make the difference in battle was *Tennessee*'s superior volume of fire. *Mutsu* carried eight 16/45s as opposed to *Tennessee*'s twelve 14/50s. *Mutsu*'s bigger guns were more likely to penetrate *Tennessee*'s armor than were *Tennessee*'s guns likely to cut through *Mutsu*'s armor. On the other hand, *Tennessee*'s larger number of guns and superior rate of fire meant she would get off at least 75 percent more shots and score 75 percent more hits at whatever range the battle was fought. So *Tennessee* would win.[12]

These calculations demonstrate that the navy assumed a meeting of super dreadnoughts would mean dozens if not hundreds of shells exchanged, with both ships coming away bloodied. Yet there was something quite unreal about who would win. The navy assumed that the shells would not penetrate too far. If one happened to penetrate to a powder magazine, the ship would be destroyed. That is what happened to *Arizona* at Pearl Harbor in December 1941. A Japanese 15-inch armor-piercing shell, rigged with bomb fins and dropped from 10,000 feet, penetrated *Arizona*'s deck armor and reached her magazine. Two such "bombs" hit *Tennessee* in the same attack. One spent itself on the barrel of one of her guns and the other penetrated a gun turret but did not explode.[13]

Tennessee's probable ability to defeat *Mutsu* did not mean she could hold her own against the kind of battleships the great powers were planning. World War I had not soured the victors on building larger navies; Britain, the United States, and Japan were engaged in a massive naval arms race even as *Tennessee* took her station in the Pacific in 1921. In their most ambitious form, the navy's new battleships would be bigger (from 63,500 to 80,000 tons compared with *Tennessee*'s 32,600 tons), faster (30 knots compared with *Tennessee*'s 21 knots), and more powerful (twelve or even twenty-four 16/50s). More realistically, the navy not only designed but began construction on six 43,200-ton battleships intended to carry twelve 16/50s, make 23 knots, and hold enough fuel to have a significantly greater range. Larger, faster, longer legged, and more powerful, these ships clearly would have outclassed *Tennessee* long before she had used up half of the seventeen years of useful life the navy gave battleships.[14]

The diplomats saved *Tennessee* from second-class status. The reality of the arms race developing after World War I was that neither Britain, Japan, nor the United States could afford to allow another country to alter the balance of naval power. So each intended to build ships to keep up with the others. But none of these nations relished the prospect of spending vast amounts of money just to keep pace with the others. In this circumstance, the United States invited the leading nations to discuss naval arms limitations.

In the winter of 1921–22, while *Tennessee* was getting used to life along the West Coast, Secretary of State Charles Evans Hughes was in Washington fashioning the most far-reaching arms limitation treaty in modern times. The Five Power Treaty that emerged from the Washington Conference limited the size of battleships to roughly that of *Tennessee* and restricted how many battleships each great power could have. For every 5 tons of battleship the United States had, Britain could have 5 tons, Japan could have 3 tons, and the smaller naval powers of France and Italy could enjoy 1.75 tons each. As a result, a whole generation of 42,000-ton battleships was stopped in its tracks. The navy scrapped seven battleships that were 11 percent to 75.9 percent complete.[15] Not only did the treaty prevent *Tennessee* from being outclassed by newer American ships, it also prevented Japan from building newer battleships and meant that until the start of World War II, *Tennessee* would not have to face any Japanese battleship more powerful than *Mutsu*.

If the Five Power Treaty assured *Tennessee* she would not have to face a superior enemy battleship, it also raised serious doubts about whether she would be able to accomplish the mission the navy had set for her. The treaty restricted the construction of fortified naval bases in the Pacific. Japan was not allowed to fortify anything outside its home islands. Britain could fortify Singapore but nothing farther east, and the United States could not fortify anything west of Pearl Harbor, its base in the Hawaiian islands. Navy strategists opposed that provision because they had planned on fortifying Guam, 1,500 miles west of Hawaii, and a base in the Philippines, 2,500 miles west of Guam. Without Guam, they argued, it would be impossible for the United States to operate in the western Pacific. But civilians, not naval officers, were calling the shots at the Washington Conference and from their perspective the ban on fortifications of naval bases made sense. Japan was going to fortify bases on the South Pacific islands it had acquired under mandate at the end of World War I, whereas an economically minded U.S. Congress was not going to appropriate the money to fortify Guam or Manila. If nothing had been done, the navy would have found itself facing a Japanese fleet with advanced bases in the Pacific and nothing but Pearl Harbor from which to operate.

From a defensive perspective, the 5-to-3 ratio and the ban on fortification of naval bases worked well. Japan could not operate in the eastern Pacific against a superior United States Fleet without outlying naval bases. But the navy considered its mission only marginally defensive. Its duty was to ensure access to the markets and raw materials essential to the American economy. Without naval bases from which to operate, that mission was in jeopardy. During her prime years, *Tennessee* and her fellow battleships in the Fleet had the power to defend the United States against any enemy but were unable to defend the worldwide commerce on which American power rested.

The navy was not content to abandon its global mission simply because the Five Power Treaty made it much more difficult to accomplish. If the United States lacked a fortified naval base in the western Pacific, the navy would figure out how to move against Japan without such a base. Beginning in 1923, the navy began holding maneuvers called Fleet Problems. Two Fleet Problems in 1924, one in 1925, and one in 1926 involved training the Fleet to move across the Pacific, seize an unfortified anchorage from which to operate, and establish itself within 500 miles of Japan.[16] In 1925 the entire Fleet went on a cruise to New Zealand and Australia, gathering valuable information on the problems of such a long-range operation and clearly demonstrating that the United States Navy had not given up the idea of protecting American interests throughout the Pacific.

Though these Fleet Problems were designed to help the navy identify and overcome the difficulties in a war against Japan, the maneuvers also demonstrated how valuable the airplane was becoming to the Fleet. In his annual report for 1925, the commander in chief of the Fleet stated bluntly: "No one could have passed through this year in active and close association with the Fleet without realizing that these air units are now, and must always be, an inherent integral arm of the Fleet." There was still basic disagreement over how the planes should be used. Aviators considered air power the primary striking force in the navy. More-traditional officers, including the commander in chief, saw the airplane as "no different essentially than the Destroyer Squadrons."[17]

The disagreement over how powerful a weapon the airplane was and how it should be used was splitting the navy and attracting public attention before *Tennessee* had gone to sea. To the battleship admirals, the airplane lacked the accuracy and power to endanger a modern battleship. If and when the airplane became a formidable offensive threat, defensive aircraft would counter it. But that was a long time in the future, they thought, and the navy need not worry about that now. Fundamental to this perspective was that the battleship was and would remain the mistress of the seas and the backbone of the American Fleet.

Air-power advocates thought differently. They believed, and argued endlessly, that airplanes would soon become so powerful that one aircraft carrier full of planes would be able to menace a division of battleships, and a fleet of carriers would be invincible against a fleet of battleships. The only wise policy, the champions of air power argued, was the construction of aircraft carriers

and the development of better planes, aerial torpedoes, and bombs. In effect, they wanted the navy to turn its attention and money away from battleships to air power. The men who ran the navy were not about to do that. Airplanes remained auxiliaries in the Fleet and scarce financial resources were spent modernizing old battleships rather than playing with this untested weapon of air power.

But people who believed in air power believed in it with a passion and when the navy's General Board said no, they took their fight to the public. In that forum the complicated question of the relative effectiveness of battleships and airplanes soon boiled down to the simplistic question of whether the airplane had made the battleship obsolete. The test of obsolescence was whether an airplane could sink a battleship. It was a debate that captured the imagination of the American people at the very time *Tennessee* was finishing her outfitting and getting ready to take her place in the Pacific.[18]

Brigadier General Billy Mitchell did more than anyone else to intensify this debate. As head of the army's Air Service, Mitchell wanted more funds for developing air power, which meant taking it from other defense programs. His congressional testimony and public declarations soon became explicitly confrontational. A battleship cost $40 million to construct and fit out, he declared. That amount of money could build 1,000 airplanes, a force sufficient to protect the United States against any attacker. Mitchell found a sympathetic audience among economy-minded members of Congress.

Even as *Tennessee* first ventured to sea, General Mitchell publicly challenged the navy for an opportunity to show that bombers had made the battleship obsolete. On the defensive in Congress, challenged by its own aviation officers, and smarting from growing public doubt about the effective-

ness of the battleship, the Navy Department reluctantly agreed to bombing tests.

Most naval officers honestly believed that aircraft could not materially damage a battleship in a realistic test — that is, in a test where the ship was able to maneuver at high speed and where live ammunition was used to keep aircraft at such an elevation that a direct hit would be pure luck. Even a direct hit, they believed, would not do much damage to *Tennessee* or one of her kind.[19] Of course, no one was going to allow pilots to drop bombs on *Tennessee* while *Tennessee* tried to shoot down the planes. The next best test was to allow aircraft to bomb the former battleship *Iowa,* which the navy was equipping with remote control devices, and the captured German battleship *Ostfriesland,* which was going to be sunk in any case. Worried that these older, unmanned ships might be vulnerable to bombs, the navy's director of gunnery exercises gave naval aircraft only a small role to play in their sinking.

A U.S. battleship would have first crack at *Ostfriesland.* If still afloat, seaplanes would attack first with 250-pound bombs and then with 550-pound bombs until one hit had been achieved by each type of bomb. Finally, the army's 1,040-pound or even heavier bombs could be used. Such a procedure assured the navy of ample test information from which it could assess the effectiveness of bombing. It also avoided any embarrassing results. A single hit by a smaller bomb was not likely to do any serious damage to a battleship, even one dead in the water and without a crew to make repairs. If the heavier army bomb should happen to sink her, the navy could point to the battleship guns that had softened her up for the bombers.

By 1921 there was too much interest in the potential of the airplane to let the navy get away with cutting aircraft out of the prime place in these tests. At the end of February 1921, when *Tennessee* was getting under way to join the older battleships for maneuvers in the Caribbean, the navy agreed to allow Billy Mitchell's airplanes to have the first strike at the *Ostfriesland*.[20]

Mitchell's public belittling of the battleship had turned this test of weaponry into a grudge match. Naval officers bragged they could stand safely on the bridge even as army aviators tried to bomb them. Army aviators declared they welcomed facing navy antiaircraft fire, which could not hit anything. Such posturing undoubtedly amused the American public, but it did nothing for the reputation of *Tennessee*. The very fact that Billy Mitchell would have his chance to sink a battleship made many people wonder if it had been a mistake to spend so much money on the battleship *Tennessee*. Not the least of these were the editors of the *New York Times,* who asked, "If the *Ostfriesland* can be disabled or sunk, the new and better armored *Tennessee* would also be vulnerable, for the power of the explosive would be increased."

It was precisely this conclusion that the navy worked hard to prevent the American people from drawing. To begin with, the officers running the test selected a site at the extreme range of the land-based army planes, which would force the planes to spend minimal time over the target. General Mitchell protested, but to no avail. Moreover, the navy refused to allow the army to drop torpedoes, a weapon many people thought was a more formidable threat than a bomb.[21] Finally, the navy worked to manage the news coverage of the tests in order to minimize reports that the battleship was doomed.

The painful truth that several naval officers recognized was that given enough time and bombs, aircraft would sink the *Ostfriesland,* with serious consequences for the image of the battleship. To lessen the impact of the tests, Captain William D. Leahy, director of gunnery exercises, tried to guide reporters into writing the proper

stories. Leahy explained that his plan was not to have censorship "in the literal meaning of the word," but rather that naval officers at the test "will endeavor to so indoctrinate the correspondents that their articles will be innocuous, without their being irritated by the feeling of actual censorship over them." This might be accomplished, Leahy suggested, if the reporters were impressed with just how unusual a privilege was being extended to them and if their full cooperation was sought in return. The officers should stress to the reporters that the bombing of these old warships was strictly a test of matériel and was in no sense a gunnery experiment, Leahy urged. As a veteran officer, Leahy understood that bomb or gunfire hits would produce spectacularly visible damage without materially affecting the ability of the ship to fight. Thus it would be better if reporters confined themselves to narrative descriptions of the tests — the more general, the better. It would be particularly objectionable if stories included any detailed descriptions of the apparent effects of the hits or if any conclusions were drawn at the time of the tests. The whole affair was supposed to be a low-key, drawn-out, even boring series of tests with no one saying anything until a joint army-navy report was issued weeks later.[22]

Leahy's hope was unrealistic. With the liveliness of the airplane versus battleship debate, there was no chance that the tests would be a low-key affair reported briefly on page 16 of daily newspapers. Reporters witnessing the tests tried to find a meaning in every bomb dropped and every comment made by army and navy observers. At first the tests favored the battleship as navy planes appeared spectacularly unsuccessful in hitting the *Iowa,* which maneuvered under remote control at a leisurely 4.5 knots. Of eighty dummy bombs dropped, only two struck the ship, apparently vindicating those who all along had said that

airplanes lacked the bombsight to hit moving ships. (Though the navy did not want any editorializing, it did bring a fast destroyer to pick up the press dispatches and rush them back to shore so that the favorable news stories could meet deadlines.)[23]

In fact, however, the test was more devastating to the battleship than was immediately apparent. Most of the misses fell close alongside. Bombs detonating below the water but close to the hull had a mining effect that could rupture the ship's unarmored bottom. On the second day of the bombing tests, army planes carrying the heaviest bombs the army had and flying at a low altitude, stove in *Ostfriesland*'s bottom and she sank. It was not a true test of air power, since *Ostfriesland* could not maneuver to escape, could not fire antiaircraft guns to ward off the low-level attack, and had no crew aboard to make repairs or assure watertight integrity. However, all that was lost on the public. The popular image was captured by a newsreel version of the test: A plane flew over the ship, dropped a bomb, and the ship rolled over and sank.[24]

The sleek, powerful lines of *Tennessee* still embraced a sense of power, but never again would she be considered the undisputed mistress of the seas. Now there would always be doubts that the pride of the United States Navy could survive a concerted attack by aircraft that were, by comparison, primitive. It was the studied conclusion of the joint army-navy board examining the bombing of the *Ostfriesland* that "aircraft carrying high-capacity, high-explosive bombs of sufficient size have adequate offensive power to sink or seriously damage any naval vessel as present constructed." That included the USS *Tennessee,* arguably the most powerful warship in the world.

In 1921 *Tennessee* would only be vulnerable if she went too close to land, because the only planes large enough to carry a bomb that could hurt her were too large to take off from an aircraft carrier. But *Tennessee* had a useful military life of seventeen years and during those years the advances in aircraft and aircraft carriers would mean she would be at risk anywhere on the high seas. Air power was revolutionizing naval warfare, and many people in the navy understood this. Some defenders of the battleship admitted that air power posed a new threat and that someday, possibly, it would become so great a threat that the battleship would no longer be of value. But that day had not come, they argued, and it might never come. They would not gamble the national security on speculation. Even after warning that airplanes could destroy any warship, the joint army-navy board concluded that the battleship remained the backbone of the Fleet and the bulwark of the nation's sea defense. The airplane had added to the dangers to which a battleship was exposed but had not made it obsolete. "The battleship still remains the greatest factor of naval strength."[25]

These conclusions did not end the debate. New voices were added to the ranks of the champions of air power, most notably Rear Admiral William S. Sims. Sims, as much as anyone, was responsible for the development of the modern American battleship, but by 1923 he was publicly declaring that the future rested not with the battleship but with the carrier-based airplane. So much pressure was placed on the navy to shift its priorities from battleships to airplanes and aircraft carriers that the secretary of the navy instituted a special inquiry under Chief of Naval Operations Edward W. Eberle. Throughout the fall of 1924, the board listened to the advocates of aviation and the defenders of the battleship and emphatically concluded that "the battleship is the element of ultimate force in the fleet, and all other elements are contributory to the fulfillment of its function as the final arbiter in sea warfare." While

admitting that aircraft posed some threat to battleships, the board concluded that for every new offensive weapon a counter weapon is developed. In this case it would be a combination of antiaircraft guns and defensive aircraft. Though it would be necessary to have enough carriers to protect the battleships, the board believed that battleships remained central to American defenses and that airplanes and their carriers would support the battleships just as did the cruisers and destroyers. The board simply refused to accept the possibility that airplanes had revolutionized naval warfare.[26]

It was too much to expect that the navy would turn its back on the battleship. To spend over $30 million to build and outfit *Tennessee* only to declare her obsolete was asking too much of any institution, especially one so bound by tradition as the navy. To expect officers who had commanded battleships to equate flimsy aircraft with 30,000 tons of steel and guns that could fire farther than anyone could see was asking them to be more imaginative than we can rightly expect. What is amazing is not that the battleship held on to her role as the primary weapon in the naval arsenal but that the navy did so little to improve battleship defenses against the constantly increasing offensive capabilities of airplanes. *Tennessee* was not obsolete in 1921 or even in 1925, when the Eberle Committee gave its report, but every year she was becoming more vulnerable to being destroyed by aircraft.

We should not make too much of *Tennessee*'s air vulnerability; sinking her would not be an easy task, at least not during her normal life expectancy of seventeen years. Only armor-piercing bombs dropped from a high altitude could penetrate her deck armor, and the probability of hitting a maneuvering battleship from a high enough altitude was so low that over six hundred bombs would have to be dropped

to score sufficient hits to sink her. As aircraft improved, however, and bombs grew more powerful and bombsights more sophisticated, *Tennessee* would have to thicken her deck armor if she was going to survive.

A more serious danger came from the very heavy bombs that fell alongside. Fused to detonate about 50 feet under the water, the concussion would rupture the bottom of all but the most sturdily built warships. The magnetically detonated torpedo that exploded as it passed beneath the ship posed an even greater threat. *Tennessee* was fortunate to have a double bottom designed at the last minute before her keel was laid down in 1917. That construction, coupled with her intricate system of watertight compartments, meant she could absorb several underwater explosions. But clearly, this was her most vulnerable spot.

The best defense was to furnish *Tennessee* with steel side "blisters" and a triple hull. Filled with sea water or fuel oil, the blisters could absorb the concussion of a bomb or torpedo. In addition, watertight compartments could be subdivided to lessen the significance of any compartment's being flooded. Those alterations took money — lots of money — and the navy always had a better place to spend its money than on *Tennessee*. In the 1920s, the navy placed a higher priority on modernizing the older battleships so they could operate with the five new battleships of the *Tennessee* and *Colorado* classes. By 1934, as *Tennessee* approached the end of her life expectancy as a man-of-war, the navy considered modernizing her and *California*. But the Navy Department was wary of making such a major commitment of time and money on the eve of the 1935 London Naval Arms Conference. If the United States, Britain, and Japan could not agree to maintain the balance of naval power established in the Five Power Treaty (as happened), American naval planners preferred to ap-

The newest and most powerful American warships were based in the Pacific Ocean where they could keep an eye on the Japanese navy. In case of national emergency, the warships could be quickly moved from one ocean to another via the Panama Canal, and every year or so the Atlantic and Pacific fleets met near Panama for combined maneuvers. In this photograph it is clear that *Tennessee* did not have much room to spare as she passed through one of the Panama Canal locks in the late 1920s. Had protective side blisters been installed, as the Japanese were doing to their battleships in the mid-1930s and as was done to *Tennessee* in 1943, she would have been too wide to fit through the locks. Although the added width would have limited her value to the navy during the 1930s, without side blisters *Tennessee* was dangerously vulnerable to torpedo and bomb attacks.[27]

ply scarce financial resources to building new, larger battleships rather than remodeling older ships of *Tennessee*'s vintage.[28] Too modern to be upgraded in the 1920s, a decade later *Tennessee* was too old to be rehabilitated.

The Japanese felt differently toward *Mutsu,* Japan's counterpart to *Tennessee.* From 1934 to 1936, Japan virtually rebuilt *Mutsu* and her sister ship *Nagato.* To reduce damage from bombs or plunging shells fired from a distant battleship, the Japanese doubled the thickness of *Mutsu*'s deck armor to 7 inches and increased the barbettes to 22 inches. To reduce the danger from underwater explosions, a triple hull and side blisters were installed. Gun elevation of the main batteries was increased from 30 to 43 degrees, lengthening the firing range to 23 miles. Antiaircraft protection was improved by replacing two of the 5 ½-inch guns with twenty 25mm antiaircraft guns. All this added 6,500 tons to *Mutsu*'s weight, but modernizing her propulsion system increased her range of operation from 5,500 to 8,650 miles while sacrificing less than 2 knots of speed. That left *Mutsu* capable of 25 knots, considerably faster than *Tennessee.*[29] By 1937, *Mutsu* was a faster, more heavily protected battleship than was the aging *Tennessee.*

The reality of weaponry is that what is state of the art one year will soon be outmoded either by an updated version of that weapon or by a totally new one. *Tennessee*'s construction was completed in September 1920, and the navy had calculated that she would have seventeen years of useful service. That would make her obsolete in 1937. In practice, she was obsolete a year earlier. But with no new battleships under construction, the United States would have to make do with what it had; thus in 1935 the useful life of *Tennessee* was redefined as twenty years. However, by 1938 the new American naval building program was just getting under way and

would not produce a new battleship until after *Tennessee* was officially overage. Again the navy redefined *Tennessee*'s useful life — twenty-six years. She would be fit to fight until September 16, 1946. Japan dealt with the outdating of its battleships by spending huge sums to remodel old ones and build new ones. The United States followed the less expensive course of simply stating that the old ships were not that old after all.[30]

On paper, it would not be an obsolete *Tennessee* having to face a modernized *Mutsu.* In practice, however, *Tennessee* was no longer able to hold her own in the type of war U.S. naval tacticians envisioned. Just as important, she was even more unprepared to fight a naval war in which the airplane would be paramount.

The Imperial Japanese Navy, like the United States Navy, had not given up on the battleship. But the addition of a triple bottom, blisters, heavy deck armor, and antiaircraft guns indicates that the Japanese navy took the threat of aircraft more seriously than did the officers who controlled the American navy. This attitude was reflected in a variety of ways during the interwar period. As the General Board debated removing torpedo tubes from *Tennessee* during the 1920s, it held to the fantasy that massed fleets of battleships would slug it out at close range in battles where aircraft were not a decisive factor. To their mind, the destroyer launching a torpedo attack was a greater threat than a squadron of dive bombers or torpedo planes. As late as 1940, naval maneuvers employed torpedo planes not as an independent strike force to cripple the enemy fleet but as an attacking force timed to launch its torpedoes in coordination with those launched by the destroyers.[31] By refusing to accept the plane as the primary threat to battleship security, American naval leaders failed to provide the stimulus to develop an adequate defense. Nowhere was this

The 5-inch 51 caliber guns (5/51s) were defensive weapons used to ward off destroyer attacks. Since they were not vital to the operation of the ship, they received minimal protection; most had only a thin splinter shield to protect them, and the forward upper guns were totally exposed. The 5/51s did not use a self-contained shell with projectile and gunpowder in it but rather a separate projectile and bag of gunpowder. Since the forward 5/51s were located close to number 2 turret, the men on those guns faced a deafening roar when the turret fired and found themselves in the unenviable position of holding bags of gunpowder while the big guns spat flame, superheated gases, and remnants of burning silk right next to them.[32]

NAVY YARD N. Y.   8-30-20   U. S. S. TENNESSEE   UPPER DECK   STBD SIDELOOK. AFT

more apparent than in antiaircraft fire.

When commissioned, *Tennessee* had only three antiaircraft guns — small 3/50s at that. By contrast, she carried fourteen 5/51s, guns that were designed to ward off a destroyer attack but that were ineffective against aircraft. Even if these guns could be brought to bear on low-flying aircraft such as torpedo planes, the detonation fuses that caused the shell to explode in front of the attacking airplane were off from two and a half to five seconds, making them virtually useless. During the years following the *Ostfriesland* sinking, the navy substituted eight 5-inch 25 caliber antiaircraft guns for

four of *Tennessee*'s 5/51s. This was not enough and her officers sought replacing two or more 5/51s with 5/25s. The General Board, preparing *Tennessee* to fight the last war rather than the next, refused to allow the change, claiming *Tennessee* needed all ten of her 5/51s to ward off destroyer attacks.[33]

Whichever gun was being used, the results of antiaircraft practice were erratic at best. Complacency had dominated the Fleet until Billy Mitchell's planes sank the *Ostfriesland*. Then the chief of naval operations ordered that "the development of a practical and effective doctrine of anti-

aircraft gunnery should now be prosecuted most vigorously, as progress in this direction to date has not been encouraging." But it took time to figure out how to fire at planes. Initially, gunners took aim at a kite pulled behind a boat, which proved very unsatisfactory. By 1923 the Pacific Fleet had developed a more realistic target: an 8-by-30-foot cloth sleeve that was towed behind an airplane. By the end of 1924, Eberle's special board had concluded that antiaircraft fire hit the target 75 percent of the time.

But the commander of the Battle Fleet was not so sanguine, noting in his annual report for 1925 that even though antiaircraft gunnery was getting better, there was still room for great improvement. That was a masterful understatement. In the maneuvers off San Pedro that spring, forty-four antiaircraft guns on eleven battleships fired twenty-two rounds apiece for six minutes and failed to hit even one of the eight towed sleeves, though they did come close to hitting one of the planes towing a sleeve.

The next day, *Tennessee* salvaged the Fleet's honor by firing on and destroying two airplane-towed sleeves. Her success may have been due to a method of improving range-finding control as the attacking aircraft approached. The technique, developed aboard *Tennessee,* allowed for more accurate setting of fuses and thus detonations. Admiral Eberle commended *Tennessee* "for the interest and ingenuity displayed in devising the methods and procedure used in these practices."[34] Such innovations, however, were matched by the improved speed, agility, and tactics of attacking aircraft. On balance, *Tennessee* and her fellow battleships were just as vulnerable to air attack as ever.

For example, in 1923–24, when Captain Luke McNamee commanded *Tennessee,* the ship was just beginning to figure out how to shoot at horizontal bombers. In 1929 she was getting pretty good at such antiaircraft firing. But now Rear Admiral McNamee, director of Fleet training, worried that the dive bomber would replace the horizontal bomber, and shooting down a dive bomber was very difficult. "When it is considered that a diving bombing attack can be developed and executed in a matter of seconds, the urgency of the defense problem begins to be apparent," he warned. A formation of dive bombers approaching out of the sun at 15,000 feet would go undetected until they began their dive, which would last only thirty-six seconds before the bombs were released. Given the time it takes a shell to reach the planes, gunners would have, at

most, thirty seconds to fire. Since they would come from different angles at the same time, "the prospects of stopping even a small proportion of them by gun fire are not good to say the least."[35] Nor did the prospects get much better during the 1930s. More time was spent on antiaircraft practice, but it was the one part of gunnery exercises that proved less than satisfactory.

In February 1935 there was a test of night antiaircraft firing that left mixed results. *Tennessee* spotted the first flight of fifteen planes coming in at 7:13 P.M., warned the Fleet, and fired for six minutes and fifty-five seconds at the planes, destroying four. Spotting another wing of fifteen planes off her starboard side, she fired for one minute but destroyed none. She then turned her attention to an unspecified number of high-altitude bombers, claiming six kills in three minutes. When eighteen dive bombers came within range, forty-five seconds of firing knocked down two. In a few minutes, *Tennessee* alone had knocked out twelve planes, and she was only one of eight battleships taking part in the exercise. But that was just practice. No real shells were fired and, for safety's sake, the attacking planes were brightly lit, allowing the ships to spot and train their fire long before they could have done so in combat. Captains of other ships wondered just how effective their fire would have been had the attack come under battle conditions.[36]

One answer became apparent in 1940, nearly two decades after Billy Mitchell's bombers demonstrated the vulnerability of battleships to air attack. Against high-altitude bombers, the 5-inch guns were successful in destroying or seriously damaging 10 percent of the attackers. Against dive bombers, the stop rate was only 1 percent. Torpedo bombers, forced to fly low in steady paths, were shot down at a 10 to 14 percent rate and damaged at the rate of 18 to 27 percent. But a pilot could increase his chances of avoiding *Tennessee*'s antiair-

craft fire by dropping his torpedo at long range. In short, the navy found that antiaircraft firing was "generally ineffective,...and does not provide reasonable security against air attack."[37]

With antiaircraft fire varying between poor and useless, it was apparent that the battleships would have to depend upon carrier-based pursuit aircraft to protect them against enemy planes. However, the navy's studies indicated that no matter how many defensive fighters were put in the air, some offensive planes would get through. "We formerly thought that by fighting in the air we could get control of the air like we can on the surface," one admiral explained in 1931, "but we find that no number of defensive airplanes can keep off all air attacks. Thence everybody, immediately there is a fight of any kind, seeks to destroy the enemy's aircraft, and the only way to do that is to ruin the flying decks of his carriers. The only way to do that is with aircraft."[38]

Within a decade of the *Ostfriesland* test, command of the air had become so important that aircraft carriers, not battleships, had become the prime targets in any naval engagement. In practical terms, this meant that if the United States and Japan went to war in 1931, the United States Navy would first try to destroy any Japanese carriers and then take on the battleships with relatively invulnerable American air power. In theory anyway, *Tennessee* and *Mutsu* would never have to exchange shell fire. Air power had made the battleship all but irrelevant in a sea battle. Or so naval aviators argued and so it was in World War II.

To the "gun club" officers of the navy, the big gun remained supreme. For them, the key to the Fleet's success was how well those big guns could be brought to bear on the enemy. That was a question of battle efficiency, and the struggle to achieve the highest level of battle efficiency provided the foremost competition in the navy.

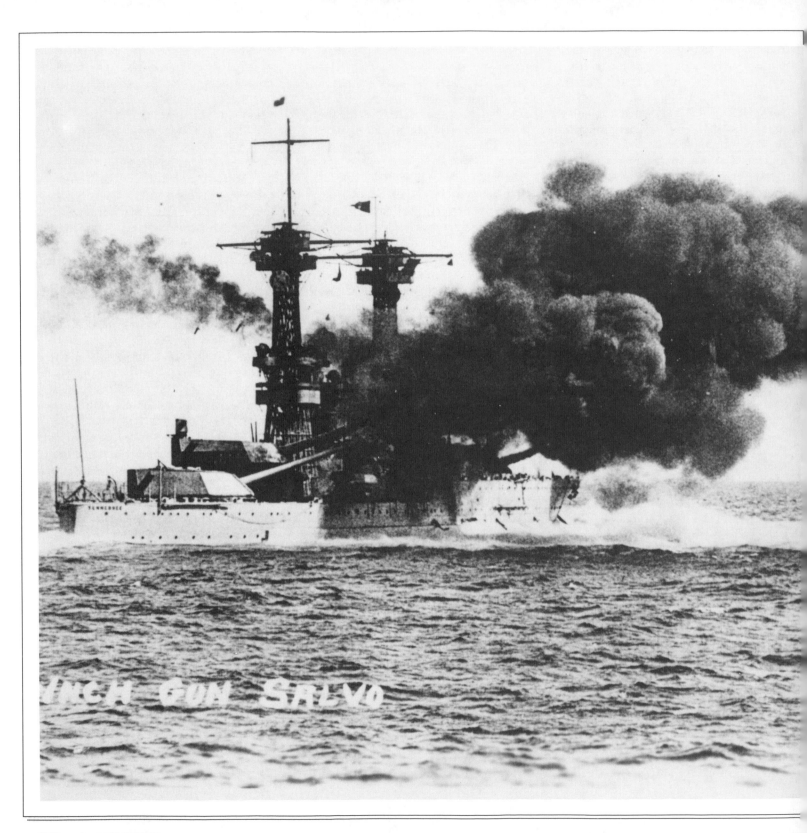

INCH GUN SALVO

CHAPTER THREE

BATTLE EFFICIENCY

In 1924, her third year in active service, *Tennessee* won the battle efficiency competition. That was the Navy Department's

The navy called it smokeless gunpowder, but it produced a great deal of smoke, especially when *Tennessee* fired a full broadside of twelve guns.[1]

way of saying she was the best battleship in the Fleet. She won it by taking first in gunnery and fifth in engineering, the two categories critical to winning a naval battle. Whether gunnery or engineering was the most important part of the ship depended on one's perspective. It was essential to hit what you were shooting at, but it was also essential to be able to steam across the ocean and engage the enemy when and where it was most vulnerable. A ship that broke down, squandered fuel, or could not sustain her designed speed materially weakened the Fleet. Predictably, the navy establishment valued gunnery slightly more than engineering, counting gunnery scores for 60 percent and engineering scores for only 40 percent of the total score in the battle efficiency competition.

Since gunners earned points for speed and accuracy, the men trained to shave seconds, then fractions of a second, off the interval between rounds fired. The more the men trained, the faster they got. And the faster they got, the less tolerance there was for error. Whether it was fourteen men

working on a 5-inch gun or more than forty on a 14-inch gun, each had to work in perfect coordination with the others if they were going to win. Should someone make a mistake, the least that would happen would be a lengthy delay in firing; the most would be that everyone would be killed.[2]

That was a point brought home to the men of *Tennessee* just before noon on Thursday, June 12, 1924. The gun crews had secured from their long-range gunnery practice and some of the men were on deck waiting for mess call. Two thousand yards away, *Mississippi* was taking her turn firing at a target barely visible on the horizon. With each firing, a tongue of flame and cloud of smoke shot out of the muzzle. A few seconds later, the roar of gunfire reached *Tennessee*. "Look at the *Mississippi*," someone yelled. Smoke and flames were enveloping number 2 turret, not pouring out of the muzzle. The men aboard *Tennessee* knew just what had happened. "When one works around a gun you figure your chances," one of *Tennessee*'s sailors was quoted after the accident. "We knew just what would happen if a charge exploded prematurely. We knew just about every man in that turret was dead." Three officers and forty-five enlisted men died that day, the greatest peacetime accident any American battleship experienced during *Tennessee*'s lifetime. Rare as that kind of accident was, the disaster was not lost on the men of *Tennessee*. A dozen years later, recruits were told the story of what had happened aboard *Mississippi* and were admonished that "every rule that is written is written in blood and someone died for it."[3]

Firing a main battery on a battleship was a very complicated, dangerous business. The danger did not come from the .75-ton shells that were next to impossible to detonate by accident. So secure were they that a ready supply of fifty-five shells was stored in the turret with continual resupply from three levels below via a shell hoist. The real danger came from the gunpowder. Each bag held 116 pounds of what the navy called "smokeless" gunpowder. Compressed into cylinders about the size of a finger, it was reasonably stable and designed to ignite only under the intense heat and pressure that would build up in the gun's breech — the heat and pressure that would come from the much less stable granulated powder that filled one end of the rather delicate silk powder bags.

These bags of powder were kept as far away from the turret as possible, five levels down in the lower handling room. The men there moved the powder from the magazine to an endlessly running powder hoist. It was a job for the least experienced men and frequently was relegated to the Filipino mess attendants. In the upper handling room, four powder bags were loaded onto the powder car for the trip up to the gun. Two bags were placed on the lower shelf and two on the upper shelf, positioned so they could be loaded into the gun with the volatile powder pointed toward the breech.

If the men in the lower handling room loaded the bags on the powder hoist the right way and if the men in the upper handling room loaded the bags on the powder car the right way, the powder man in the turret could lever them onto the loading tray the right way. If any one sailor put them in wrong, the whole process came to a temporary stop. If any of the handlers ruptured a bag, the command of "silence" was given and everything stopped until the gunpowder had been immersed in water. In combat, such errors could prove fatal. In practice, they cost the gun crew points that could mean losing a competition — and in the navy, competition was everything.

As the big gun fired, the barrel recoiled 2½ feet into the turret faster than the eye could see. Antirecoil brakes promptly returned it to the normal position and the barrel, if elevated for a long-range shot, dropped to a horizontal position to allow loading of the gun. Compressed air blew hot gases and smoldering remnants of the silk powder bags out of the muzzle. The gun captain pulled open the breech plug and with a large wet towel wrapped about his forearm, wiped off the breech mechanism. With fresh powder coming in, it was important not to have any telltale pieces of burning silk in the barrel or on the breech. The tray man unfolded and swung into position a long tray that would hold the shell and powder bags as they were rammed into the gun chamber. As soon as it was in place, the shell man rolled one of the 1,500-pound shells onto the tray and the rammer man immediately pushed it into the gun with his electric rammer.

By this time, four more bags of powder had come up the elevator, and the powder man opened the powder-car doors. As soon as the rammer was clear, he levered two bags of powder onto the loading tray, tripped a latch, dropping the two bags from the upper level, and then levered them into place. The rammer pushed the four bags of gunpowder into the breech to precisely the

right spot. The primer man had already placed a new cartridge the size of a medium-caliber bullet into the breech mechanism. When the loading tray was folded away, the plug man, assisted by compressed air, swung the breech plug shut, and the primer man placed his foot on it to make sure it was secure. Everyone stepped back and the gun was ready to fire. The whole process took twenty seconds, as little as fifteen seconds for a first-rate gun crew and even less if it was short-range firing, because the gun barrels did not have to be lowered and raised.

During those fifteen to twenty seconds, an airplane launched from a catapult at *Tennessee*'s stern circled the target fifteen to twenty miles away, radioing back where the earlier rounds had fallen. In the fire-control center, men recorded the speed and direction of the target, the speed and direction of *Tennessee,* the amount of time it took for the shell to travel the distance between *Tennessee* and the target, and how long it would take the next round to travel that distance. They then calculated the proper bearing and gun elevation for the next shot. On the order to fire, an electronic charge fired a bullet into the granulated powder. When the powder bags were properly loaded, the bullet ignited the granulated powder. The heat and pressure it built up within the gun chamber in turn ignited the smokeless gunpowder. Rather than expend its energy in a single blast, the gunpowder "burned" rapidly, with the expanding gases forcing the shell out of the muzzle ever faster. The longer the barrel, the more time the gases had to push the shell and the higher the speed of the shell when it left the muzzle.

In this complicated process, any malfunction by man or machine produced results ranging from inconvenience to disaster. If the rammer man pushed the gunpowder so there was more than 4½ inches of space between the breech and the powder bag, the burning granulated powder might

The men who loaded powder and shell in the top of the turret were only part of a large, complicated network of men, elevators, and hoists that had to work flawlessly if *Tennessee* was going to maintain the volume of fire necessary to survive in battle. Note that the 14-inch shells are stowed throughout the various levels of the battery. It was the gunpowder, not the shells, that was likely to explode from a random spark or small fire.[4]

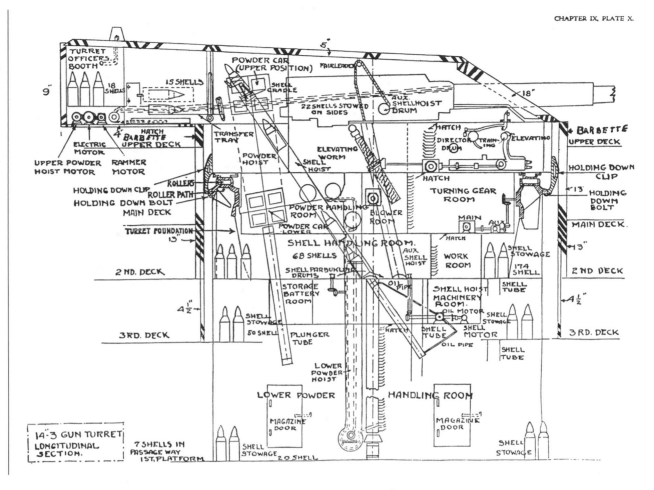

not generate sufficient pressure to ignite the "smokeless" powder. That was called a hangfire. A tray man could pull back the loading tray before the last bag of powder had fully entered the gun chamber, causing the rammer to rupture the bag against the breech. An overeager powder man could lever the powder onto the tray before the shell had been loaded. At best this would cause a long delay while the bags were lifted off. At worst the rammer would already be in motion and before anyone could stop it the powder bags would have slid into the gun without a shell. That was called a bale of hay and required the delicate task of pulling the powder out of the gun. If a powder-car door was left open, a bag could fall out. If the powder bags were not loaded properly into the powder car, closing the door might rupture them. If the breech was not securely fastened, the exploding gunpowder would rush back into the compartment. If the compressed air did not work right, burning remnants from the powder bags might ignite the next bag of powder as it was rammed into the chamber. Apparently this was the problem aboard *Mississippi*.

Though the silk bags burned rapidly, the linen labels on those bags burned more slowly. Usually the labels were removed before firing, but survivors aboard *Mississippi* testified the labels were still on, and others said there was a problem with the compressed air. The combination proved lethal as powder and spark came together. There was a puff of smoke, a small amount of flame, and then a blinding flash like a continuous streak of lightning. With a 1,500-pound shell at one end of the gun barrel and nothing at the other, the smoke and flame rushed into the turret, burning and suffocating the gun crew.[5]

Tennessee maneuvered closer to her stricken colleague and sent a boat with medical personnel and supplies. But *Mississippi,* only an hour away from San Pedro, raced home, radioing ahead for assistance. As soon as she passed the breakwater, she dropped anchor to await the approach of the hospital ship *Relief.*

The fire had been extinguished and a rescue party was bringing out the dead. But as two sailors carried out the body of an ensign, his hand brushed against the firing button. The gun roared and the recoil crushed four men in the rescue party. Fortunately the gun was pointing out to sea rather than toward the city and the shell fell harmlessly into the ocean, but not before it caused some panic aboard the steamer *Yale,* which it narrowly missed.[6]

Not long after this event, *Tennessee* put to sea for more firing of her main batteries. The compressed air on a gun in the number 1 turret aboard *Tennessee* failed. When the breech was opened, the gases poured into the compartment (called a "flareback") just as fresh bags of powder were coming up the powder car. The turret officer, Lieutenant junior grade L. S. Sabin, reached for the sprinkler valve to flood the compartment. Before he could turn the valve, the gun captain, J. C. Novatny, gave the command of "silence," and each man stood quietly at his position while Novatny grabbed the powder-hoist man by the seat of the pants and threw him out of the way, closed the elevator doors, and sent the powder back down. He then turned on the auxiliary compressed air and secured the compartment, brought the powder back up, and loaded the gun for another round.

Novatny's quick reaction not only avoided a disaster but permitted the gun to fire with only a time delay. Lieutenant Sabin believed Novatny deserved a commendation and recommended him for a meritorious mast. The tobacco-chewing coxswain said he "didn't want no commendation" and did not know what he would do with his tobacco if he had to go before a meritorious mast where the ship's officers and crew would be gathered to hear the captain praise his quick action. Sabin gave Novatny the choice of swallowing his tobacco during the mast or spitting it out before, but he was going to get the recognition he deserved.[7]

Powder was passed from the magazine to the lower handling room where it would be loaded on the powder hoist for its trip to the upper handling room. The scuttle was designed so that when one side was opened, the other would be sealed, preventing a fire in the lower handling room from spreading to the magazine. Unfortunately, bags of powder frequently stuck in the scuttle, and the men inside the magazine would often reach in to give the bag a push. Ensign Joseph E. Wilson tried that in 1926 and had four of his fingers nearly severed as the scuttle door closed on his hand. The inquiry into the accident concluded that Wilson had violated standard procedure but in the press of time during target practice had responded with a natural impulse. Wilson's action was understandable but not excusable, and the navy denied him compensation.[9]

The most common problem was breaking powder bags. During practice, *Tennessee* used heavy-duty bags that could withstand repeated drills. The men became used to these rugged bags and it was impossible to persuade them that they had to treat the bags gently in order to learn how to handle the real bags. Inevitably, when it came time to use the more delicate silk bags, rough handling ruptured some of them. When that happened, everything stopped until the gunpowder was immersed in water. Not until 1939 did *Tennessee* solve this problem by ordering a durable but delicate-looking fabric that convinced the men to treat each bag gently during practice.[8]

One of the obstacles to training the men to be gentle with 116-pound bags of gunpowder was the rotation of men in and out of a gun crew. It was routine in the navy to have 40 percent of the men aboard a ship transfer off during any year. In *Tennessee*'s case, 40 percent was the lowest rate she experienced during the 1920s; at times, it rose as high as 60 percent. In the mid-1930s, transfers off of *Tennessee* dipped to 34 percent. But in those years, as many as 10 percent of the crew transferred within the ship from engineering into the deck force or vice versa. Add to this a few men who moved from one gun to another and it is clear that during most of the interwar years, *Tennessee* annually shifted nearly half the men in her gun crews.[10] That turnover rate posed a serious problem for maintaining the levels of speed, accuracy, and safety the navy expected.

The situation was not any better when it came to the ensigns and lieutenants junior grade who were in charge of the guns. No sooner were they experienced in their positions than they were transferred to another post. Upon occasion, such transfers required junior officers to step into roles for which they were not fully prepared. Lieutenant Sabin, who had been commanding turret number 1 when there was a flareback, reported aboard *Tennessee* in 1922 as an ensign assigned to be the junior gunnery officer of turret 1. No sooner had he moved in than his turret officer transferred out, leaving him in charge of a gun about which Sabin had only read. An intense training course by the division chief taught him enough to survive in that post. The navy understood the problem but believed frequent transfers were the only way to give a young officer the variety of experience necessary for him to grow.[11]

Commanding officers might complain, but their complaints had little impact. In 1928 *Tennessee*'s commander, Captain George Pettengill, tried to keep aboard some of the younger officers he had just trained. He selected six ensigns of the Class of 1927 to remain aboard, not because they were better than the others but because they had acquired specific skills the ship needed. Of the six he selected, two were in line to become turret officers, one was in training in range finding and plotting, one was a main battery spotter, a fifth was an aviation gunnery observer, and the sixth was the assistant radio officer, valuable in communicating with spotting aircraft.[12]

The chiefs and the veterans on the guns trained the new men, but there was not enough time to develop a high level of gunnery proficiency. Though a sailor might complain that there was constant drill, *Tennessee*'s schedule was in fact always cluttered and lacked the kind of gunnery practice that would allow the ship to reach her peak level of performance. To begin with, one quarter of her time was spent in maintenance and upkeep. In the 1920s, this meant entering the navy yard at

Bremerton, Washington, for up to three months of overhaul every year. By the 1930s, this was cut back to once every eighteen months, something that saved a little money and a great deal of time. But even when not dedicated to maintenance, men in the gun crews were responsible for sweeping and "holy stoning" the deck, removing rust, chipping off old paint and applying a new coat, and generally waging a battle against the impact of saltwater on exposed equipment. They could not devote their day to gunnery while other men made the ship look good.

The annual war games and fleet concentrations provided an excellent opportunity for Fleet maneuvers and tactical training but not gunnery practice. What most irritated commanders was the continuous visitations to various West Coast cities in order to help them celebrate some civic event. Though it could be a pleasant diversion, as when *Tennessee* was the guest of honor at Vancouver, British Columbia, just weeks after entering the Pacific, the cruise north and the time spent there did not improve gunnery performance. It took direct action by two former *Tennessee* captains to bring these visitations under control in the 1930s. Richard H. Leigh and Luke McNamee had risen to the rank of vice admiral and each in his turn as commander of the battleships in the Battle Force prohibited his ships from participating in local civic celebrations during periods allotted to gunnery tactics or upkeep.[13]

In spite of these obstacles, the men did practice. Again and again they went through the motions of loading and pointing their guns. Even in dry dock, 5-inch gun crews were known to practice their aim by training on paper cutouts of ships. Some people in the navy argued that pride in one's shipmates, ship, service, and country as well as the realization that a good practice in peacetime was the surest way to stay alive in wartime should be enough to moti-

vate the men. But the reality in the navy was that more material incentives were necessary to get the men to do their best. So the Navy Department awarded an "E" for excellence to each gun crew that scored high enough in competition. An "E" was painted on the gun, and each member of the gun crew wore an "E" on his uniform. The navy also paid a cash bonus as high as $10 per man.

Whether it was the money or pride that motivated the men of *Tennessee,* they did very well, winning a variety of awards throughout the 1920s and 1930s. Of course, things did not always go right — as in 1934, when *Tennessee* fired at the wrong target by mistake, discovered her error, corrected the fire, and earned a commendation anyway for shifting to and hitting the proper target with the limited ammunition that remained.[14] What is interesting is not that *Tennessee* earned her share or even more than her share of gunnery "E's" but rather her lack of consistency in performance. One turret might rate highest in the Fleet while another would rank near the lowest on any given practice. The disparity was particularly apparent on the 5-inch guns. In a short-range practice in 1940, *Tennessee*'s best 5-inch gun scored a perfect four hits for four shots in each of two sets, one fired in 17.1 seconds and one in 16.7. By contrast, *Tennessee*'s worst gun took 23.4 seconds to score three hits for four shots and in the second set reduced its time to 17.2 seconds but could only manage one hit. Another gun was 100 percent accurate but took an incredibly long 23.4 and 26 seconds to make those hits.[15] A failure of equipment could explain some of the disparity, but most of the effectiveness of gunnery rested with the training of the gun crews.

In 1938 the ship's newspaper carried an unusually large number of editorials urging the men to perform well. It would not be easy to match last year's performance, the

CAPTAIN'S INSPECTION PARTY

U.S.S. Tennessee 1924
Turret ONE - Lt. (j.g.) Sabin
SRBP 100% HITS
Pointers, Trainers, GUNNERS MATE
AND Turret J.O. (Ens. Stafford)

Left: The captain's primary responsibility was to maintain his ship at the highest possible level of battle efficiency. A secondary and time-consuming duty was to foster good relations with the public. Participation in civic events, opening the ship to the public, and giving civic leaders tours of the ship were important ways the navy sought to cultivate popular support. Here Captain Frank Brooks Upham escorts several civilians on an inspection of a few of the men aboard ship during the mid-1920s.

Above: When firing at a cloth sleeve pulled by a small ship, there was little doubt if you hit it. A 14-inch shell made a large hole. Here the key men in number 1 turret pose with the evidence of their 100 percent accuracy.[16]

gunnery officer commented in the *Tennessee Tar*. "We have had many shifts of personnel. It has been necessary to train new men. Some of them never have seen a big gun fired before. Many men, more experienced, have been shifted to the more important stations. They have had to learn to man their new posts." But lengthy drilling had convinced the gunnery officer that the ship could do well if the men did not let up.

> When we start down the range, let's have every man at his station, alert, surefooted, and true eyed. To the load crews we say, "Give us good loads. Make them sure and fast." To the pointers we say, "Split the bull with every pull of the trigger. Don't miss a buzzer."
>
> It's all over but the shootin' now. Our long period of training has ended. And we are ready for the race.
>
> When we make our run, we want four hits, one run, no errors.
>
> Give it to us boys!

And give it to them they did. A record fifteen guns earned an "E," including all four main turrets. But the lack of continuity that comes with shifting men could be seen in the fact that only seven guns that scored an "E" in 1938 had scored in 1937, while six guns that had scored in 1937 failed to score in 1938.[17] The key to battle efficiency lay with the men. Or as the old naval adage put it, "Men fight, not ships."

The most dramatic shift in the performance of *Tennessee*'s guns came with the advent of extreme long-range or indirect fire. When it was commissioned, the conventional wisdom was that *Tennessee* would engage the enemy at around 20,000 yards. In 1922 *Tennessee* fired a long-range practice in which spotters perched atop her cage mast accurately directed gunfire up to 25,000 yards. The next year *Tennessee* was the first U.S. battleship to engage in indirect fire where a spotter aircraft tracked the target at 38,000 yards and directed *Tennessee*'s fire beginning at

35,000 yards. She never saw her target. By 1927 repeated practices of indirect fire had proven its value. Though it would be better to be able to see the target from the ship, hazy weather would often mean targets as close as 18,000 yards would be obscured. So *Tennessee* regularly practiced firing at targets 18,000 to 20,000 yards away but out of sight. To make sure that all the spotting was coming from aircraft and not a particularly sharp-eyed spotter aboard ship, *Tennessee* fired over Santa Barbara Island at a completely obscured target. She proved she could do that in 1925; in 1926 she proved she could hit such a target even when her own speed and heading were changed in the midst of firing. By 1927 the procedure had developed to the point where several battleships could fire simultaneously and the chief of naval operations ordered that every battleship in the Fleet be involved in indirect-fire practice every year.[18]

Indirect fire required spotter aircraft, and there had been talk about installing aircraft aboard battleships even in 1917 and 1918 as *Tennessee* was being built. A few battleships already carried planes that would fly off platforms constructed on top of turrets. Their value was very limited, as these planes were not equipped for water landings and had to land ashore. The General Board held over fifty hearings from August 1918 to May 1919 on the issue of aircraft on battleships and, in spite of strong opposition from many officers, recommended in June 1919 that as many battleships and cruisers as could carry airplanes should be equipped as soon as possible with fighting, spotting, and short-distance reconnaissance planes. When *Tennessee* joined the Fleet the following June, her officers presumed she would be outfitted with two aircraft, but that did not happen for more than four years.[19]

The delay was partially the result of the time it took to develop a catapult that could

The catapult is aimed toward the side of the ship and a sled is fired forward. At the end of the catapult, the sled stops and the plane continues. This 1925 photograph shows a Vought VE-7 observation plane.[20]

In 1928, *Tennessee* had a second catapult installed on her number 3 turret. By the end of the 1920s, two catapults and three observation planes were standard for American battleships.[21]

launch the planes and partially because of staunch opposition by battleship officers who did not want catapults and planes cluttering their ships. Not until spring 1922 was a functioning catapult ready for installation. But it was 60 feet long and 4 feet wide and weighed 15 tons, so big that many officers believed it would get in the way of *Tennessee*'s primary purpose, which was to fire her guns. Willing to consider the value of spotter aircraft in long-range firing, these battleship men were annoyed by the efforts of the Bureau of Aeronautics to turn the battleships into aircraft carriers. Aviators made no secret of their intentions. They wanted to get as many aircraft with the Fleet as possible and if that meant putting them aboard battleships, so be it.

The aviators lost this battle, and in March 1922 the General Board ruled that the mission of aircraft aboard battleships was to help battleships do what they were designed to do: destroy the enemy with their big guns. Thus the first plane put aboard was to be a spotter. The second plane could be a combat plane designed to protect the spotter or shoot down an enemy spotter. No plans were made for placing attack aircraft such as torpedo planes aboard. Undaunted, the aviators responded that each battleship should have two pursuit planes, one spotting plane, and one torpedo plane. The aviators' refusal to take no for an answer did not convert the General Board, but it did persuade some "gun club" officers to delay authorizing installation of catapults and planes aboard battleships.

Though spotter aircraft eventually proved invaluable, there were many problems in getting the plane and the ship to work well with each other. Initially, the most irritating problem was the inability of planes and ships to communicate clearly by radio. The radios were so bad that more often than not a salvo from the main battery knocked out contact. When battleships of the Fleet gathered, there were insufficient radio frequencies to service the spotter aircraft — eleven aircraft spotting for eleven battleships had to share seven channels.[22] Moreover, with more than one battleship firing at the same time it was very difficult to tell which shells came from which ships. Gradually radio technology improved, and constant practice established a spotting doctrine that proved reasonably reliable.[23]

One problem that was never totally resolved was the limitations that rough weather and combat situations placed on launching and recovering aircraft. Both maneuvers were dangerous. The plane was held firmly to the catapult by a launching car. The catapult was rotated toward the wind and an explosive charge accelerated the car and plane from 0 to 50 miles per hour in less than 60 feet. At the end of the track, the car abruptly stopped and the plane was catapulted into the air where, more often than not, it flew. When it came time to land, *Tennessee* made a sharp turn, her massive size knocking down waves and making a smooth landing surface for the pontoon-equipped planes. As the ship slowed to a near stop, the plane taxied close to her where a boom lowered a line that the second man aboard attached to the plane. (By the 1930s, the aircraft taxied onto a sea sled where a hook on the pontoons would attach to the sled and drag the plane along permitting *Tennessee* to keep up a reasonable speed.) If everything went smoothly, touchdown to hoisting aboard could be accomplished in less than two minutes. But even such a brief pause would be very dangerous in wartime if an enemy submarine was present. At any time, the whole process of launching and recovering aircraft was very hazardous, and crashes were common.[24]

The benefits that came from spotter-directed indirect fire far outweighed the inconvenience and dangers associated with having aircraft aboard. In 1924 *Tennessee* had a catapult installed on the quarterdeck and two spotter aircraft assigned to the ship. In 1925 she successfully catapulted fifty planes, the second highest number in the Fleet. In 1928 *Tennessee* had a second catapult fixed atop the number 3 turret and carried a third spotter plane. Battleship purists may have cringed at the sight of catapult and aircraft atop a 14-inch gun turret, but aircraft aboard battleships had come to stay.[25] Only spotter aircraft were permitted, however. *Tennessee* never had a pursuit plane aboard. If one was needed to protect her spotters or to shoot down an enemy spotter, it would have to come from an aircraft carrier that would accompany the battleships.

From the perspective of launching and recovering aircraft in rough weather or when enemy submarines might be present, it made sense to have the spotter aircraft stationed aboard carriers rather than battleships. But the naval aviators aboard carriers wanted to attack enemy ships, not serve as an auxiliary arm to a battleship, and they were content to allow the battleship to do her own spotting. Similarly, commanders of battleships did not want to depend upon aviators outside their command for something as vital as spotting. Besides, if the gunnery officer aboard ship and the spotter in the air were to work well together, they needed to live and work together aboard the same ship. Only then would each truly understand the problems confronting the other.[26]

Indirect fire increased *Tennessee*'s effective gunnery range by nearly 50 percent. But that long-range firing uncovered a flaw in her 14-inch 50 caliber guns: The shells did not land where they were supposed to. Firing at the older long range of 20,000 yards, a three-gun salvo formed a tight pattern when it landed. But with fire undertaken at 30,000 yards, there was an erratic dispersion of shells that created patterns as great as 1,000 yards between shells. First discovered in 1926, it was of utmost concern to the navy. So great was the dispersion of shells that it would take two *Tennessee*s to have the same effective long-range fire as one of the newer *Colorado*-class battleships. Put another way, at the extreme long ranges, the combined fire of *Tennessee* and her sister ship *California* would be only as effective as *Tennessee*'s alone was once considered to have been. It took the navy seven years of examining every possible cause before ordnance specialists solved the problem by improving the equipment designed to prevent tilting that came from the trunnions, the cylinders that supported the turret when it turned. In 1934 performance in the extreme long-range firing was satisfactory.[27]

All this was of only marginal interest to the men who worked below in engineering. While the gun crews were engaged in practice for their annual gunnery competition, the electricians, water tenders, machinists, and firemen who tended the equipment of *Tennessee* were themselves in constant competition. The ship's efficiency was measured by performance during certain trials such as smokeless runs, but unlike the gun crews, who suffered no penalty if they made a mistake during practice, the engineering force was involved in competition all the time by a continuous monitoring of fuel-oil consumption and investigation of any material breakdowns or malfunctions of the engineering equipment.

How the efficiency rating worked can be seen in examining *Tennessee*'s engineering efficiency score for December 1935. That month she was under way 118.2 hours. Her electric motors produced a total of 495,556 revolutions of her propellers for an average speed of 8.9 knots over 1,052 engine miles steamed. The navy had allocated *Tennessee* 87,233 gallons of fuel, but she actually consumed 99,233 gallons, for an economy score of 87.907 (87,233 ÷ 99,233.) That month she spent 625.8 hours sitting at port and for this she was allowed 58,198 gallons and used 62,016 for an economy score of 93.844. If she had been able to conserve just 3 gallons an hour while sitting in port, she could have raised her efficiency rating from 93.8 to 96.8.[28]

This kind of incentive prompted a variety of energy-saving activities, some reasonable, some not. A good crew would coordinate its actions with the engineering staff to avoid wasting electric power: An anchor line might be snugged up before a second generator was turned off or a supply officer would tell the engineering officer that he would not be loading supplies that day so the electric-powered boom would not be in use and a second generator need not be activated. Desalinization of water required steam, and to conserve steam and thus fuel oil, each sailor was limited to one or two pails of fresh water daily for bathing and washing underwear. In times of close competition, the allotment could be cut in half. On *Tennessee*'s first shakedown cruise to Cuba in 1921, the engineering officer installed water meters throughout the ship to identify which group of men was using too much water. Of course, any unreported oil that could be brought aboard (called "gravy") made the efficiency figures look that much better. A good chief water tender supervising the oil being pumped aboard for his boilers might strike a deal, swapping anything from ice cream to pure grain alcohol for a little off-the-record oil.

While the ship was under way, great attention was paid to steaming at the most economical speed. That meant setting and maintaining a speed that would allow the most efficient use of the boilers. If five boilers were optimum for 13 knots and six boilers for 16 knots, either of those speeds would be efficient. But cruising at 14 or 15 knots would mean lighting the sixth boiler without fully using the steam it generated. Unfortunately, when in formation, the

Though San Francisco Bay is scenic (here *Tennessee* passes Alcatraz), it is also treacherous, earning the nickname "sands-can-shift-so." Entering the bay in June 1937, *Tennessee* found that a shrimp fishing boat had strung its nets illegally in the channel she normally took to her anchorage. Captain John T. G. Stapler, against the strong objections of his navigator, decided to stop the motors, glide over the nets, and make a hard right turn into the channel. But there was not enough room. When he realized his mistake, Stapler ordered the ship to back full, but it was too late. Quietly and gently *Tennessee* slid onto a sand bar. It took two days and several tugs to get her afloat. Captain Stapler, who had been in command only a few weeks, soon found himself overseeing the gunboats of the South China Patrol.[29]

speed was set by the flagship, which was usually a geared-turbine ship rather than an electric-drive ship such as *Tennessee*.[30]

Whatever speed was selected, good economy meant as few changes as possible. If *Tennessee* was supposed to cruise 500 yards behind the lead ship, the goal was to keep within 480 to 520 yards with as few changes in propeller revolutions as possible. Captain Frank Brooks Upham encouraged this by establishing a contest in the mid-1920s to see which watch officer could score the fewest number of changes in propeller revolutions. One young officer who had a close friend in engineering fed his friend distances to the lead ship every minute for fifteen minutes each hour. From these figures, the officer in engineering calculated the rate at which *Tennessee* was closing on or falling behind the ship and ordered adjustments in fractions of a revolution, say three-tenths of a revolution. Since it was less than a full revolution, it

was not counted on the revolution change counter on the bridge, and when Captain Upham came to the bridge at 8:00 A.M. and asked how many revolution changes the young officer had ordered, he was astonished to hear that there had been none.

But was that conservation? To hold her position, the ship had increased and decreased her speed in fractions of a revolution rather than a full revolution. Upon reflection, the young watch officer decided to tell the captain, who was impressed and thought it a good idea. However, when the young officer in engineering told the engineering officer, he labeled it plain cheating.[31]

It was just this issue of tricks of competition rather than efficiency that prompted many people in the navy to object to the engineering competition. In a drive to win the engineering competition, a captain might reduce heat and freshwater allotments aboard ship to a level that hurt morale and the ship's overall efficiency. In one

case, a commander of one ship (not *Tennessee*) turned off machinery that was essential to her safe operation. Though such excesses were apparent, most officers supported the competition as the only way to persuade commanders to run a tight ship. This was particularly true for preventing equipment from malfunctioning (a "casualty"). It was impossible to keep everything aboard running at 100 percent efficiency. Yet that is what the navy expected. Virtually every time something went wrong, the ship received a penalty that lowered her efficiency score.

To see what kinds of things went wrong and what penalties were assessed, consider the seven casualties *Tennessee* experienced from 1934 to 1937.

January 1934. A nut worked loose in an obscure corner of a piece of machinery that was not easily seen. The resulting temporary derangement could only have been avoided by the most minute inspection and was not due to any fault of personnel, said Captain

JUNIOR OFFICERS U.S.S. Tennessee — JUNE 3, 1922

Schaffer A.C. Cook "Willy" Schindler "Steve" Cooke Joe Rockwell "Bolder" Meyers "Stool" Roberts "Cliff" Kelsh "Tommy" Thompson "Slim" Flickem "Sol" Wise

"Sady" Sabin Hamilton Kate Power Frank Eggers "Chappie" Chappelle "Robb"? Rice Len Jacobi Downing Westfall C.J. Walker

_ JUNIOR OFFICERS _ JUNE 1922 _ U.S.S. TENNESSEE.

William W. Smyth. The commander of the battleships disagreed, saying that those nuts were known to work loose and a quicker reaction time by the attending crewman could have minimized the casualty.

January 1934. In a high-speed maneuver with the Fleet making a 40 degree turn, a defective fuse blew, resulting in the loss of the rudder angle indicators. Thinking he had lost steering, the helmsman shifted to engine-room steering. But there was a new master compass aboard that was being tested by the manufacturer, and it could not tolerate more than a 7.5 degree lag before causing the gyros to tumble. With the loss of the gyros, it was impossible to steer from the engine room. The commander of the battleships stated that with proper foresight, the officers aboard would have anticipated something such as this and prevented something such as this and preven-

tive actions could have been taken.

September 1934. While at sea, *Tennessee* was conducting listing control drills by transferring oil. While doing so, the ship heeled and some air got into one of the oil lines, disrupting the suction and causing the ship to slow down. Captain Milton Davis said it was a worthy experiment and that should mitigate any penalty. The commander of the battleships agreed it was a worthy experiment but said the casualty should have been prevented.

May 1935. A 30-gallon bubble of water sitting in the middle of a bunker of oil pumped aboard ship went undetected until it was sucked into a boiler causing smoke. Not our fault, said Captain Milton Davis. Yes, it is, said the commander of the battleships.

May 1935. The helmsman misinterpreted an order and transferred the steer-

ing from the bridge to the trick wheel rather than to the conning tower. The trick wheel was in a hard-over position and when connection was made, it tried to turn the rudder over and shorted out the motor, causing *Tennessee* to sheer out of formation. No excuse, said Davis. Penalty assessed, said the commander of the battleships.

June 1935. Steering control was lost for one minute because of improper adjustment of the contact screws. This casualty was directly attributable to personnel error.

July 1935. A tube in the boiler that was installed ten years earlier wore out and sputtered fuel, causing smoke. No signs of wear were apparent on the tube from outside. Though no fault was attached to the ship's personnel, the commander of the battleships assessed a penalty anyway.

November 1937. While testing a new oil-ratio sprayer that was believed to be more

Left: For junior officers fresh out of the naval academy, life aboard *Tennessee* was a combination of pressure to perform well and an enjoyable life among good friends at the start of a career.

Right: The men aboard ship were expected to make repairs on broken equipment and replace parts that were wearing out before they caused a casualty. When a section of pipe from an oil-cooler saltwater line was removed and needed brazing, it was taken to this blacksmith's shop. But at 4:00 on a Friday afternoon, the shop had closed. That would not have been a problem except that no one replaced the pipe or passed the word that the pipe was gone. On Saturday someone opened a valve, and the electric-motor room was flooded with saltwater, seriously damaging one motor.[32]

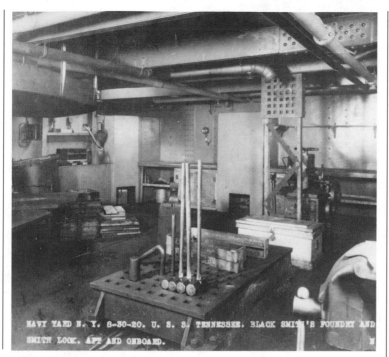

NAVY YARD N. Y. 8-30-20. U. S. S. TENNESSEE. BLACK SMITH'S FOUNDRY AND SMITH LOOK. AFT AND ONBOARD.

economical, *Tennessee* was called upon to suddenly increase speed. The sprayer failed and she made smoke for several hours. Captain E. A. Wolleson urged a smaller penalty, since it was the result of a worthwhile experiment. The penalty was not reduced.[33]

It was the navy's policy in these cases to lower a ship's efficiency rating from .1 to .3, on the rationale that only a penalty would force the officers and men to pay stricter attention to the details that would enable a ship to achieve the highest possible level of efficiency. As with the gun crews, if the engineering force performed well, they received the "E" recognition — this time a red "E" painted on the ship's funnel and an "E" worn on the uniform. Of course, there was also the cash award to the men responsible for the "E." When *Tennessee* won an engineering "E" for 1940–41, 365 petty officers and enlisted men received awards of $10 each, a hefty amount for a young sailor earning only $36 a month.[34]

Beyond the problem of competition and

casualties, the engineering force confronted the endless battle of periodic repair and installation of new equipment. But usually there was not enough money to repair everything that needed to be repaired and install the new equipment that needed to be installed — in part because of a statutory limit of $300,000 per ship per year in repairs and improvements. Most of that money could be chewed up in the normal overhaul required aboard a ship with so many moving parts. Furthermore, putting something new aboard was not simple.

In 1928 *Tennessee* sought an additional 5-inch 25-caliber antiaircraft gun. The gun without the ammunition hoist to supply it was useless, and the 5/25 ammunition would not fit on the existing 5/51 ammunition hoists. But the navy did not have enough money to install the gun and the hoist. In addition, George Pettengill, *Tennessee*'s commander, wanted a new battle phone system. As *Tennessee* prepared to enter Bremerton for her overhaul, a struggle developed over what work would

be done and who would do it. The Bureau of Construction and Repair wanted Pettengill to use his own crewmen to put in the phone system rather than employing expensive private contractors. Pettengill claimed he lacked sufficient skilled electricians to do both that job and complete normal electrical maintenance. He knew full well that items not repaired during overhaul caused casualties later and would cost him points in his pursuit of an engineering "E" and the battle efficiency award. With the Bureau of Construction and Repair and Pettengill each refusing to do the work, a compromise was reached that left some things undone. The bureau would install the new 5/25 gun, and the *Tennessee*'s crew would rig some kind of system by which ammunition could be transferred to the gun. The crew would make various repairs to the electrical system aboard ship, and the new phone system would be postponed to some unspecified time. In the following year's overhaul, The bureau would install the permanent ammunition hoist. It was not an ideal solution, but it was the kind that all sides could live with and was typical of a navy that had too little money to keep its first-line ships in top condition.[35]

Whatever was or was not done during overhaul, only by the greatest attention to the smallest details could a ship achieve the level of battle efficiency the navy demanded of her. And only by a public competition was it possible to motivate officers and men alike to pay attention to the details. Those who scored well were honored and paid for their diligence. Those who fell short were held up to the ridicule of the better ships in the Fleet. Because the failure of one man to perform flawlessly meant the loss of points for the group, the system created much peer pressure for each man to do his part. Ultimately it was the men, not the ship, who were responsible for *Tennessee*'s battle efficiency.

CHAPTER FOUR

LIFE ABOARD A PEACETIME BATTLE-SHIP

A thousand or more men tended the machinery

designed to make *Tennessee* a superior weapon of war. They lived in cramped quarters, had little privacy, and were subjected to the strictest regimentation. Officers told them when to work, when to play, when to bathe, when to do their laundry. But it was not enough if the sailor obeyed all the regulations that governed his life. Every shipmate was part of a community, and the officers and enlisted men who made up that community expected him to be a good citizen, to enjoy his life aboard, to love his new home, to be proud of *Tennessee*. There was no room for the obedient sailor who remained an individualist — he had to become part of the *Tennessee* team.

The men in this community had several things in common. Most of them were young, virtually all were white in a navy that did not recruit blacks, few had any idea about life aboard a battleship before they joined the navy, and as often as not they were aboard *Tennessee* less by choice than by capricious assignment. This was invariably the case for the new recruits who

The crew of the captain's gig in 1925 pose for a photograph showing the brass work aboard their boat. To many sailors, the nice thing about having boat duty was that it meant more opportunities to get away from the ship and be on their own.[1]

might comprise a draft of two, four, or six dozen men fresh out of boot camp, unless they were held aboard a receiving ship for a few weeks to make sure they did not carry any communicable diseases. When *Tennessee* needed men, someone in the Bureau of Navigation authorized a draft from the training camp at Hampton Roads, Newport, Great Lakes, or San Diego, where someone else picked names off a list and ordered them shipped to San Pedro, California. That is how three dozen men whose names began with "B" arrived on the same day in the mid-1930s.

Once aboard, they might be given the opportunity to volunteer for the deck crew or the engineering force, but unless they had a particular skill, the new men were put where they were needed as arbitrarily as they were selected for service aboard the ship in the first place. A petty officer led the men through a maze of ladders, hatches, and passageways to the compartment that housed their newly assigned division. Each division was responsible for a particular task, such as manning one of the main batteries, tending to the boilers, or making electrical repairs. These men who worked together also lived and ate together. For the new sailor aboard ship, life revolved around his division.

Unlike sailors on older battleships, each man aboard *Tennessee* had the luxury of a private locker large enough to hold all the clothing that the navy had issued him: hats, jumpers, trousers, dungarees, underwear, shoes, socks, leggings, overcoat, and so on. There was also room for a few personal items such as a hairbrush, scrub brush, whisk broom, towel, and personal hygiene supplies. There was no room in the locker for civilian clothes aboard and though some men kept civilian clothes ashore either in a locker or at a friend's apartment, the navy disapproved of any practice that encouraged men to think of themselves as something other than part of a team.[2]

In addition to a locker, the petty officer assigned each man a place to hang his hammock. The hammock aroused strong feelings among sailors. Some liked the way it let them rest comfortably even in rough weather while men in bunks or cots were tossed back and forth. And there were those who liked the space left in the compartment once the hammocks were taken down and stowed. But most men viewed the hammock as something to be avoided. Some hated it so much that they sought to transfer off *Tennessee* to a smaller ship that was equipped with bunks. Others looked forward to the day when they worked themselves up to a petty officer's rating so they could have a cot instead of a hammock (even though the cot had to be folded up every morning and reassembled every night). With hammocks and cots stowed every morning, there was no place to lie down during leisure time after a meal. And if a sailor, exhausted from the day's labors and perhaps too late a liberty the night before, wanted to turn in early, he could not do so because hammocks were not to be hung until the order was given at 7:30 P.M. To do so earlier was a breach of regulations that could earn the violator a deck court-martial with subsequent extra cleaning duties or even loss of liberty.

For the sailor resting comfortably in his hammock on a Saturday night, there was the problem of shipmates returning from liberty. Each hammock was identical except for the owner's name carefully stenciled on it. But in a dimly lit compartment and after several hours of partying, finding one's own hammock could prove to be difficult and the sailor who took the first hammock he found simply created more turmoil among his shipmates who came aboard later.

The navy brass were aware of these problems and experimented in the 1920s with installing bunks aboard *Oklahoma* and *California, Tennessee*'s sister ship. Morale aboard those ships increased so dramati-

cally that the commander of the Fleet's battleships recommended that bunks be put aboard other battleships as well. But skeptics worried that bunks crowded compartments and cut down ventilation. Their opposition and a lack of funds meant *Tennessee* did not convert to bunks until World War II.[3]

In defense of those who feared that bunks would cut down on the flow of air through the ship, ventilation was a constant problem. The fans usually pumped sufficient amounts of fresh air to most parts of the ship, and there were several dozen portholes that could be opened. When ready for battle, however, the air induction vents were closed lest an enemy bombard *Tennessee* with poison gas that the fans would spread through the ship. And in rough weather, when hatches and portholes were closed and men were forced to stay below deck, the ventilation system could not handle the load, and the air became so thick you could see it, a condition that was not helped by men who became seasick. In cold weather, there was a steam heating system that worked well to warm the air; however, it dried out the air so fast that it caused discomfort among the crew. On those cold, foggy mornings when the ventilation fans had blown damp air into the compartments, a couple of hours of dry heat were welcome. Whether the men got that heat depended on the captain. If he was more interested in winning the engineering or battle efficiency competition than in the comfort of his crew, he would forego heating the air in order to conserve oil. In a close competition, the oil used to heat the ship could mean the difference between winning and losing.[4]

A close engineering competition could affect the men's bathing habits as well. Oil was used to make the steam that was condensed to make fresh water for the boilers, laundry, galley, and washrooms. The less water used to bathe, the less oil burned. Even in the best of times, the bathing facili-

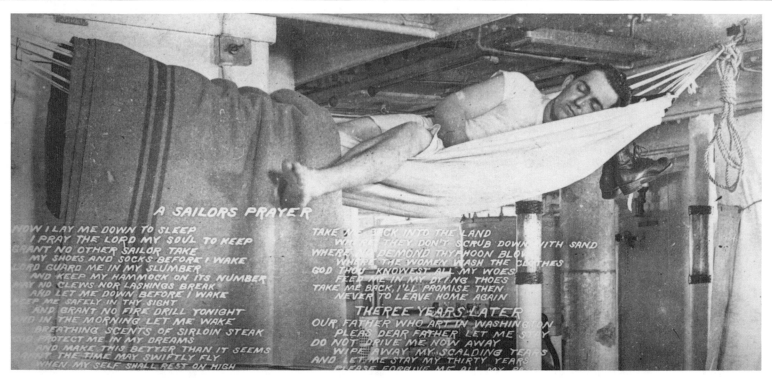

A SAILORS PRAYER

NOW I LAY ME DOWN TO SLEEP
I PRAY THE LORD MY SOUL TO KEEP
GRANT NO OTHER SAILOR TAKE
MY SHOES AND SOCKS BEFORE I WAKE
LORD GUARD ME IN MY SLUMBER
AND KEEP MY HAMMOCK ON ITS NUMBER
MAY NO CLEWS NOR LASHINGS BREAK
AND LET ME DOWN BEFORE I WAKE
KEEP ME SAFELY IN THY SIGHT
AND GRANT NO FIRE DRILL TONIGHT
AND IN THE MORNING LET ME WAKE
BREATHING SCENTS OF SIRLOIN STEAK
PROTECT ME IN MY DREAMS
AND MAKE THIS BETTER THAN IT SEEMS
GRANT THE TIME MAY SWIFTLY FLY
WHEN MY SELF SHALL REST ON HIGH

TAKE ME BACK INTO THE LAND
WHERE THEY DON'T SCRUB DOWN WITH SAND
WHERE NO DEMOND TYPHOON BLOW
WHERE THE WOMEN WASH THE CLOTHES
GOD THOU KNOWEST ALL MY WOES
FEED ME IN MY DYING THOES
TAKE ME BACK, I'LL PROMISE THEN
NEVER TO LEAVE HOME AGAIN

THEREE YEARS LATER
OUR FATHER WHO ART IN WASHINGTON
PLEAS DEAR FATHER LET ME STAY
DO NOT DRIVE ME NOW AWAY
WIPE AWAY MY SCALDING TEARS
AND LET ME STAY MY THIRTY YEARS
PLEASE FORGIVE ME ALL MY PAST

This photograph from the early 1920s showing a sailor asleep in his hammock provides a glimpse of a sailor's bedding, clothes, and shoes as well as the mess tables stowed directly above and behind his head. The accompanying "Sailors Prayer" reflects the usual gripes of a battleship sailor:

Now I lay me down to sleep
    I pray the Lord my soul to keep
Grant no other sailor take
    My shoes and socks before I wake
Lord guard me in my slumber
    And keep my hammock on its number
May no clews nor lashings break
    And let me down before I wake
Keep me safely in thy sight
    And grant no fire drill tonight
And in the morning let me wake
    Breathing scents of sirloin steak
God protect me in my dreams
    And make this better than it seems
Grant the time may swiftly fly

When my self shall rest on high
In a snowy feather bed
    There I long to rest my head
Fly away from all these scenes
    From the smell of half done beans
Take me back into the land
    Where they don't scrub down with sand
Where no demon typhoon blows
    Where the women wash the clothes
God thou knowest all my woes
    Feed me in my dying throes
Take me back, I'll promise then
    Never to leave home again.

THREE YEARS LATER
Our Father who art in Washington
    Please dear Father let me stay
Do not drive me now away
    Wipe away my scalding tears
And let me stay my thirty years
    Please forgive me all my past
And things that happened at the Mast
    Do not my request refuse
Let me stay another cruise.[5]

ties and procedures aboard *Tennessee* shocked many a new recruit. In the morning between breakfast and mustering the crew or in the evening after work or after dinner, the men had the opportunity to bathe. That meant being issued a bucket and going to the washroom, where each sailor filled his bucket with fresh water and heated it at a steam outlet. With practice he would be able to wet himself, soap up, rinse down, brush his teeth, and, finally, wash his underwear with only that allotment. All of it took time, and it was not unusual to see men lined up, waiting for access to the washroom or, just as likely, waiting for a shipmate in his division to finish with a bucket so he could use it. The situation became even worse if the captain sought to conserve oil and cut the freshwater ration to a half bucket twice a day. Cold, saltwater showers were, of course, always available.[6]

If the bathing facilities were inadequate, the toilet facilities were primitive. There were no modern toilets, only 54-foot-long troughs. One served as a urinal; another was very much an indoor privy — just a board with holes cut in it. A current of seawater carried the excrement into the ocean or the bay, as the case might be. That same current also carried crudely built toilet-paper rafts set afire by practical jokers and allowed to drift beneath the unsuspecting sailor sitting downstream. After his first visit to the facilities, one horrified recruit swore he would never again answer a "call of nature" aboard ship during his four-year enlistment. Almost as annoying was that these facilities were located in the bow (hence their being called the "head"); thus men living or working at the stern had to walk the length of the ship to relieve themselves, something that was impossible if the ship was in a battle-ready condition with watertight hatches closed. Even during routine times, the trip to the head took men away from their work details for an annoyingly long time — annoying to their officers, that is.[7]

Chief petty and commissioned officers, of course, lived better than the enlisted men. Chief petty officers had their own quarters, a spacious compartment designed to hold about 150 chiefs, but *Tennessee* had less than half that number during peacetime. Junior officers (ensigns and lieutenants junior grade) received accommodations according to their seniority. There was one stateroom for two officers, seven staterooms that held three officers each, and a large bunk room that could accommodate as many as twenty officers. All shared a common junior officers' mess. The heads of navigation, gunnery, engineering, and medicine, who were lieutenant commanders or commanders, shared a cabin and ate in the officers' mess, which included the lieutenants, each of whom enjoyed a stateroom. The captain had his own stateroom; the executive officer his own cabin. All of these officers enjoyed freshwater showers, bunks, and meals prepared specially for them and served by Filipino mess attendants. Part of the officers' pay was intended for their rations, and how well they ate depended on how much they agreed to contribute to their commissary fund, which was supervised by an officer acting as treasurer.

By all accounts, the enlisted men ate well if not as well as the officers. During the 1920s, fresh vegetables were frequently in short supply, something that was always a problem on longer cruises. But a change in naval policy meant more fresh produce by the 1930s, and the food that was prepared was generally good and ample. When *Tennessee* loaded supplies, she took aboard beef, pork, and chicken by the hundreds of pounds, potatoes by the ton, and large amounts of fresh vegetables, including an amazing number of cucumbers.[8]

The men ate in their compartments at tables seating ten, which they set up in the space available once the hammocks were taken down. No Filipino mess attendants

Item	Price	Item	Price	Item	Price
Book, memo	.20	Garter paris	.25	223	.65
BLADES Razor		Ham deviled	.05	800	.65
Gillette 6	.35	Ink writing Libbys	.15	Shaving stick colg.	.25
Gillette 12	.65	Jams asstd	.10	Shoe polish black	.07
Vic	.25	Laces shoe black	.05	Shoe polish tan	.07
Everready	.35	Laces shoe white	.05	Shoe shining outfit	.35
Durham Duplex	.35	Lead pencils	.15	Soap boxes Ivory	.20
Blanco Kaki	.15	Matches	.06	Soap hand paste	.10
Bon Ami	.10	Milk Evp.	.05	Soap Ivory	.07
Brushes, nail	.20	Oil 3in1	.25	Soap fairy	.07
CAKES		Papers cig. white	.05	Soap palmolive	.07
Fautasies	.35	Papers cig. brown	.08	Soap Coleo	.07
March Mellow Sand	.10	PAPER WRITING		Soap Life buoy	.07
Sugar wafers	.10	Highland line	.30	Soap lava	.07
Graham squares	.10	Highland small emb.	.40	Soap P&G	.07
Chesse wafers	.10	Highland large emb.	.50	Soap P&S	.10
Valley creams	.10	Peanut butter	.15	Soap Woodbury	.20
Bauquet	.30	Peanuts salted	.15	Soap cuticra	.20
Candy hard	.20	Peanuts large	.25	Soap powder lux	.10
CANDY MRS. SAYLORS		Peaches Td	.15	Sponges bath	.20
1 Lbs. Boxes	.65	Pineapple	.15	Stroppers twinplex	3.30
1/2 Lbs. Boxes	.35	Pen holds	.03	Strops auto strop	.35
candy bars asstd.	.05	Pens fountain US	1.00	Strops army & navy	.75
Cards greeting	.10	Pencils lead	.025	Tablets	.10
Cards pinachle	.35	Pencils art point	.75	Tablets large	.15 & .20
Cards playing	.35	Padlocks yale	1.00	Edgeworth	1.50
CIGGARETTS		Padlocks Comb.	.85	Prince Albert	.15
Piedmont BR. AM.	.08	Pipes Briar no. 10	.65	Bull Durham	.08
Piedmonts L&M	.13	Pipes Wellington	.50	Lucky Strike	.15
Fatima	.10	Pipes corn cob	.05	Mailpouch	.08
Chesterfields	.13	Plums	.15	B&B Chewing	.75
Camels	.13	Pork & Beans	.05	Star chewing	.75
Lucky Strike	.13	Powder talcum	.15	Tooth brushes	.30
Cigars		Raisins sun maid	.05	Tooth brush holder	.30
Lonodras	.10	Razors		Tooth paste Pebeco	.35
Pefectos	.10	Gillette New style	3.10	Tooth paste pepsodent	.35
Nashionals	.15	Gillette Old Style	.75	Tooth paste Farhams	.25
Rio Tan	.10	Auto strap	3.10	Tooth paste colgate	.20
Robert Burns	.12	Durham Duplex	.60	Tooth powder	.20
Polish silver	.20	Gem & Everready	.65	Witch hazel	.15
Envelopes	.10	Shaving Brushes			
Garter EZ	.35	102 & 103	1.00		

here — the men were served by "mess cooks," regular sailors in the division who did no cooking but spent three months waiting on tables. Even as the bugler sounded reveille at 5:00 A.M., the fifty or so mess cooks aboard were in the galley filling their large, brass coffeepots. They lugged these down ladders and through passageways to the compartment where their ship-

mates were sitting half asleep on top of lockers. They hung the pot on a large hook and the men helped themselves. Once the hammocks had been stowed, tables and benches were taken down from their overhead stowage areas and set up. The mess cook and his striker (an assistant) walked to the scullery for the knives, forks, spoons, plates, and bowls necessary for the meal.

-:M-E-N-U:-

Cream of Tomato Soup
Salted Petites
Celery en Branch　　　　Sweet Pickles
Roast Young Tom Turkey
Cranberry Sauce　　　　Giblet Dressing
Baked Virginia Ham　　　　Green Peas
Mashed Potatoes　　　　Brown Gravy
Combination Salad　　Thousand Island Dressing
Silver Cake　　　　Pumpkin Pie
Fruits in Season　　　　Ice Cream
Cigars　　　　Cigarettes
Black Coffee

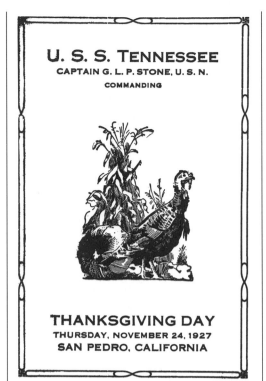

U. S. S. TENNESSEE
CAPTAIN G. L. P. STONE, U. S. N.
COMMANDING

THANKSGIVING DAY
THURSDAY, NOVEMBER 24, 1927
SAN PEDRO, CALIFORNIA

Left: The price list from *Tennessee*'s store in 1923 provides insight into a sailor's life. Though the list does not tell how popular each item was, it reveals some details about life aboard ship. Some men shaved with straight razors, while others used the new safety razors. Tobacco use was common, with some men smoking cigarettes, some cigars, some pipes, and some rolling their own; several chewed tobacco. That the ship carried ten different brands of soap indicates that how one washed in a bucket of water was a very personal thing. All items have been retyped here as originally spelled.

Above: On holidays, special meals were planned complete with souvenir menus like this one on Thanksgiving Day, 1927. Sailors were encouraged to send home such menus as well as copies of the ship's newspaper. [9]

By 7:15, they were carrying breakfast from the galley to the compartment. When the meal was over, the men washed their utensils in soapy water, and the mess cook returned them to the scullery for steam cleaning.

Three times a day, seven days a week, for three months, the mess cook followed this routine. For his extra effort and to compensate him for the uniforms he was bound to ruin, he was paid $2 a month in addition to his regular pay, which was usually $36 or $54 a month. How soon you got your food and whether you could get seconds on choice items depended on how hard the mess cook worked, so it was important to select a good man and keep him happy. The respect of his shipmates was important, but cash was appreciated even more; thus every payday the men tipped the hard-working mess cook.

So many men carrying coffee, dishes, and tureens of food through passageways meant spillage and breakage. But it could not be helped. What could be avoided was the policy of carrying buckets of soapy water from the scullery to the mess tables where the men would wash their own utensils. All *Tennessee* needed was a dishwasher.

The opening salvo in the battle of the dishwasher came in 1925 when the commander in chief of the Battle Fleet questioned the wisdom of having men wash their dishes by hand throughout the ship when the installation of a dishwasher such as those used ashore could obviate the practice. Aboard *Tennessee,* Captain G. L. P. Stone was particularly incensed by the situation. It was wasteful of fresh water and cleaning material and much more so in labor and time. He wrote the Bureau of Construction and Repair that "the washing of the dishes in water which is unclean is not, in any sense, satisfactory in the interest of the contentment, efficiency and health of this command." Lest the bureau ignore his request for a dishwasher, Stone added, "It is requested that the receipt of this letter be acknowledged, that the Commanding Officer be advised of the action the Bureau will take, that the machine be furnished at the earliest practicable moment, and, finally, that it be treated as an urgent matter."

Stone's request was endorsed by his superiors, including Richard H. Leigh, *Tennessee*'s first commander, who was now chief of staff to the commander in chief of the Battle Fleet. But Stone's fury and the sympathetic endorsement of his superiors did not move the Bureau of Construction and Repair. A dishwasher was a good idea, the bureau replied. In fact, originally *Tennessee* had been provided with a dishwasher, but it was removed during construction (presumably to make room for something else). As soon as money came available, the bureau assured Stone, it would authorize the installation. Since it would cost about $10,000 to purchase and install an appropriate washer, the money would probably never be available.

It was a matter of priorities. The navy had $10,000 to spend on increased sanitation and crew comfort if it chose to do so. But *Tennessee* was also seeking a hydraulic gasoline stowage system, and the bureau chief asked the commander of the Battle Fleet if he intended to make installation of the dishwasher a higher priority than the gasoline stowage system. She was, after all, a warship, not a cruise ship, and in the choice between more efficient gasoline stowage to fuel the airplanes coming aboard *Tennessee* at that time or a more sanitary method of washing dishes, the former won. Stone made another request in 1927, but this time it did not get past the commander of the Battle Fleet. Again in 1932 and 1933, the captain of *Tennessee* made requests. However, though policy was to install a dishwasher, the money was not forthcoming.[10]

Washing dishes was just one more duty in a navy apparently obsessed with cleanliness. Sweeping, scrubbing, polishing, and washing took up a good amount of a sailor's day. After the morning coffee and before breakfast, the men swept down their compartments, wiped all ladders, polished the bright work, and, on some days, washed their clothes, hammocks, or bedding. At least once a week they would carry their bedding on deck for airing. There was also the weekly task of carrying the tables and benches from each compartment to the deck where they were scoured with sand and canvas. Breakfast was served at 7:15, after which they had an hour to relax or clean up before being mustered for inspection. The rest of the morning was spent in drills or in doing repairs and maintenance on the ship.

The men finished their morning drill and work at 11:45, at which time they broke for lunch and a little relaxation. From 1:00 to 4:30 there were more drills or maintenance work, after which they turned their attention to light duties about the ship. Dinner was at 6:00, followed by free time. After the sweepers had again swept down all the compartments, hammocks could be hung at 7:30. First call sounded at 8:55, and the smoking lamp was put out. At 9:00, all hands turned in and kept quiet. At 9:05 the bugler played taps and the men were in

their hammocks, not to get out except for urgent calls of nature.

In a typical day at sea, the men spent 8 hours sleeping, six hours eating and relaxing, six hours in drills and repair work, and about four hours cleaning the ship and themselves. Though this was no more demanding than what a civilian would put into a job and work around his home, the difference was that the *Tennessee* sailor had little choice of what he would do and when he would do it. He ate when the navy told him to eat or he did not eat at all. He could not stay up late and read if he wanted to. He had to do laundry as often as the navy said he should, and he swept, scrubbed, polished, and mopped when and where his officers told him.

Except for cruises, *Tennessee* worked a five-day week, rarely staying out more than Monday through Friday and frequently remaining in port and heading out only for day maneuvers. Friday afternoon the captain inspected below decks, and Saturday morning he reviewed the deck crews. After that there was liberty.[11]

Sunday was a quiet day aboard ship. The married men were ashore with their families, and many single men had liberty. With no drills scheduled, the men had time to relax and play cards, joke, or tend to personal business, at least until the church pennant was raised. Six feet by two feet of dark blue with a white Latin cross on it, the pennant was positioned just above the American flag — testimony to the navy's recognition that though there is no state religion, God is higher than the state. When the pennant went up at 10:00 A.M. each Sunday, horseplay, noisemaking, card playing, and smoking stopped. The men aboard ship did not have to attend what the navy called "divine services," though they were encouraged to do so. If they desired, they could bring family and friends aboard for the services and then have them stay for lunch.

For most men, life aboard *Tennessee* revolved around their division. Men who ate, worked, and lived with the members of their division had little reason to mix with men from other divisions. This was particularly true of the marine detachment aboard ship, seen here at inspection during the late 1920s.[12]

By the 1930s, chaplains in the Fleet had coordinated their efforts and established 10:00 as the church hour throughout the Fleet. Thus when the chaplain aboard *Tennessee* was Catholic, the Protestants aboard could travel to another ship for services and vice versa. No provision seems to have been made for Jews, though occasionally national Jewish leaders persuaded the Navy Department to encourage ship commanders to facilitate leave for their Jewish crew members during Passover.

Sometimes a chaplain would lead his flock to shore where they would attend a prominent local church. Though this might have been a welcome change for the men, the apparent motive of these chaplains was to put "the personnel of the navy in a very favorable light in the estimation of the public" in general and in the minds of prominent civic officials in particular. Such public relations through religion reached its peak in June 1934, when the Fleet visited New York and the chief of chaplains organized a Fleet Sunday service. St. Patrick's and St. John the Divine cathedrals were selected, and more than three months of planning and publicity within the Fleet went toward assuring a turnout of two to three thousand men at each church. At St. John's, *Tennessee* supplied six officers and 223 enlisted men, more than any other battleship. Catholic attendance at St. Patrick's was less impressive, however, with only two officers and seventy-eight enlisted men. Though the chief of chaplains complained that *Tennessee* "had fallen down in the Catholic church party," the 309 officers and men who attended one service or the other made up nearly one-third of the ship's crew.[13]

The chaplains believed divine services would help foster a unified and contented crew — shipmates who prayed together stayed together. *Tennessee*'s officers, on the other hand, worked to establish the same

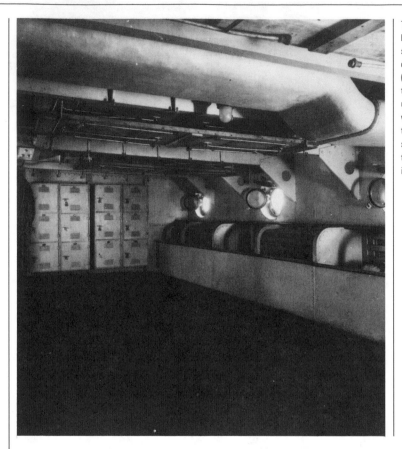

The floor was dark-red linoleum, but everything else was battleship gray. With the hammocks down and stowed in the "nitting" (which was now a chest rather than the webbing used initially) underneath the port holes, there was ample room for setting up the tables and benches seen stowed overhead here. Everything a sailor possessed had to fit into the locker assigned to him.[14]

sense of unity and contentment by providing recreational activities aboard ship — shipmates who played together stayed together. Though liberty was highly prized and frequently given, the goal was to create a ship so comfortable that a man with a three-hour liberty on a weeknight would prefer to remain aboard ship rather than rush to get away from her. After dinner and before the hammocks were hung, men might take a cup of coffee on deck to talk or listen to the band concert that was held almost every evening. Movies were almost always available. Some men preferred to remain in their compartment, playing cards or listening to the centralized radio system installed in 1936. Though the lighting below decks was generally poor (she had to burn oil to make the steam to generate the electricity, and the more oil she

burned, the less likely she would be to win the engineering efficiency competition), reading was a popular pastime.

From the day she was put into service, *Tennessee* had a good library. As the education level of the crew increased during the 1930s, men increasingly stopped by the library to pick up a book, usually a mystery. During several weeks in 1938, the library loaned out 2,000 mysteries, two hundred Book-of-the-Month Club selections, and one classic. Such usage, as well as adding two hundred books or more a year and keeping them until they had worn out, required more space; so in 1939 the library was remodeled with steel shelves and a new passageway entrance. At the same time, the library set out to increase its stock of technical books, apparently in the hope that it would improve the skills of the crew.[15]

In San Pedro, there was usually a dance on Saturday nights for which one of the battleships would supply the band. Occasionally, *Tennessee* sponsored her own dance, usually ashore but by the late 1930s aboard ship. When *Tennessee* traveled to Bremerton for her three-month overhaul and the men were far away from their usual haunts, the Navy Mothers Association brought dozens of young women of the right character to ship dances. But if attendance is any indication of popularity, the men of *Tennessee* enjoyed the "smokers" more than anything else. A ring was set up, the ship's band played, cigarettes were liberally distributed, and boxing matches in a variety of weight classes took place between the best from *Tennessee* and another battleship.

All of these diversions were essential to the maintenance of morale, but the Navy Department did little to support them. Most of the money for these events came from the ship's service fund. This was money that comprised the profits from the photo shop, tailor and pressing shop, cobbler shop, barber shop, laundry, and soda fountain or "gedunk" stand, where the men could get ice cream, sandwiches, and soft drinks. The $15,000 a year these enterprises generated paid for dance decorations, cigarettes at the smokers, motion picture projection equipment (the Navy Department supplied the films), new books in the library, sheet music for the band, paper for the weekly ship newspaper, the *Tennessee Tar,* even extra polish for cleaning bright work aboard ship. The centralized radio system came out of the ship's service fund as did various athletic trophies awarded to members of the crew. The ship's service fund also paid for the equipment and uniforms for athletic teams.[17]

It is hard to overestimate the importance of athletic competition to the men and officers of *Tennessee* and the other ships in the Fleet. The avowed purpose of athletic competition was to encourage as many enlisted men as possible to exercise, stimulate ship loyalty, and provide a pleasurable diversion from the routine of shipboard life. However, friendly athletic competition could get out of hand. In 1924, critics complained that in order to win, the best athletes aboard ship were given light duties so they could train. Battleships left their number one team ashore when the ship put out to sea in order not to interfere with its practice. It was not unknown to try to induce a good athlete to transfer ships in order to build a strong team. Professionalism in Fleet athletics, especially boxing, became a serious problem by the early 1930s, and sailors who were also professional boxers were barred from ship competition.

Another major problem was the time consumed in the athletic competitions. By the mid-1920s, a typical year involved *Tennessee* in eleven boat races, thirty-two track meets, four sailing races, three boxing meets, three wrestling meets, twenty-two baseball games, three football games, eleven basketball games, three swimming meets, one rifle meet, and three tug-of-war meets. If *Tennessee* achieved a divisional championship, she had to participate in a couple more events in that category. So time consuming were all these contests and the practice required to prepare for them that when the Fleet cruised to Australia in 1925, all hands looked upon it as an escape from the rigors of athletics. Unfortunately it did not work out that way, since the Australians assumed there would be some athletic events. *Tennessee* had to quickly put together a football team. By the 1930s, commanders regularly worried about the time spent on athletics; in 1934 the commander in chief of the Battleship Force curtailed

Athletic competition served the dual purpose of raising morale and providing good exercise for the men. These photographs of shipmates cheering on their team and of the pulling crew give testimony of how athletics could achieve both goals.[18]

athletic events in order to find enough time for gunnery practice.[19]

Concern over too much emphasis on athletics was not shared aboard *Tennessee* in 1934, a year she won the iron man trophy. Gunners coveted a gunnery "E" for excellence, engineers an engineering "E," and everyone a battle efficiency "E." But the iron man was something special. It went to the Fleet battleship that had the best percentage of victories in all the sports under competition. In 1934 those were baseball, basketball, boxing, wrestling, sailing, boat racing, swimming, rifle, pistol, officers' tennis, officers' pistol, and golf. After *Tennessee* won the iron man trophy, its likeness appeared on the masthead of the *Tar* for the next year. And when she lost it, a solemn procession including mourners carried it to the victor. *Tennessee* won the iron man three times in the 1930s.[20]

Critics of this much time and energy spent on athletics complained that the victors employed only a small number of talented men in the competition and that most men aboard ship did not receive the benefits of exercise. During 1933–34, the number of men from a battleship who participated in intership athletics ranged from a low of 175 to a high of 350; aboard *Tennessee,* the number was 288 out of about 1,500 men who served aboard ship at one time or another that year. But *Tennessee*'s intraship athletics program in which men from one division competed against those from another division involved another 864 men.[21]

That the participation rate was so high aboard *Tennessee* during 1933–34 testifies to the effectiveness of Captain William W. Smyth, who exhorted his men to enter every event and score some points even if they could not finish first. "To Captain Smyth we owe no uncertain measure of our success," the *Tar* stated in a special twelve-page iron man edition. "He was on the sidelines during our games, he offered

This 1927 issue of the *Tennessee Tar* reflects three items important to many captains: a high rating on an admiral's inspection, sports, and a good disciplinary record showing few men absent over their liberty.

encouragement and lastly but not least he had a belief that our teams could stand up with the best of them and win." To Captain Smyth and his fellow battleship captains, the value of athletic competition was not just physical conditioning and a diversion for the men. Its value lay in the belief that "good athletic teams meant good gun crews, good healthy appetites, and good morale and a happy ship." Sadly, Captain Smyth died of a cerebral hemorrhage in May 1934, two months before *Tennessee* won the iron man. It was left to the athletic officer to drive home the point that "every time we go on the range or a target prac-tice, every time we go to sea for a cruise, every day spent in port or in overhaul, and finally, every time we are inspected should be regarded by all hands as an opportunity to demonstrate to the rest of the Fleet that the *Tennessee* is setting the pace."[22]

The Fleet brass commended that spirit but decided something had to be done to curb the excesses of athletic competition. Since the late 1920s, they prohibited the practice of leaving men ashore to train when the ship was under way. And when the ship was in port, only rifle and pistol teams could be quartered ashore for training. No men were to be excused from their duties between 8:00 A.M. and noon during weekdays in order to train. Finally, civilian coaches were prohibited.[23] Apparently these regulations did not solve the problem of men being drawn away from their duties aboard ship so they could train. Consequently, the commander in chief of the battleships limited required competition to only those sports that could be practiced or held aboard ship. This excluded baseball, basketball, football, and swimming. If a captain wanted to participate in any of those events, he could do so; but the point system used in them limited a ship's chances of winning the iron man trophy. Baseball, basketball, and swimming were brought back a year later at a reduced weight in the overall scoring, but football remained a problem, since the season conflicted with fall gunnery practice.

That gunnery practice was more important for a battleship than football practice is obvious. But many officers believed that they could have both. When Admiral E. C. Kalbfus, the commander in chief of the battleships, polled his captains after one year without football, he found them split seven to seven whether football should be restored. In fall 1936, the second year of only voluntary football, eight of fourteen battleships fielded teams. At every game the 4,500-seat stands in San Pedro were filled to capacity. For the play-offs between *New Mexico* and *Pennsylvania,* 11,000 people jammed into stands designed to hold only 9,000. Bolstered by this show of popular support and privately favoring restoration of football, Admiral Kalbfus once again asked his captains what they thought and once again he found them almost evenly divided over the return of football. Captain Laurence McNair of *Tennessee* reported that he and most of his officers definitely opposed the inclusion of football in the iron man competition. The need to keep men aboard for gunnery practice along with the expense involved,

McNair concluded, outweighed the advantages brought from its popularity. Faced with such strong opposition, Kalbfus relented and left it up to each captain. If they wanted to field a team, they could earn 10 points per victory (a rather small incentive).[24]

Sports, books, movies, dances, and smokers all were officially sanctioned methods to make the sailor's life easier. Officially frowned upon but tolerated were the informal ways men had of making life more comfortable. A sailor who controlled what someone else wanted — food, extra clothing, pure grain alcohol, ice cream — could trade it for something he needed or wanted. Such bargaining was against regulations, of course, but some regulations were enforced more than others. One that was widely ignored was the practice of tipping for services rendered. Just as a tip encouraged the mess cook to work harder, a tip got the sailor a better haircut. And better service might be had from the cobbler or tailor if a small tip was given.

Extra cash could make life a little easier by allowing a sailor to splurge on a cake of Woodbury soap at 20 cents rather than Life Buoy at 7 cents or, for those with a sweet tooth, buy a one-pound box of Mrs. Saylors Candy for 65 cents. Cans of peaches and pineapple could be purchased for 15 cents and, in the hands of a talented fermenter, turned into an intoxicating if not always tasty drink. Getting drunk was one way to forget the cramped quarters, lack of privacy, and strict regulations that characterized life aboard ship. But for most men, liberty offered the greatest relief from navy routine.

Perhaps that is why the navy used the failure of men to return from liberty on time as a measurement of morale. A crew that found living conditions commodious, shipmates congenial, and regulations reasonable would not be absent over liberty (AOL), be absent without leave (AWOL), or desert. It was the unhappy sailor who stretched

liberty an extra hour or two or even a day, or who did not come back at all. Though it sounded good in the abstract, this method of measuring morale was not very reliable because it made no distinction between the sailor who missed a streetcar and got back to ship twenty-seven minutes over liberty and the sailor who stayed away for days, went AWOL, or deserted.[25]

Desertion was the most serious offense. Unfortunately for *Tennessee,* her desertion rate was usually above that of her fellow battleships and frequently near the top.[26] The navy made several efforts to explain why men deserted but only from the records available, not from interviews; in most cases, the reasons for deserting were not known. The conventional wisdom in the Fleet and in Washington was that a man deserted either because something pulled him away or something pushed him away. The pulling force was usually home or family. Sailors who were homesick or whose families needed them simply left if they were unable to get leave.

The force that pushed sailors into desertion was an inability to adapt to navy life. Perhaps a sailor felt he had been treated unfairly by a petty officer, or maybe he could not get along with his shipmates, or perhaps the regulations and regimentation aboard a battleship proved intolerable. Once on liberty, such a man might decide to just stay away. Sometimes, forgetting his unhappiness in drink, a sailor would find himself over liberty and be afraid to return to face the wrath of captain, division officer, or petty officer. The navy gave such a man ten days to get back to the ship on his own before he was classified a deserter. And if he voluntarily returned in less than thirty days, he would not be tried as a deserter but simply as absent over liberty and receive a far less serious punishment. But for some men, the fear of officers, shipmates, or navy life was great enough to prompt them to risk desertion.

Seaman Second Class Edward Diebel, Jr., was one such sailor. A shy, quiet young man who in 1921 had been aboard only a few months, Diebel found it difficult to make friends among his shipmates. Not that he was a troublemaker or picked fights, far from it; he was most unassertive. He just never fit in, was never "one of the guys." One June day, Diebel wanted a bath. Rather than go to his petty officer to have a bucket issued so he could take the customary sponge bath, Diebel took a coffeepot that was not in use. Perhaps he was afraid of his petty officer or perhaps he did not want to bathe with his shipmates. Whatever his reasons, he was discovered washing himself while standing over a coffeepot full of water.

He was reported to his petty officer, who told him that he would have to go before the If there was a police force aboard ship, it was the Master at Arms (MAA) staff, who led inspection tours, handled prisoners, and even inspected before hammocks were hung in the evening. Armed with a badge and sidearm, they escorted ashore the crew member who received a bad conduct discharge, bought him civilian clothes, gave him the money he had coming, took his uniform from him, and sent him on his way.[27]

Whenever a navy ship crossed the equator, the men who had not done so before (called "polly-wogs") were summoned for humiliation and physical abuse before King Neptune and his court. This photograph of King Neptune's court heralding the passage of *Tennessee* across the equator in 1925 documents that there were a few black members of *Tennessee's* crew. The muster rolls indicate that they were not mess attendants (who were all Filipino) but were assigned to one division or another. It is likely that as the years passed and blacks were not recruited, the number aboard ship dropped until blacks were recruited for the mess attendant branch shortly before World War II.[28]

captain for this breach of regulations. Word of this bizarre incident spread rapidly through the ship, and two men, upset by his activities, accosted him and shoved him against a bulkhead. A petty officer intervened and broke up the confrontation, but the smaller, totally intimidated Diebel cowered, sobbing, in the corner. He was ordered into his hammock where he was when taps sounded. But at 3:00 the next morning, a crewman saw him on deck, fully dressed, heading to the stern. When the crew was mustered, as they were every morning after breakfast, Diebel was missing. A thorough search of the ship revealed he was not aboard. A court of inquiry concluded that fearing his shipmates and the punishment he would certainly receive, Diebel had jumped overboard when *Tennessee* was less than 5 miles from the coast of Mexico. A strong swimmer, Diebel apparently believed he could reach shore. Few on board thought it likely, and the navy ruled he had died in the line of duty. Statistically he was never counted as a deserter.[29]

To the navy, this was another example of the kind of young man who should never have been recruited. Most commanders understood how important it was for petty and division officers to handle their men properly; but these commanders also believed that the best way to cut down on desertions was to recruit a better-quality sailor. They were correct. Desertions reached their highest rate aboard *Tennessee* in 1927, when nearly 6 percent of the crew jumped ship. In 1928 the desertion rate began to drop and continued to fall until the mid-1930s, when it regularly showed a rate of less than 1 percent. Some attributed the decline to the lack of jobs available to young men during the Great Depression, which made life aboard *Tennessee* look much better than it had when jobs in the civilian sector were plentiful and well paying.

But it appears that the depression did less to discourage desertion than it helped to improve the quality of the men recruited. In 1927 the navy recruited poorly educated men — more than a quarter had not completed elementary school and less than half had any high school. On the navy's aptitude test, 72 percent scored 50 or higher. During the next three years, improved recruiting brought in men with higher test scores and better education. In the fiscal year ending June 1930, 83 percent of the recruits were scoring 50 or higher, only 12 percent had not completed elementary school, and 60 percent had some high school. In the next year, when the full impact of the depression was felt, the quality of recruits increased dramatically. The percentage scoring above 50 on the navy's test climbed from 83 to 95. The percentage of recruits who had not completed elementary school dropped from

12 to 3.5. And the percentage who had some high school jumped from 60 to 76. As the depression continued to deepen, the quality of recruit rose further. By 1933, nine out of ten recruits had completed some high school and only 2.5 percent had not completed elementary school. And on the aptitude test, 99.3 percent were above the 50-point mark.

Put simply, by the 1930s the navy could be very picky about whom it enlisted. In 1935 there were 203,070 applicants and the navy took only 10,754, or 1 in 20. By 1936 it had more than 6,000 men on a waiting list to get in. It was not uncommon for a local recruiter to insist upon a statement from the police department or the sheriff attesting to the good character of the recruit.[30]

The 1930s also brought a slight change in the racial makeup of the crew as the navy again began recruiting African-Americans. As a result of the navy's earlier whites-only recruiting policy, there were scarcely a half dozen blacks aboard *Tennessee* during the 1920s, scattered throughout the ship in different divisions. These men were veterans from the Great War who had remained in the navy. The black men the navy accepted during the 1930s were placed only into the mess-attended branch of the service and were intended to replace the Filipinos, who were being gradually retired from service as the United States prepared to give the Philippines their independence. The first contingent of blacks came aboard for training in June 1935, but only three remained. Each year after that, the number of black mess attendants increased and the number of Filipinos decreased. By the end of 1940, there were twenty-seven African-American and nine Filipino attendants aboard.[31]

With the influx of blacks aboard *Tennessee,* racial segregation became more apparent. At one point, the chief of the mess attendants, who earned the same pay as a

chief petty officer but whose rating was technically different, tried to move into the chiefs' quarters. The chiefs moved his belongings into the passageway and that was the end of that. The *Tar* reflected this segregation when it published the names of men being promoted. In December 1935, nine men were promoted. Normally the *Tar* announced the promotions by grade, listing those rising to first class and then those rising to second class. But this time it listed the Filipinos going to first class, then the Filipinos to second class, and finally one African-American rising to first class, thus drawing a distinction between the Filipinos and the single black sailor who moved from second class to first class.[32]

By 1937 there were sufficient blacks aboard to warrant a short announcement under the headline "COLORED BLUEJACKETS' BALL. Tonight, in the Eagles' hall, Bremerton, the colored boys from the *Arizona, Oklahoma,* and *Tennessee* will entertain their friends at a Colored Bluejackets' Ball." By 1939 the mess attendants fielded a softball team that played the all-white E Division during a stop at Guantánamo, with the winner to play the all-white Fifth Division for the softball trophy. Though there were still at least nine Filipinos in the mess attendants' division, none of the fourteen names on the softball team was Filipino. Even though all-black and all-white teams were allowed to compete in intraship sporting events, when *Tennessee* traveled on to New York for the World's Fair, black and white sailors did not celebrate together. The *Tar* told members of the crew that they would find a friendly welcome at the Soldiers' and Sailors' Club of New York and at the William Sloane House YMCA and the Brooklyn Navy YMCA. Though no mention was made of these being for whites only, the *Tar* announced that "enlisted colored men are welcome at the new YMCA Building located at 180 W. 135 Street. This is right in the center of Harlem. There will be adequate facilities and entertainment at this branch for any of the colored men who wish to avail themselves of it." The *Tar* also announced a reception for "colored" sailors at the A.M.E. Church and the "Sixth Annual Ball honoring colored sailors of the United States Fleet."

A more blatant form of racism was apparent in the humor column of the *Tar*, which printed a dozen or so short jokes each issue, with racial stereotypes not being uncommon:

"Say Johnsing," commented Rastus, looking up from his paper, "it says heah dat in Sumatra a man kin buy a wife for foah dollars."

"Foah dollars!" gasped Johnsing, "Ef a niggah's got foah dollars he don't need no wife."

"Rastus, are you a married man?"

"Nossah, Boss, ah earns mah own living."

Ironically, in the midst of such "humor," the chaplain wrote an editorial on prejudice, denouncing it as injurious both to the recipient and to the one who holds the narrow view. "It is quite a common thing for people of one nationality, religion, or creed to have a prejudice against those of another. There is no condition that is so fallacious and harmful as this.... [T]he most fundamental of truths is that all people, en masse, are alike and the percentage of good, bad, and indifferent persons in each class differs very slightly. This is statistically true." When he wrote that "all people" were alike, *Tennessee*'s chaplain was thinking of European-Americans, not African-Americans. Reflecting the institutionalized racism within the navy, the chaplain confined his condemnation of prejudice to questions of nationality, religion, or creed and said nothing of race.[33]

With so many recruits available and so few slots to fill (whether reserved for Americans of European or African ancestry), the navy hoped to avoid recruiting any troublemakers. Inevitably some men enlisted who could not adjust to navy life in general and discipline aboard *Tennessee* in particular. Division officers had the first responsibility to make sure that these men toed the line. If at all possible, minor infractions — such as hanging clothing in an unauthorized place, failure to take clothing down on time (called "clothing adrift"), smoking out of hours, or having a dirty hammock — would be taken care of by a firm warning. Men who did not respond to the warning or broke more important regulations were taken before the captain's mast, where the commanding officer heard the charges and awarded punishment typically including the loss of liberty or extra police duties ranging from two to twenty-four hours. If he felt the charge serious enough or the man a habitual offender, the captain ordered the case to be tried at a deck court-martial or a summary court-martial aboard ship. During the troublesome recruiting years of 1925–1928, one in six *Tennessee* sailors went before a deck or summary court martial. A decade later, the rate had fallen to one in sixteen.

Serious infractions were relatively rare aboard ship. Occasionally there was a fight, a case of theft, someone operating a still, or serious insubordination. These cases, because of their infrequency, stand out in the deck logs — for example, in 1927 a sailor was given a general court-martial for his gross misconduct on shore, assault, indecent language and actions, and lying to the commanding officer at the captain's mast. More common were the less serious cases of neglect of duty, failure to carry out an order, or concealing a venereal disease. These warranted a summary court-martial with penalties as varied as reduction in rating, solitary confinement on bread and water for ten days with full rations every third day, or loss of substantial portions of pay for up to six months.[34]

When troublemakers showed up, the captain would do what he could to reform them. He might tolerate immediate and unauthorized punishment being inflicted on a sailor — for example, one sailor reported to sick bay with a broken nose and a "contused" left eye after being struck while "returning" another person's gear to that person's locker. More likely, however, the captain would dispense swift and certain punishment tempered as much by the character of the person being punished as by the nature of the offense. The Navy Department set maximum penalties on certain offenses and prevented the captain from invoking penalties such as reducing the rating of a sailor whom a different captain had promoted or taking away more than a certain amount of a man's pay. Periodically, the commander of the battleships in the Fleet published a schedule of punishments to prevent "widely divergent punishments for similar offenses." But in practice, the captain retained almost total power over what he would tolerate and how severe he would be in punishment.

A man whose offense was serious (theft or homosexuality) would be given a bad conduct discharge, as might the sailor who frequently got into trouble. Typically, a bad conduct discharge occurred aboard ship no more than once or twice a month. Occasionally, one of *Tennessee*'s captains cleaned house, and the rate would jump to four or five a month. But even at the smaller rate, the sight of a shipmate being escorted ashore and banished from the navy kept before the crew the fact that certain behavior would not be tolerated. A favorite form of punishment for a good sailor who always got drunk on liberty or who came back late involved sentencing him to a bad conduct discharge but suspending the sentence for six months. If the sailor committed any infraction during that probationary time,

the captain could invoke the discharge without any further trial. The navy kept no statistics on whether such a threat worked. But *Tennessee*'s captains invoked it frequently enough to indicate they had faith in it as a reform measure.

If a troublemaker could not be reformed, he could be transferred to another ship. With more than half the crew turning over each year, it was relatively easy to ship a malcontent to another ship where, it was always possible, he would find a situation more to his liking and therefore perform better. A draft of forty men came aboard *Tennessee* from *New Mexico* on May 14, 1927. Before the year was out, twelve of them had deserted, indicating that the captain of *New Mexico* had dumped his malcontents on *Tennessee*.[35]

The most common infraction was absence over liberty. It made no difference what year it was or how good the crew was, invariably 10 to 12 percent of the crew would fail to get back from liberty on time. This was the case in 1927, when desertion was a problem, and in 1936, when desertion scarcely existed. To be AOL meant certain punishment; the only way to avoid being caught was to climb up the anchor chain. The punishment was sure to be extra police duty and loss of several liberties. The longer a man was AOL, the greater the penalty. In 1937 *Tennessee*'s schedule of punishments called for the captain to deprive a sailor of two liberties if he was AOL less than two hours and one additional liberty for each additional hour up to six hours. If he stayed out six hours to thirty days, he would be taken before a deck court-martial where, for every day AOL, he would be docked five days pay and placed in solitary confinement for two days. If he was AOL longer than thirty days, he was sent ashore for a general court-martial on the charge of desertion, though even here leniency was shown to those men who turned themselves in within six months and especially to the young sailor who had less than six months service when he started his unauthorized absence.[37]

Hidden in the relatively minor penalty of

a loss of a couple liberties was a bad mark on the sailor's conduct report for that quarter of the year. In the lean days of the 1930s, when few men were leaving the service, advancement was difficult to achieve and a bad conduct report could have major consequences on a sailor's chances for advancement.

A sailor entered the navy as an apprentice seaman. In four months, he automatically advanced to seaman second class or fireman third class, which were comparable grades. After that, movement was slow. It was possible for the smart sailor with an unblemished record to achieve a third-class petty officer rating in four years. Achieving a "rating" meant completing a self-study course and passing an examination. The division officer oversaw this part of the education and might order a man to study, threatening to deny him liberty if he did not do so.

There were many jobs aboard ship that could not be learned from books, and there was more than one way to get a rating. Veterans reported that there was a seasoned deckhand who was a master with ropes and knots but who could not pass the written test for promotion because he was functionally illiterate. With the silent approval of the division officer, the man signed up to take the test and appeared with his hands wrapped in bandages, claiming he was suffering from burns; he dictated the answers to a yeoman. He passed the examination and was promoted to chief boatswain's mate.

Having taken the self-study course and passed the examination, the enlisted man waited for an opening in the grade he sought. Inevitably there were more men qualified for promotion than there were spaces to fill. This is where the conduct record became particularly important. A man who scored high on a test but who had a blemished conduct record would be passed over for promotion in favor of the

man with a lower test score but a better conduct record. To make a rating (to be advanced to petty officer third class), an enlisted man would need a proficiency rating of not less than 3.5 out of 4.0 for the quarter preceding advancement. But he could not get a 3.5 proficiency if he had a conduct rating of less than 3.5. One absence over liberty or one sobriety offense would give him a conduct rating no higher than a 3.0 and block his promotion for at least three months.

Considering test scores, proficiency rating, conduct rating, and especially length of service, the captain established a priority list for men seeking ratings. Whether the man advanced, however, depended on how many slots the navy had open. In 1938, for example, out of 134 rates available in the Fleet, *Tennessee* was granted 14, second only to *Pennsylvania,* which received 15. In some branches, however, only one place was open, making advancement very slow. One tactic the men employed was to transfer to a branch where the chances of advancement looked better — a seaman, for example, might move over to become an electrician, because the demand for skilled men in that area was greater. In the mid-1920s, when turnover was large and advancement easier, only about 2 percent of the crew made such shifts. By the mid-1930s, when advancement was very difficult, 8 percent of the crew so shifted.

A major incentive to seek advancement was the increase in pay that went with it. The monthly pay for a new recruit was $21, which rose to $30 after four months. A sailor might work his way up to $36 and even $54 during a four-year enlistment. If he achieved a petty officer rating, it would almost certainly be during his second enlistment and he would be paid $60 plus a $6 bonus for his length of service.[38]

Earning $66 per month, the navy thought it appropriate for a man to take on

family responsibilities. But during the 1930s, it took an enlisted man so long to achieve a petty officer rating that the Navy Department feared sailors would marry and try to support a family on $54 or even $36 a month. The Navy Department responded by requiring each captain to determine whether a sailor had complaints of nonpayment of debt against him or domestic troubles before allowing him to reenlist. As the *Tar* explained, "If a man, earning but $36 a month, undertakes to become a benedict, it is but natural for his superior officers to suspect that he lacks enough common sense to even be considered a half-wit; and that perhaps he is not desirable material for retention in the Naval Service."

Because most men aboard at any given time were in their first enlistment and in the lower pay grades, only a minority were married. But for those who were married, life aboard *Tennessee* offered special problems. More often than not, she was in her home port of San Pedro, and sailor and family were together. When she went to Bremerton for a three-month overhaul every eighteen months, married men frequently packed up their family and sent them up north to be with them, remembering to pack the coats and boots not needed in San Pedro. But when the Fleet went on maneuvers or paid a special visit to the East Coast, the time away from home was long. In 1939, when *Tennessee* participated in Fleet Problem XX in the Caribbean and then visited the New York World's Fair, she steamed 16,098 miles and was away from her home port for 119 days. After maneuvers off Hawaii in 1938, which kept *Tennessee* from San Pedro for six weeks, the *Tar* published a cartoon as she headed home, showing a sailor hugging his wife while two kids look on, saying, "Mamma! Who's that man?" The caption is "Back to Pedro (Reckon they've forgotten?)"

For a few, being at sea meant hearing of

tragedy by naval radio. On April 2, 1938, while off Lahaina, Hawaii, the *Tar* reported:

> D. H. Spraggins, CFC, received a dispatch yesterday informing him of the sudden death of his 2½ year old son, Sonny Boy.
>
> A message was also received by S. E. Shrider, S1c of the death of his newly born baby boy at the Seaside Hospital, Long Beach.
>
> The ship's company's sincerest and most heartfelt sympathy goes out to our shipmates and their wives.[39]

Though *Tennessee* was a warship, death did not often touch her, and those who died aboard did so in ways associated more with a factory than a warship: For example, Seaman First Class Flavill H. Coop was climbing a "sea ladder" strung over *Tennessee*'s side just before Christmas 1932 when he lost his grip and fell back into the launch, fatally fracturing his skull; a printer, sweating profusely, leaned against an electrical switch and was electrocuted.

When a shipmate died, more likely than not it would be ashore and unrelated to naval duty. Electrician's Mate First Class Eilert Madsen was riding on a ferry when he cursed a woman accompanying a sailor from another ship to a hotel. The sailor knocked Madsen down and fractured his skull. Madsen died a week later, and the navy tried the other man for manslaughter. John Barker was a machinist's mate second class who had just transferred aboard *Tennessee*. In his previous duty in China, he had met and fallen in love with a Russian émigré woman. Despondent over their separation, Barker went AOL on December 31 and shot himself on January 3, 1935. Seaman First Class John A. Clark and several men from *Tennessee* liked to take the train up to Los Angeles on Saturday night and drink at a bar called Joe's Café. On March 21, 1936, Clark got drunk and the bar owners let him sleep it off in a rear booth. Not totally sober when he awoke, he took a woman companion to the neighboring Yorkshire Hotel, sat down in the window, and fell 12 feet to the roof below. He died of his injuries nine days later.[40]

By the mid-1930s, automobiles and motorcycles were killing sailors at an alarming rate. *Tennessee*'s only death in 1934 was automobile related. Later that year, the motorcycle placed two more shipmates in the hospital. After her six weeks in Hawaii in 1938, *Tennessee* returned home, her crew saddened no doubt by the realization that two of their shipmates had lost children during the cruise but happy to be home with family and friends again. She had been home less than two weeks when the motorcycle claimed the lives of two more *Tennessee* sailors, Fireman First Class Herbert Harold Amex and Machinist's Mate Second Class John Arthur Geer. On a Sunday morning, they failed to see a car coming and smashed head on into it.

That was enough for the commander of Battleship Division Two, which included *Tennessee*. From December 1935 to March 1938, he reported, there were eighty-eight deaths in the entire United States Fleet, with thirty-nine, or 44.2 percent, being the direct result of motor vehicle accidents. Indeed, more than one out of ten men admitted to sick bay were put there by a car or motorcycle. To put a stop to such reckless behavior, warning posters began appearing aboard *Tennessee* and once each week division officers lectured the men on safe motor vehicle operation. These lectures did not help Donald Benson Palmer, machinist's mate second class. He enlisted in January 1936 and served continuously aboard *Tennessee* until November 1939, when he drove his motorcycle into an Arden Milk truck at the corner of Pica and Seventh Street in Long Beach.[41]

If death aboard ship was rare, nonlethal accidents abounded. Men slipped on decks, fell down ladders, and fell out of hammocks. Hands and feet were injured loading ammunition, and punctures and lacerations were common for the men who worked around machinery. Occasionally, a man fell overboard or out of a small boat but was picked up in a matter of minutes. The greatest danger from the ocean came from a man foolish enough to go on deck during rough weather when a "green wave" (a wave that has not broken but is pure water) could wash him overboard or bash him against the ship. And there were accidents associated with exploding shells. In 1927 a primer on a 5-inch gun exploded, injuring three men. In 1928 someone set the fuse on a 5-inch shell to zero seconds so that it exploded as soon as it emerged from the muzzle. The shards seriously injured one member of the gun crew and slightly injured four more. But such events were rare.[42]

The health of the crew was more often affected by the ventilation system. During a lengthy storm, the air below deck would be thick enough to slice, and in rough weather, men would be pouring spilled soup out of their shoes. Since smoking was common in the living/sleeping quarters, nonsmokers could not escape it, though this was not considered a health issue at the time. The biggest problem was high temperatures when *Tennessee* cruised in southern waters. On her initial cruise in Cuban waters, the temperature at certain places below deck reached 130 degrees. On a cruise to Panama thirteen years later, the same problem existed, with the temperature in the boiler room hitting 170 degrees while temperatures at the various operating stations below deck never dropped below 88 degrees and reached a high of 160 degrees, sending six men to sick bay.[43]

With their cramped quarters and shared coffee cups, one man's disease often spread to the shipmates in his division. During

Though discipline aboard any battleship was strict, exceptions to the regulations could always be made. Cinderella, a mixed-breed dog, was smuggled aboard *Tennessee* in 1935 by a kind-hearted sailor who found her in San Pedro. There was an order prohibiting pets on the ship and eventually Cinderella was ordered ashore. But when the executive officer came to get her, she reportedly sat up and begged, softening his heart as well as that of the captain, who issued a special order allowing her to remain.[44]

1927, twenty to fifty men reported to sick bay each month and stayed there from a day and a half to five days, usually suffering from some respiratory infection or tonsillitis. Routine care also had to be given to the teeth of the crew, and a dental office did a brisk business fixing teeth, filling 643 and pulling 479.[45]

In all of these areas, *Tennessee* was a reflection of the society in which she existed. When football fever swept American colleges, it also swept the Fleet and *Tennessee*. And just as some people worried that athletics were playing too large a role on campus, some in the navy worried that athletics were taking too much time in the Fleet. Also, the quality of men who served aboard *Tennessee* was directly related to the state of the economy. And what killed the men aboard her more than any other cause was society's infatuation with motor vehicles and (possibly) alcohol. Even the

status of dental hygiene in society was reflected in the amount and kind of dental treatment given sailors. But nowhere were the interrelations between society and the ship more apparent than with the problem of venereal disease. The navy was quick to state that no man joined the navy with VD. Yet the disease always put 10 to 15 percent of the crew in sick bay, sometimes more. Gonorrhea, syphilis, and chancroid were prevalent enough to warrant medical officers to label them the greatest menace to the navy. VD had been such a serious and obvious problem during World War I that Captain Leigh had to reassure the mothers and fathers of Tennessee that their sons would remain pure in body while serving aboard his ship. It was a promise easier made than kept. When the recruits from *Tennessee* entered boot camp and, later, when they came aboard ship, they were told what venereal disease was and how to avoid it:

Abstain from sexual contact with anyone who might have it. Captain Leigh ordered 500 copies of the navy pamphlet "The Girl" and another 500 copies of "Shore Leave." The next year brought the navy training film "Fit to Win," which was reported to make for a good evening's entertainment.

Standing orders required a sailor who did not heed such warnings and was exposed to venereal infection to report the contact and submit to treatment with a chemical prophylaxis. If he did not do so, became infected, and sought to conceal the infection, the recommended punishment was two months' confinement imposed by a summary court-martial, a penalty greater than all but the most serious infraction a sailor might commit. In addition, while infected he was denied liberty and for every day on the sick list, he was docked a day's pay and his tour of duty was extended one day. To catch men who tried to conceal their affliction, the medical officer was authorized to examine the crew at will.

Sermonizing and threats of punishment did not stop the spread of venereal disease aboard *Tennessee.* By the start of 1921, when she was still in New York, *Tennessee*'s VD rate had climbed to 70 per 1,000 men aboard ship, a very low rate compared with the 137 to 337 cases per 1,000 that characterized the battleships in the Pacific. But it was high compared with the rate aboard the battleships in the Atlantic and it continued to get higher, reaching 91 per 1,000 in June and 99 per 1,000 in September, after *Tennessee* joined the Fleet in southern California. The worst rates of infection came when she visited Caribbean ports where venereal disease was commonplace. During those cruises, the navy often made special efforts to keep crewmen and prostitutes apart by restricting overnight liberties and heavily patrolling red-light districts. Though such efforts proved reasonably effective in preventing massive outbreaks of VD aboard ship, the ongoing infection of one-tenth or as many as one-quarter of the crew remained unsolved. Some officers who tried to attack the VD problem found their hands were tied by the indifference of most ship commanders, who considered venereal disease one of the natural afflictions a navy had to tolerate, and by the social conservatism that dominated public policy during the 1920s.

The Roaring Twenties are often remembered as an age of loosening morals reflected in the speakeasy, bathtub gin, the flapper, and jazz. However, it was also an era of social orthodoxy, reflected in Prohibition, the revival of Christian fundamentalism, and the conservative American Social Hygiene Association. The forces of orthodoxy condemned the sexual openness they perceived in society and denied that VD was a problem — nice people did not get VD, they did not talk about VD, they did not need to worry about VD. The American

Social Hygiene Association forced the U.S. Public Health Service and state public health organizations to abandon their most effective anti–venereal disease programs, and as a result, syphilis and gonorrhea flourished across the land.[46] The conservative solution — if we can call it a solution — was to urge people to avoid sexual promiscuity.

At times the navy bowed to this prevailing wind. When state courts ruled the navy's anti-VD film, "Fit to Fight," obscene in 1920, navy officials scrapped it and prepared the apparently less objectionable "Fit to Win" in 1921. When "decency" campaigns across the country forced state public health departments to stop the distribution of chemical prophylaxis lest its very effectiveness in preventing VD lead to increased promiscuity, the navy refused to issue to men going on liberty chemical prophylactic kits (a small tube filled with an ointment to be injected into the sailor's penis immediately after intercourse) because "such methods imply or lead to the assumption that exposure to venereal disease is expected to occur and thus conflict with moral and educational measures."[47]

Even a special naval board established in 1925 to explore the VD problem began its report with the proclamation that it was "fundamentally true that the Navy's venereal disease problem is as bad as it is, largely because of the lack of suitable training and proper restraint of children in the homes of the United States and because of defective social hygiene in high as well as low levels of society in practically all communities."[48] Until American society changed its promiscuous ways, many of the men it would be providing to the navy would be "wanting in the finer qualities of moral and ethical character" — that is, they were going to have sex with prostitutes who were likely to be infected. Moral education and indoctrination would have to be continued, the Navy Department's board on venereal disease concluded, but these would have little effect on the VD rate.

There were those in the navy who were not content to wait for society to reform or for human nature to change. In 1922 the navy decided an ounce of prevention was worth a pound of cure and resumed issuing chemical prophylactic kits as men went ashore but did so quietly to avoid adverse public reaction.[49] The navy's own VD board concluded that the service had to confront VD in the Fleet through a program of diversion and treatment.

No one in the navy thought they could persuade sailors on liberty not to think about sex. Nor did the special board on VD believe that it was possible or even desirable to prevent sailors from fulfilling their sexual urges. Instead, the men needed to be directed away from illicit sex with infected women. One way to do this was to keep sailors from standing on street corners "following with their eyes every young woman who passes, until, after a time, curiosity, imagination, and desire have so stimulated sex feelings that before the evening is over they will endeavor to satisfy their desires." Adequate recreation measures would divert the men from street corners, reduce contact with prostitutes, and lower the VD rate. Another tactic the board recommended was to make the men so contented with life aboard ship that they would not be in a hurry to get off and stay off, thus falling into the hands of prostitutes. The baseball, football, and basketball facilities constructed in San Pedro, the smokers held on the docks, and the band concerts and films shown at night were morale-boosting efforts from one perspective, but for those responsible for crew health, they were effective means of keeping sailors away from prostitutes.

The second part of the navy's diversion tactic was to provide an alternative outlet for the men to satisfy their sexual urges. Official policy was to indoctrinate the men in "the moral and physical evils of incontinence." But the board could not "overlook the fact that the female of the species as well as the male is activated by strong emotions arising from the sex instinct." Nor could it deny that in larger American cities it was commonly felt that young single women "are entitled to freedom in social and sexual as well as business relations.... Such women are not necessarily promiscuous in their relations with men." Clearly distinguishing this kind of woman from the professional prostitute or the "loose woman," the board urged more opportunities for men on liberty "to form associations and enduring friendship with young women of good moral character." Unless this happened, the board warned, the men would turn to prostitutes and "the venereal disease problem must to that extent be more difficult to solve."[50] Obviously, Navy Department officials could not announce that they hoped sailors would shun the local taxi dancer in favor of the "girl next door." But that is what the board's plan of diversion amounted to.

The dances the Fleet sponsored in San Pedro almost every Saturday night and the special dances put on by *Tennessee* helped morale and were designed to lower the VD rate. And when the Navy Mothers Association brought five dozen nice young women to a dance at Bremerton, everyone assumed morale would go up and the commander in chief of the Fleet could be confident the VD rate would not rise. Bremerton was always a problem because the men were away from their established social circle and some sought out prostitutes.

In spite of the moralizing, education, diversion, and alternate sexual outlets, many men continued to become infected. How many is not clear, since the navy's figures only reflect those who received treatment by navy doctors. Physicians ashore did "a land office business" treating sailors who sought to avoid punishment by concealing their infection.[51] The loss of liberty and pay and the extension of service for infected men was an understandable policy. While on the sick list because of VD, a man gave his ship no service, so he deserved no pay; in addition, the days in sick bay should not be counted in his years of service. But the fact remained that these regulations encouraged men to conceal the disease and that made treatment more difficult.

The venereal disease board hoped to bring more men in for treatment by reducing the punishment, but commanding officers had little sympathy for the person who acquired VD. It was bad enough that the high rate was taking trained men away from their jobs and thus lessening the efficiency of the crew; the naval establishment was not prepared to let this go unpunished. A few reforms were implemented, however. The captain gained authority to grant liberty to an infected sailor and hold an infected sailor blameless if he had reported his exposure promptly and received supervised prophylactic treatment. On the other hand, any man who contracted a venereal disease and who had not received the prescribed treatment at the time of his initial exposure would be charged with disobedience of General Order 69, tried by summary court-martial, and could be confined for as long as two months and then given a bad conduct discharge.

All this did no good. VD rates remained high during the late 1920s and into the 1930s, both for the Fleet as a whole and *Tennessee* in particular.[52] This was to be expected. Though the reform-minded efforts of the VD board reflected the best thinking of public health officials in the land — educate the men, provide alternatives to sailors seeking out promiscuous women, treat those exposed, and punish those who do not cooperate — knowing what to do and doing it were very different things. In society and in the Fleet, effective implementation of a strong anti-VD plan was lacking. Society in general and the officers of the Fleet in particular learned to live with VD rather than to confront it. Aboard *Tennessee,* the ship's service store sold a large variety of condoms at near cost. When used properly, the condom was the most effective method of preventing transmission of a venereal disease. But in spring 1933, a new officer was put in charge of the ship's service store and, for some reason, discontinued the sale of condoms. The result was an increase in the VD rate aboard ship.[53] Nor did captains severely punish sailors who acquired the disease and were eligible for a summary court-martial and two months' confinement. In the seven years following the summary court-martial provision published in General Order 69, 7 percent of *Tennessee*'s crew was on the sick list due to misconduct, which usually meant with a venereal disease. Yet during the same time, less than 2 percent of the crew received summary courts-martial for any cause.[54]

The attitude in the Fleet began to change in 1934, when the commander of the battleships increased anti-VD efforts, complaining that "the measures practiced for the last two decades have permitted venereal diseases to continue to exist to an excessively high rate." Shipboard lectures about VD increased, more posters appeared, the men were encouraged to participate in athletics, overnight liberties were canceled when out of the country, condoms were given to the men, and the chemical prophylaxis was administered as soon as possible after exposure. Increased inspections of the men to discover concealed infections were coupled with restrictions on an offender's liberty and other forms of punishment. But none of these efforts seemed to do much good, as the men "appear indifferent to the dangers of exposure." Such indifference was most apparent in a class of men who were "repeated venereal addicts" and "make up our excessive

number of sick days." The solution was to give them undesirable discharges and get them out of the navy.[56] The number of discharges of men aboard *Tennessee,* however, shows that *Tennessee*'s captains did not follow this suggestion.

By 1935 the Fleet had turned its attention to treatment, establishing clean, modern, and convenient prophylactic centers ashore in San Pedro so men could receive treatment as soon as possible after exposure. But it was a half-hearted effort. Though the centers were open twenty-four hours a day, they treated only 8 men per 1,000 while on-board treatment stood at 117 per 1,000. Medical officers lamented that line officers were more interested in their gunnery and engineering efficiency scores than in the health of their crews. One medical officer concluded that "a long, hot shower using plenty of soap" would prevent many venereal infections. But no enlisted man on a battleship ever got a hot shower, much less a long, hot one. If the navy really wanted to get serious about VD, some medical officers believed, it should hold commanding officers responsible for the VD rate of their men just as it held them responsible for how the men performed in gunnery or engineering.[57]

The Navy Department would not go that far, but eventually it altered its policy when the public attitude toward VD began to change. The catalyst was Thomas Parran, who was appointed U.S. surgeon general in 1936 and carried his anti-VD campaign to a national forum. To stop VD, local authorities had to find the cases, treat them, identify the contacts that might have been infected, and educate the public to the dangers of these diseases. Pressured by naval medical officers and Surgeon General Parran's campaign, the secretary of the navy issued General Order 97, which removed any punishment for a man who came forward for treatment no matter how long he had been infected.[58]

These efforts brought a dramatic drop in the VD rate in the Fleet starting in 1934: The Fleet's VD admission rate held steady at 13.5 percent from 1930 to 1933, it dropped to 10.5 percent in 1934, to 9.2 percent in 1935, to 7.1 percent in 1936, and to 6.3 percent in 1937, less than half of what it was just four years earlier. With the removal of the misconduct charge for infected men, sailors who found they were infected and would previously have concealed that infection came forward, raising the admission rate to 7.1 percent in 1938 and 8.3 percent in 1939. The real infection rate was probably slightly higher, since some commanders apparently stuck to the old policy of punishing men who were infected, and in July 1940, the secretary of the navy had to send out another letter saying revival of such punishment was not approved.

The most dramatic drop in VD admissions came in 1941. For the first five months of 1940, the rate was 6.2 percent. For the first five months of 1941 it was 4.1 percent. This one-third reduction came with the transfer of the Fleet to Hawaii in May 1940, a place where the prostitutes were inspected for disease, the army maintained excellent prophylactic stations, and overnight liberty was rare. In July 1940, the Fleet VD admission rate was 47 per 1,000 sailors. But *Tennessee* had not yet joined the Fleet in Hawaii and had spent a few months at the navy yard in Bremerton, Washington. With her crew exposed to the prostitutes who derived their livelihood from the naval trade, the admission rate aboard *Tennessee* rose to 162 per 1,000 men, more than three times the rate for the ships in Hawaii.[59]

President Franklin Roosevelt gave the order that kept the Fleet in Hawaiian waters. His decision had nothing to do with venereal disease and everything to do with a world that was on fire. It was the start of *Tennessee*'s transition from peace to war.

CHAPTER FIVE

FROM PEACE TO WAR

Tennessee was designed to fight, but she was built so the United States would not have to fight. As with the rest of the navy, *Tennessee* was first a deterrent, then a combatant. The theory was that if the United States had enough ships and the will to use them, a potential enemy would not dare start a fight. The enemy that the navy had in mind was Japan, and as a warning for Japan to restrain its expansionist ambitions, the navy kept most of its ships and all of its modern battleships in the Pacific. A more obvious show of interest in the western Pacific came in 1925, when the Fleet cruised to New Zealand and Australia. Regularly during the 1920s and 1930s, American ships practiced War Plan Orange ("Orange" was the code name for Japan), which called for the Fleet to steam across the Pacific, seize Japanese-held islands for naval bases, and confront the Japanese navy thousands of miles from the continental United States.

This display of American naval power convinced Japanese expansionists that their future as a great Asian power required a navy large enough to hold the western Pacific against the United States Navy. So in the 1930s, Japan began a secret naval building program. As Japan built ships, *Tennessee* and the other aging battleships across the Pacific fell behind their Japanese counterparts. To hold her own in combat, *Tennessee* needed protective blisters on her sides, thicker armor on her decks, and better antiaircraft guns with which to defend herself. But a nation preoccupied with the Great Depression was not ready to rebuild its navy or build new ships to replace the older ones.[2]

Consequently, it was a relatively weak United States Navy that faced Japan in 1937, when the Sino-Japanese war erupted. Unlike earlier confrontations in which the Chinese capitulated, the "China incident" dragged on and grew until in 1941 it became the Pacific war (what Americans call World War II). Many naval officers strongly opposed Japan's Asian expansion, especially when Japanese naval aircraft attacked and sank the USS *Panay,* a wooden gunboat stationed on the Yangtze River. Chief of Naval Operations William D. Leahy believed it was time to rein in the Japanese by getting the Fleet ready for combat and putting it to sea. But cooler heads prevailed, especially that of Secretary of State Cordell Hull, who was not about to be dragged into a war with Japan over China. The Japanese apologized, paid indemnities, and gave assurances that such an "accident" would never happen again.[3]

There was bloody warfare in China, but that did not affect the officers and men aboard *Tennessee,* who occupied themselves with engineering, gunnery, and athletic competitions. Except for overhauls and Fleet exercises, *Tennessee* and her fellow battleships followed a relaxed routine of a few days at sea during the week and weekends in port. Once in the 1930s, Admiral Joseph Reeves, commander in chief of the Fleet, shook up his command on a Saturday morning by ordering the Fleet to sea without any warning. Men raced to fire up boilers, and the ships went to sea not knowing what world crisis had taken place. But by and large, the Fleet remained in a relaxed condition.[4]

Though the United States took no overt action to stop Japan in China, American moral support for China and verbal opposition to Japanese expansion prompted Japanese strategic planners to seek self-sufficiency in raw materials, especially oil, before the Americans cut them off. The closest source of oil to Japan was the Dutch East Indies. That Japan would need that region if it was going to achieve economic self-sufficiency was no mystery to American naval and diplomatic officers. It was also clear that though the United States Navy could do little about Japan in China, the long supply lines between Japan and the East Indies were vulnerable to naval pressure. When Japan turned south, the United States began the game of battleship diplomacy.

Roosevelt's first move came in spring

1939, when Adolf Hitler's armies occupied Czechoslovakia and a general European war seemed likely. Britain and France began to shift some of their military forces from Asia to Europe, leaving a power vacuum in Southeast Asia where the French held their colony of Indochina and the British a strategic naval base at Singapore. All this took place just as the Fleet was about to visit New York City for the opening of the World's Fair. Though the Japanese were not planning an imminent attack against Southeast Asia, Roosevelt wanted Japan to know that the United States considered the future of Southeast Asia and the South Pacific much more important than that of China. As a demonstration of this concern, the president ordered the Fleet to turn around and return to the Pacific. Roosevelt allowed one battleship to represent the Fleet at the opening of the fair, *Tennessee.*[5]

The Navy Department did not record whether the officers and men aboard ship paid any attention to international events. The men who read the daily news summary prepared from radio reports and distributed aboard ship had a good idea of what was happening in the world. It is probable that some men shunned the after-dinner card games, movie, or band concert to sit on deck and mull over current events.[6] But there was no sense of urgency. *Tennessee* was not left behind while the Fleet went to war or even to confront an enemy. Franklin Roosevelt was sending a message to Japan that he hoped would make a war less likely. The Fleet was going home, and some married men aboard *Tennessee* may have wished they too were going. They had not seen their families since leaving the Bremerton Navy Yard three months earlier.

On the other hand, there was plenty to keep them busy in New York. As the only modern battleship at the fair (the other two battleships were *New York* [1914] and *Texas* [1914]), *Tennessee* was a popular

Tennessee spent most of her time in the Pacific, occasionally moving into the Caribbean for Fleet maneuvers and from time to time venturing back to New York City. Her last voyage to New York was in 1939, when she helped celebrate the opening of the World's Fair. As the newest American battleship at the fair, she was singled out for a special visit by the Crown Prince of Norway, complete with gun salutes and the crew standing inspection.[7]

attraction, with hundreds of visitors coming aboard daily, as many as 1,900 on one day. Ashore there were the usual sights New York had to offer, as well as the special parties and receptions that marked the opening of the fair. Over a quarter of the men attended a special naval dance at the swank Hotel Astor. And then there was the fair itself, which most men toured and a few saw as they marched in the opening ceremony parade. Of course, life was not all partying. Ammunition had to be loaded and drills conducted. *Tennessee* was, after all, a warship, and war was fast approaching.[9]

The European side of World War II began with the German conquest of Poland in September 1939, but it was not until the German spring offensive in 1940 that the world saw just how formidable Hitler's new war machine was. German troops overran Denmark and Norway in April; it was only a matter of time before they took the Netherlands as well. With the Dutch East Indies orphaned and the British on the defensive, Franklin Roosevelt and Cordell Hull feared that an opportunistic Japan would expand into the South Seas. Secretary Hull sharply warned Japan that the United States considered a Japanese attempt to dominate Southeast Asia and the South Seas as far more provocative than Japan's domination of China. To back up these words, Roosevelt flexed his naval muscle.

At that time, the United States Fleet was completing Fleet Problem XXI in Hawaiian waters. Fleet Problem XXI involved moving across the Pacific to attack the Japanese in their home waters. Of course, the Fleet never actually moved close to Japan but practiced going from the West Coast to Hawaii. By early May, the exercise would be complete and the ships would return to their home ports in California. Roosevelt, however, decided to hold the Fleet in Hawaii, 2,500 miles closer to Japan, as one more naval action designed to deter Japanese expansion.

While the Fleet tarried in Hawaiian waters, the situation in Europe deteriorated beyond anyone's expectations. German armies forced the British into a massive flight from the Continent at Dunkirk and soundly defeated France. With France broken and Britain bracing for a German invasion, the United States was the only power left to hold Japan in check. As a result, what started as a temporary naval demonstration became a permanent transfer of the Fleet. No one in Washington could be certain whether stationing the battleships at Pearl Harbor would actually deter Japan from its South Seas ambition, but Roosevelt was certain that to withdraw the ships would only encourage more Japanese expansion.[10] The Fleet had to stay at Pearl Harbor.

Fleet commander Admiral James O. Richardson thought the transfer of his ships to Hawaii a mistake. All the tugs, targets, and ammunition his ships needed to maintain battle efficiency were on the West Coast. Since no one in Washington could say whether the Fleet would remain at Pearl Harbor for two months or two years, Admiral Richardson was reluctant to transfer the requisite equipment and ammunition when he might have to send it right back. Once the support ships and equipment arrived, it became obvious how inadequate were the facilities in Hawaii. The anchorage at Lahaina was too exposed to be safe, and Pearl Harbor was too small for efficient movement of large ships. Air and surface operating areas were too restricted and congested. Facilities were lacking, whether in the form of a range-finder calibration range, repair shops ashore, or housing for the men who serviced the Fleet. Finally, if war should come, the Fleet based at Pearl Harbor was not prepared to move against Japan without first assembling a supply train on the West Coast and possibly even returning to the mobilization ports located there. Richardson's protests did not move Roosevelt except to convince him to relieve Richardson of his command. The president did not worry that the Fleet was not combat ready or that the training facilities in Hawaii were meager. He was re-enforcing diplomatic language with a naval demonstration, a mild form of "saber rattling," and if he pulled back from the naval demonstration, it would make the diplomatic warnings useless.[11]

Tennessee missed these first chaotic months in Hawaii. Since she was scheduled for overhaul at the Puget Sound Navy Yard in Bremerton, Washington, in April, her officers and men spent the summer working aboard ship and enjoying extensive liberty. It was not uncommon for married men to bring their families to Bremerton during overhaul periods, so the married men of *Tennessee* had a few months to be with their loved ones before joining the Fleet at Pearl Harbor in August. From Bremerton, *Tennessee* steamed south to her home port of San Pedro, where the sailors had a week to put their personal affairs in shape before saying good-bye to friends and family and heading for Hawaii.[12]

From the enlisted men's perspective, the Hawaii they saw upon arrival in August 1940 had too many sailors and too few shops, bars, restaurants, and recreational facilities. Men used to weekend liberties were stuck with Cinderella liberty (liberty that ended at midnight). Fully aware of the morale problem, the navy built baseball and softball fields, basketball, tennis, handball, and volleyball courts, and four swimming pools. Within a year, a Fleet recreation center was open. The men of *Tennessee* took full advantage of every opportunity to relax. Swimming parties of fifty men or so proved very popular, and the weekend liberties at Nanakuli meant relaxing with a large beach, free beer, lots of good food, comfortable cots in tents with wooden floors, and no one telling the campers when they had to get up.

But softball games, rowing races, and swim parties in the Hawaiian paradise did little to ease the pain of separation that the married men felt. Officers and chief petty officers might afford to bring their families to Hawaii if they could find housing for them. But most married men simply had to endure. Eventually a rotation system was established where ships took turns returning to their West Coast ports. *Tennessee* was back at Long Beach by November 14, 1940, stayed through Thanksgiving, and spent Christmas in Bremerton. She did not leave California for Pearl Harbor until January 20, 1941. After that, it was six months before she was home again. Gunner's Mate third class R. A. Carl, Jr., said good-bye to his three-month-old son, whose birth he had missed; he would not see the child again until he was nine months old.[13]

Sporting events were most certainly not a satisfactory substitute for feminine companionship. Prominent women in Honolulu organized dances for enlisted men every two weeks at Moana Park Pavilion. A battleship supplied the band, the navy distributed the invitations, and the whole affair was carefully planned and controlled. Each dance was only from 8:00 to 11:00 P.M., and there were three times as many sailors as women. Sailors were encouraged to "cut in" during a dance, but only at the sound of a whistle. With over 10,000 battleship sailors alone swelling the ranks of enlisted men in Hawaii and the dance hosting only 300 at a time, this plan was only a drop in the bucket. *Tennessee* organized its own dance at the Roof Garden of the Alexander Young Hotel. "Because of the great number of ships present and the comparative difficulty in securing the attendance of the ladies," only men from *Tennessee* were permitted to attend.[14]

President Roosevelt could not afford to worry about the inconvenience his order had caused to officers and men. If his deli-

cate game of deterrence was successful, he would keep Japan from expanding into an area over which the United States would go to war. As such, his transfer of the Fleet to Pearl Harbor was not an attempt to pick a fight with Japan. Quite the contrary, Roosevelt had been careful to avoid appearing so belligerent that Japan would respond in a blustering manner, escalating tensions. The president had not denounced Japan or even made a public announcement. He had ordered Admiral Richardson to say the Fleet would remain for a period of time and only gradually did Japan realize that the transfer was permanent.

From Tokyo's point of view, no matter how discreetly the Fleet transfer was made, it still was an attempt to deny Japan the economic self-sufficiency Japanese leaders believed was necessary to survive in a hostile world. Though the power of the Fleet was not what it once was, it was sufficient to make it impossible for the Japanese navy to strike south and leave the Japanese home islands undefended. As such, it was the first clear military challenge to Japanese expansion and the first real step toward war. Roosevelt did not believe that his Fleet transfer would lead to war. But nations go to war less by deciding on it than by taking actions that close off alternative courses of action. As the alternatives disappear, leaders frequently find themselves resorting to war as the only option left. This does not mean that wars are inevitable, only that it is easier to stumble into a war than plan far enough ahead to avoid one. Nor does it mean that one side or the other cannot be the aggressor, only that no nation sees itself as the provoker in the dispute but rather as the provoked.[15] In this case, the United States was responding to threatened Japanese expansion. In Tokyo, Japanese expansion into the South Seas was viewed as a response to the economic threat posed by the United States. Neither side wanted a war, but both sides were moving toward one.

Ironically, as *Tennessee* settled into the routine of her new base at Pearl Harbor, Chief of Naval Operations Harold R. Stark scrapped the War Plan Orange that had been the basis for the Fleet's transfer to Pearl Harbor. Worried that the Fleet would be dragged into a Pacific war when it needed to confront the German threat in the Atlantic, Admiral Stark drafted and President Roosevelt approved a plan wherein the navy would stand on the defensive in the Pacific while waging war aggressively in the Atlantic. Submarines and cruisers would harass Japan's supply lines, but the battleships would not be sent across the Pacific. If *Tennessee* was going to engage the Japanese, it would have to be because a Japanese fleet had come across the Pacific.[16]

Shortly after he transferred the Fleet to Hawaii, Roosevelt began to prepare the nation for a global war against the Axis powers of Germany, Italy, and Japan. Raw materials were stockpiled, weapons of war built, and men trained to fight. Aboard *Tennessee,* that mobilization meant a change in the makeup of her crew. *Tennessee*'s complement rose from about 1,000 at the time of the transfer to Pearl Harbor to over 1,400 a year later, a 40 percent increase. And the number of men transferring off the ship also rose as the navy moved men to new posts ashore and at sea. Where one-third of the crew typically had transferred in a year during the 1930s, in *Tennessee*'s first year at Pearl Harbor there was a 100 percent transfer rate, though some of these men came aboard for a brief training stint and were then transferred. Looked at another way, in 1938 and 1939, half the crew had been aboard more than nineteen months. By the end of 1940, half the crew had been aboard less than nine months.[17]

This rapid flow of men on and off ship disrupted the cohesive community that had developed during the 1930s. More-over, as the demand for personnel increased, the navy could not be as selective as it had been. The consequence of these developments was an increase in breaches of discipline aboard *Tennessee.* In the year before the transfer to Pearl Harbor, there had not been a single desertion from the ship. In the year after the transfer, there were ten. In the late 1920s and early 1930s, 2 percent of the crew underwent deck courts-martial for relatively small breaches of discipline. By the late 1930s, the rate had fallen to less than one-quarter of that, half of 1 percent. In the year following the transfer, as new men came aboard, the rate increased to 1 percent and continued to rise until it peaked at 3 percent in 1943 before *Tennessee* set off for combat in the Pacific.

Not only were there many new faces aboard ship and conditions more crowded, men from the naval reserve were appearing in larger numbers. With years of shore duty, they often brought to *Tennessee* ratings higher than a man who had completed four or more years aboard ship when promotions were hard to get. Here was an opportunity for friction, especially if the old salts believed the new man was not worth the rating he wore on his sleeve. But it was a short-lived problem. By spring 1941, any sailor who had sufficient years of service, a clean conduct record, and passed the test received an advancement in rating. During the winter of 1940–41, two or three times as many men received advancements in their ratings aboard *Tennessee* than had been the case a year earlier and still there remained more openings than there were men qualified to fill them. With so many unfilled positions at higher ratings, the navy made sure that anyone who needed time to study for an examination would get it and even offered an additional examination in the hope of finding more sailors who would pass it.[18]

The Fleet was also getting ready for war. In June 1941, it practiced different levels of readiness so a ship could call on full power from all boilers in a much shorter time than normal. The important questions were how much oil did that consume, how many men needed to be on duty, and how hot would it get in the boiler rooms if boilers were kept in a state of readiness so that they could produce steam with thirty minutes, fifteen minutes, or even five minutes notice? And while at anchor, what would it take to keep all boilers at half power so a battleship could get under way in a half hour? These were not routine tests but engineering exercises for a Fleet that assumed it could be called upon to move fast with minimal notice.

Tennessee's engineering officers discovered that if the navy was prepared to burn the oil, they could keep the boilers in a state of readiness by increasing the number of men on an engineering watch by about 40 percent and having those men work in a temperature of 96 degrees, levels of men and temperature that could be sustained indefinitely.[19]

As *Tennessee* prepared for war, American and Japanese diplomats labored in a futile effort to find a common ground on which to build peace. With diplomacy dead in the water, Japan pushed south and occupied the southern part of French Indochina in July 1941. The Roosevelt administration responded by cutting off oil exports to Japan; Britain and the Dutch East Indies did so as well. By November, Japan was running out of oil and had to either surrender its dream of being a great Asian power or invade the Dutch East Indies to get the oil Japan needed to fuel its war machine. Taking the East Indies, however, meant leaving the home islands vulnerable to attack by the American warships massed at Pearl Harbor. Roosevelt had placed the ships there for precisely that reason. For more than a year they had been an effective deterrent, but now Japan was dominated by an all-or-nothing mentality and the ships at

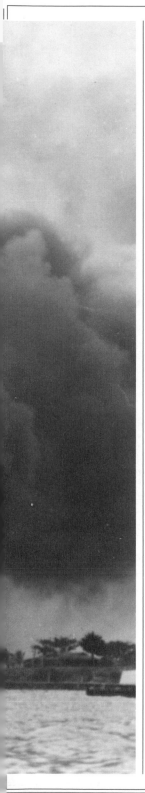

Arizona burns furiously, with *Tennessee* directly behind her and *West Virginia* alongside *Tennessee*.[20]

Pearl Harbor changed from being a deterrent to a target. From Tokyo's perspective, more was to be lost by capitulating to American demands than by going to war with the United States.[21]

The seriousness of the situation was clear to diplomatic and naval personnel. Twice during 1941, Pearl Harbor went on a high state of alert as diplomatic tensions mounted. But nothing happened and it was impossible to stay on alert all the time, at least before a shooting war had started. Moreover, a Japanese attack on Pearl Harbor was so difficult and dangerous that Americans and Japanese both presumed it to be foolhardy. The likelihood that Japanese ships would be detected before they could attack, the difficulty in training aviators to attack in the cramped quarters of Pearl Harbor, the absence of an aerial torpedo that could be dropped in the harbor's shallow waters, and the danger that while the attack was taking place American aircraft would find and sink the Japanese carriers combined to make a Japanese attack on Pearl Harbor an act of desperation.[22] For the men who continued their daily routine aboard *Tennessee,* war may have been seen as a possibility but not as imminent, and a Japanese strike at Pearl Harbor was about the furthest thing from their minds.

Diplomatic negotiations collapsed on November 26, 1941. What Japan was willing to concede was too little for Franklin Roosevelt or Cordell Hull, and what the president and secretary of state asked of Japan was too much for the Japanese government. War was now unavoidable, and intercepted Japanese messages indicated it could come any day. The American navy lost no time warning its ships and bases throughout the Pacific: "This despatch is to be considered a war warning," the message stated bluntly. "An aggressive move by Japan is expected within the next few days." Naval intelligence tracked Japanese warships and troop transports heading south and predicted an attack at Borneo, the Isthmus of Kra, or possibly even the Philippines. What naval intelligence did not know was that Admiral Nagumo Chuichi's aircraft carrier task force had already begun its secret journey across the Pacific. On December 7, 1941, it reached its target.[23]

Tennessee was not prepared for what was about to happen. Along with her fellow battleships, she had sat along Battleship Row in Pearl Harbor since Friday, November 28. The navy's war warning either had not been passed on to her captain, Charles E. Reordan, or had not been taken seriously by him. In any case, the ships were not ordered to sea or even ordered to keep steam ready so they could get under way in minutes. Reordan and his executive officer, Commander Colin Campbell, were both ashore on liberty at their residences that Sunday morning in December. The ranking officer aboard was Lieutenant Commander J. W. Adams, and about the last thing on his mind was a Japanese attack.[24]

In all respects, it was a perfectly normal Sunday morning aboard *Tennessee.* Down in the ship's brig was Mess Attendant Second Class H. C. Johnson, serving a three-day sentence on bread and water for neglect of duty and failure to carry out an order of the chief steward. In the windless anchor room, a quiet place to sleep once the ship got busy, was Chief Storekeeper J. C. Bradford. He had come aboard from liberty at 5:00 A.M. and stopped by the galley to pick up a sandwich from the night cook. The night cook was not supposed to do that — his job was to prepare meals for the men coming off watch. But if he liked you and you could do something for him (a chief storekeeper could always do something for someone), he would make you a sandwich. On deck, Jim Beddingfield was in charge of a cleaning detachment preparing for an admiral's inspection the coming week. Below in the junior officers' wardroom,

Lieutenant Junior Grade Ed James was getting ready to go ashore. He was going to a ballgame but had said he was attending church ashore in order to get permission to leave the ship earlier. Chiefs were allowed to sleep until 8:00 A.M. on Sundays, and at least one was asleep in his bunk. The marine color guard was on the fantail, and the clerk of the marine detachment was filling out the morning report in the detachment's office. Throughout the ship, men were storing mess tables and were getting ready for liberty. On the bridge, officers and men could see planes in the distance — on this beautiful morning with a light breeze, visibility was 40,000 yards.

Just before 8:00 A.M., a Japanese plane dropped to 75 feet above the water and released a torpedo that punctured *West Virginia*'s side, slamming her violently against *Tennessee*. The deck officer sounded general quarters and recorded in the deck log at 7:58: "Attacked by enemy planes (Japanese)." The impact of the *West Virginia* crashing into *Tennessee* knocked Chief Water Tender Richard Fife out of his bunk. He, like others, thought the ship had been rammed. Some assumed a loading hatch or boat had fallen or a winch had collapsed. Few if any of the men below decks guessed it was a Japanese attack. Even the sound of the "general quarters," or

battle stations, alarm provoked disbelief and exasperated expletives for the fool who ordered a drill on Sunday morning. It did not take long for the truth to set in.

By the time men got on deck, they saw Japanese torpedo planes skimming just above Pearl Harbor's waters, dive bombers dropping from the sky, high-altitude bombers releasing their loads from 10,000 feet, and fighter planes strafing the ships. Smoke, fire, and Japanese planes filled the air. No time to think, just react. The 5-inch 25 caliber antiaircraft gun crews blasted away, pouring out 760 rounds at the attacking Japanese planes. The 5-inch 51 caliber guns could not be aimed high enough to

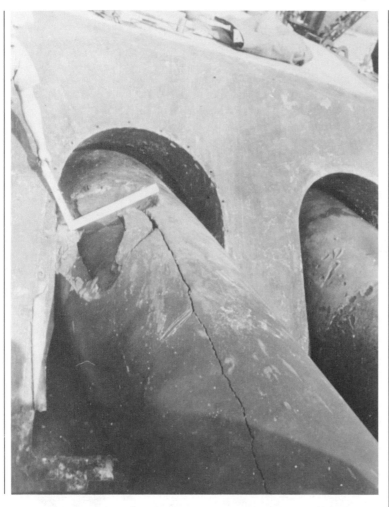

Left: On December 10, *Tennessee* was still trapped, blocked by the sunken *Arizona* to the right, pinned by *West Virginia* whose decks are awash right next to her, and blocked by *Maryland* just to the left. *Maryland* is next to the capsized *Oklahoma.*

Right: One of the bombs that hit *Tennessee* detonated on a gun barrel, destroying the gun but doing little other damage to the ship. A sailor marks the spot of impact.[25]

shoot over the *West Virginia,* so marines from one of those guns rushed to an unmanned 3-inch 50 caliber gun and began firing it even though they had never worked on such a gun before. Throughout the ship, sailors set up and manned 50 caliber machine guns, firing a total of 4,000 rounds at the low-flying Japanese planes.

Meanwhile, chaos surrounded *Tennessee. West Virginia* listed badly and hemorrhaged oil onto the burning waters. As soon as she could get up steam, *Tennessee* kept her screws turning at a 5-to-10 knot rate so the wash would drive the oil away. Lieutenant Commander Adams wanted to bring the captain aboard, but the ship's boats

were sunk or burning. Intense heat from burning oil and burning ships ignited bow and stern awnings that had given shade to the men in the peacetime navy. As the heat grew, the many layers of paint *Tennessee* had accumulated over the years began to burn in the after crane room, and Adams ordered three magazines flooded lest the heat cause an explosion. It became so hot that no one could reach the ship's doctor's office to retrieve the morphine stored there, and the wounded lying on mattresses and cots in the passageway outside sick bay had no relief from their pain.

Back in June, *Tennessee* had demonstrated it was feasible to keep steam oper-

ating in the boilers so she could get under way in fifteen minutes or less. But even after the war warning of November 26, no one ordered that level of readiness aboard *Tennessee* or any of the other battleships in Pearl Harbor. When the attack began, *Tennessee* had only one boiler burning to generate electricity and was unable to heed the order to get out of the harbor as fast as possible. *Nevada* was the only battleship to get under way during the attack and it took her the better part of an hour to get up steam. *Tennessee* did not try to get out until 10:30 A.M., after the attack was over. By then it was too late. Almost as soon as the first torpedo struck *West Virginia,* that battleship began listing to port, pulling taut the two steel cables and six hemp lines that held her to *Tennessee.* Prompt counterflooding of compartments on *West Virginia*'s starboard side allowed her to settle on the bottom, but in doing so she wedged *Tennessee* tightly against docking quay F6. *Oklahoma,* forward and outboard of *Tennessee,* gently heeled over and capsized, pinning *Maryland* just as *Tennessee* was pinned.

Arizona, moored directly astern of *Tennessee,* blew up at 8:20 A.M., when a bomb penetrated the deck armor next to the battleship's number 2 turret, detonating the forward magazine. The explosion was so great that it blew out fires aboard the repair ship moored next to her and lifted *Tennessee* in the water. *Arizona*'s burning foremast tumbled onto *Tennessee*'s quarterdeck and a cloud of black smoke shrouded her so the men on the bridge could see little of what was happening on deck and gunners could not see aircraft approaching. Smoke did not stop the Japanese bombers. Flying at 10,000 feet, they dropped converted 15-inch armor-piercing shells weighing 1,500 to 2,000 pounds. Falling from nearly 2 miles up, these bombs easily sliced through battleship deck armor, as the destruction of *Arizona* showed.

It was *Tennessee*'s good fortune that neither of the two bombs that hit her did significant damage. The first carried away part of the signal mast, punched through the catapult above turret 3, and penetrated the 5-inch armor on the top of the turret at a 75-degree angle. But the bomb burned rather than exploded. The concussion from the impact killed two men in the turret, and several others were burned by the fire or were poisoned when they inhaled the fumes. But sailors extinguished the flames in only three minutes, and though that gun was put out of commission, it was the only thing damaged. A second bomb struck the center gun barrel of turret 2, destroying the barrel but not harming the ship. The shards raked *West Virginia*'s bridge, killing that ship's captain, but no serious casualties resulted aboard *Tennessee*.

It was 10:00 A.M. before Captain Reordan could get aboard, and by then the attack was over. The damage to the Fleet was extensive: *Arizona* destroyed, *Oklahoma* capsized, *West Virginia* and *California* sunk in shallow water, *Nevada* run aground to avoid sinking in the channel. *Tennessee*, still fit for duty, had lost two of her twelve guns, one catapult, one crane, and all her boats; four men were dead and nineteen critically or seriously injured. Her superstructure was scorched and punctured by fire and shell, but such cosmetic damage to the ship did not affect her propulsion, power, and fire-control systems. By the standards of a battleship designed to take massive punishment, the Japanese had scarcely laid a glove on *Tennessee*.

Some of this good fortune may have been due to the effectiveness of the ship's antiaircraft fire, which many men aboard believed had forced Japanese high-altitude and dive-bombing pilots to miss their target. But luck plays an important role in battle, and it was only by chance that the two bombs that had hit her dead center either did not explode or spent their fury on the barrel of a gun. *Tennessee* was also fortunate enough to be moored inboard and sheltered from the brutal impact of Japanese torpedoes.

Though she survived the initial attack, *Tennessee* was still in great danger. *Arizona,* astern of her, burned furiously while *West Virginia,* leaning against her port beam, poured thousands of gallons of fuel oil into the flaming harbor. Even with *Tennessee*'s propellers washing the flames away, the heat was so great that hundreds of welds ruptured. As *Tennessee* sat battling for her life, reports of a Japanese invasion began to circulate. At 12:10 P.M.: "Enemy transport reported 40 miles off Barber's point. Parachute troops landing on Barber's point." At 12:46 P.M.: "Various planes coming in, many friendly, others uncertain as they turn away." But there was no invasion nor more attacks. Admiral Nagumo had withdrawn his forces, worried that the American carriers at sea might surprise his ships while the Japanese planes were attacking Pearl Harbor.

It took two days for *Arizona* to stop burning and another seven days to demolish the concrete moorings and free *Tennessee*. An

Right: By December 9, *Arizona*'s fires had burned themselves out, but *Tennessee* was wedged tightly in place by the sunken *West Virginia*.

Below: While *Tennessee* was at Bremerton Navy Yard during January and February 1942, yard workmen repaired the damaged parts of the ship but concentrated on improving antiaircraft defenses. Air-search radar was installed, and fire-control radar was fitted to the main batteries and to the 5-inch antiaircraft gun directors. *Tennessee*'s 3-inch and 50 caliber antiaircraft guns were removed and 1.1-inch and 20mm guns were installed. Splinter shields were constructed around her 5-inch antiaircraft guns. Finally, her old 14-inch Mark 4 guns were replaced with the improved Mark-11 model.[26]

inspection of the ship revealed that the intense heat had warped every piece of hull plating above the waterline. Over the next four days, repair parties welded 1,500 cracks and 2,000 weakened rivets, placed a patch atop turret 3, and covered all but twenty of the portholes. At 4:00 P.M. on December 20, *Tennessee* headed for the West Coast and more extensive repairs. Accompanied by *Pennsylvania, Maryland,* and four destroyers, she encountered no Japanese ships, though nervous sonar operators, soundmen, and lookouts thought they saw the enemy everywhere. On December 29, she pulled into Puget Sound.[27]

As soon as *Tennessee* dropped anchor at the navy yard, dozens of civilian workers began around-the-clock repairs that grew even more comprehensive once she entered dry dock. They replaced the hull plating warped by fire and the wiring melted by the intense heat. When *Tennessee* emerged two months later, her aft cage mast was gone, her portholes were covered over, and more antiaircraft guns bristled from her superstructure. For the men aboard, however, the biggest changes came inside. For most of *Tennessee*'s life, her crew complement ranged from 1,000 to 1,200 men. By the middle of 1942 there were over 1,700 men aboard and by the end of the war the figure was well over 2,000. The only way so many men could sleep was to have multilevel bunks in place of the hammocks that had been strung from the overhead. The bunks meant no room for mess tables, so a cafeteria-style food service replaced the practice of mess cooks carrying food to the men in each division.

Many of the men aboard *Tennessee* when she emerged from the Puget Sound Navy Yard on February 25, 1942, had never slept in a hammock or eaten at division tables and had no idea how the ship had changed. They were new recruits, men who had joined the navy after the Pearl Harbor attack and spent twenty-one days in boot

War brought a dramatic change in the way *Tennessee* looked. Before World War II her high cage masts provided a striking silhouette (left). After being repaired in January and February 1942, her appearance changed somewhat — a cage mast had been removed and more antiaircraft guns installed (bottom, left). The "ultimate rearmament" of 1942–43 made *Tennessee* look like a modern battleship. Her cage masts were gone, her two smokestacks had been merged into a single funnel, even her deck was modified with a raised area amidships to provide a better field of fire for two more twin 5/38s (right). When she emerged from Bremerton in May 1943, *Tennessee* carried eight twin 5/38 gun mounts, ten quadruple 40mm gun mounts, and forty-three 20mm guns for a total of ninety-nine antiaircraft guns.[28]

camp, just long enough for their vaccinations to become effective. The first 250 men, mostly apprentice seamen from the naval training station in San Diego, came aboard on January 5. Another 150 recruits joined them during the next few weeks. Aboard ship, these men had to learn their jobs and find their sea legs. For seven of them that was a painful experience. During a storm they ventured on deck where a large wave promptly slammed them into the superstructure. Until the recruits learned their job and all the men learned to work together as an efficient crew, *Tennessee* was not fit for combat even though her wounds had

been healed. Fortunately, most of the officers who oversaw the training of the crew were veterans. Only eighteen of the fifty-one ensigns and two of the nine lieutenants junior grade aboard were new to the ship.

With her repairs completed, *Tennessee* reached San Francisco on March 3, 1942. No one was taking any chances on another surprise attack. Torpedo nets shielded her sides, and half the antiaircraft batteries aboard ship were manned at all times. Sentries posted on deck took their job seriously. When a civilian motorboat approached too close to *Tennessee* and failed to heed a challenge, a sentry fired warning shots and the

boat quickly changed course and stood clear.

Sailors were admonished to watch what they said, since "loose lips sink ships." Not everyone got the word, however. One young ensign activated from the naval reserve sat in the bar at the St. Francis Hotel discussing the prospective movements of Task Force One, to which *Tennessee* was attached. The navy's investigation resulted in the ensign's being relieved of duty and later recalled to active duty for purposes of standing general court-martial.

Task Force One, under Vice Admiral W. S. Pye, contained the available Pacific-based battleships and a screen of destroyers. In effect, it formed an expensive patrol force guarding the American coast from a possible Japanese attack. In April *Tennessee* steamed 1,000 miles west into the Pacific on patrol but found nothing. In June, following the decisive American victory at the battle of Midway, *Tennessee* and Task Force One steamed into the Pacific on the chance that the surviving Japanese warships might try to sneak around and attack the West Coast. But the Japanese had retired to their home waters, so *Tennessee* returned to San Francisco without seeing action. These weeks provided ample opportunity for gunnery practice and engineering tests, but with the war raging at Midway and Savo Island near Guadalcanal, *Tennessee* was definitely on the sidelines.

More than the attack on Pearl Harbor, where ships were not free to maneuver and were caught by surprise, the battle of Midway demonstrated the destructive power of the aircraft carrier. The American and Japanese ships never saw each other, but their aircraft pounded one another at ranges that made the big guns of a battleship irrelevant. Able to make only 21 knots, *Tennessee* was too slow to catch a Japanese aircraft carrier or to keep up with the fast, 31-knot aircraft carriers in the United States Navy. *Tennessee* was not only too slow to use as an offensive weapon against the Japanese navy, she was also too vulnerable to Japanese air attack to use almost anywhere. On August 2, 1942, she participated in an antiaircraft test in which American fighters and bombers simulated a carrier-based attack. Though her newly installed tracking radar on the 5-inch guns picked up the planes at 35,000 yards and tracked them all the way in, there were so many planes involved that it "was impossible to oppose all attacks by gun fire." The only solution was to increase her armor and her antiaircraft armament.

Once again she steamed to the Puget Sound Navy Yard and on August 26 began an overhaul that became known as an "ultimate rearmament." The aft cage mast had been removed in January. Now the remaining cage mast and the conning tower were removed for a lower, more compact superstructure that would afford a freer fire zone for antiaircraft guns. The old 5/51s, relics of a day when battleships needed to ward off attacking destroyers, were finally removed, as were the 5/25 antiaircraft guns, and replaced with a large number of 5-inch 38 caliber 40mm and 20mm guns positioned so that every angle from which an enemy plane might attack was covered by guns of different sizes and ranges. To protect her from torpedo attack or bombs falling close aboard, 8-foot-wide blisters bulged from her sides. Filled with water or fuel oil, the blisters absorbed the shock of an exploding torpedo or bomb, leaving the inner hull free from damage. There was nothing new about such blisters; during the 1930s there had not been enough money in the budget to make the changes.

Overseeing the eight months of *Tennessee*'s rearmament was Captain Robert Haggart, a naval academy graduate who had minimal service on battleships but who understood the problems of fitting out. Haggart's major problem was to keep a sense of discipline in his men when the war was so distant. Unable to live aboard ship, the men were quartered aboard a converted ferry and in navy yard barracks. Nevertheless, they were a command, and officers held inspections, granted liberty, and punished men who broke the rules. Even while in dry dock, however, *Tennessee* was on guard against saboteurs, with at least two 20mm and two 50 caliber machine guns manned at all times. When a report of unidentified aircraft came in, *Tennessee* closed her watertight compartments as best she could and activated all her antiaircraft guns, or at least those that were operative. On December 3, 1942, reports of a possible enemy attack resulted in all guns being put on alert as well as an additional 30,000 rounds of 20mm ammunition being brought aboard. When the attack never materialized, the ammunition was returned to shore.

On April 14, 1943, repairs were almost completed and the ship's company returned aboard. A few more tests were run, one more dry docking was done, and fuel was taken aboard along with over 2,000 14-inch shells and tens of thousands of rounds for the 99 5-inch 38 caliber, 40mm, and 20mm guns. On May 8, *Tennessee* got under way and conducted extensive gun and engineering tests. She was, in most respects, a new ship. She looked different, most of her crew members were not aboard when the war began, and she had a new mission — the navy intended to use *Tennessee* and the older battleships to pulverize the Japanese-held islands the marines were about to storm. *Tennessee* was well equipped to do that. The big problem was not going to be the equipment but the men. Since the United States had never fought this kind of amphibious war, the men aboard the new *Tennessee* would have to learn how to fight it. That would take time.

The added weight of armament and blisters slowed *Tennessee* down. On her speed run, she could make only 20 knots rather than the 21 knots she was able to make before the war. Since she was going to be used against stationary targets, the loss of speed was unimportant. Here civilian engineers work with the officers and men of the engineering force in *Tennessee*'s propulsion control room as the remodeled ship goes through her final tests in May 1943.[29]

get Sound Navy Yard.   12 May 1943.
Propulsion control room.

B.S.# 54769

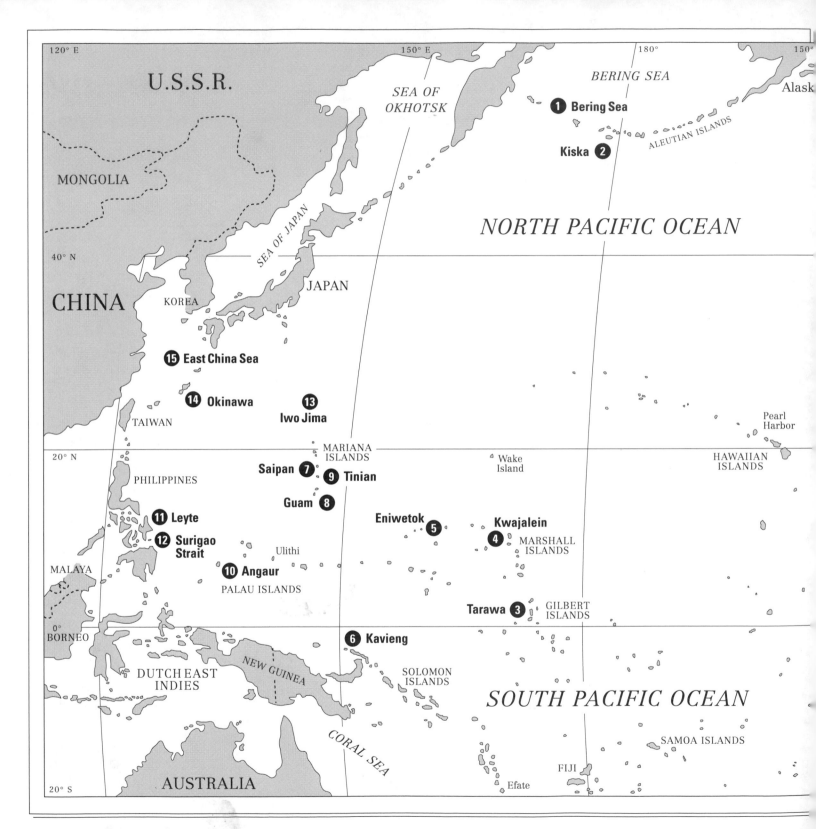

U.S.S.R.

BERING SEA

Alask

SEA OF
OKHOTSK

1 Bering Sea

2 Kiska

ALEUTIAN ISLANDS

MONGOLIA

NORTH PACIFIC OCEAN

SEA OF JAPAN

40° N

JAPAN

CHINA

KOREA

Pearl
Harbor

15 East China Sea

14 Okinawa

13 Iwo Jima

TAIWAN

MARIANA
ISLANDS

Wake
Island

HAWAIIAN
ISLANDS

20° N

PHILIPPINES

Saipan **7** **9** Tinian

Guam **8**

Eniwetok **5** Kwajalein

11 Leyte

4 MARSHALL
ISLANDS

12 Surigao
Strait

Ulithi

MALAYA

10 Angaur

PALAU ISLANDS

Tarawa **3** GILBERT
ISLANDS

0°

BORNEO

6 Kavieng

DUTCH EAST
INDIES

NEW GUINEA

SOLOMON
ISLANDS

SOUTH PACIFIC OCEAN

CORAL SEA

SAMOA ISLANDS

FIJI

20° S

AUSTRALIA

Efate

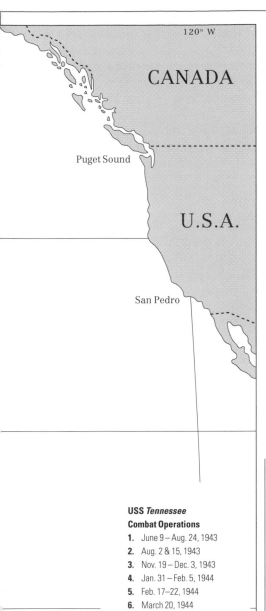

120° W

CANADA

Puget Sound

U.S.A.

San Pedro

USS _Tennessee_
Combat Operations

1. June 9 – Aug. 24, 1943
2. Aug. 2 & 15, 1943
3. Nov. 19 – Dec. 3, 1943
4. Jan. 31 – Feb. 5, 1944
5. Feb. 17–22, 1944
6. March 20, 1944
7. June 14–22, 1944
8. July 19–21, 1944
9. July 23 – Aug. 7, 1944
10. Sept. 12–20, 1944
11. Oct. 17–29, 1944
12. Oct. 24 & 25, 1944
13. Feb. 16 – March 7, 1945
14. March 26 – May 3; June 10–23; Aug. 8 – Sept. 2, 1945
15. July 4 – Aug. 7, 1945

CHAPTER SIX

LEARNING HOW TO FIGHT A NEW KIND OF WAR:

FROM KISKA TO SURIGAO STRAIT

The American strategy in the war against Japan had already been hammered out when the new _Tennessee_ emerged in May 1943. Admiral Chester Nimitz, the officer behind naval strategy in the Pacific, planned to invade the Gilbert Islands and then have his forces fight their way north and west through the Marshalls, Carolines, and Marianas. At that point the central Pacific would be secured and the navy could help General Douglas MacArthur retake the Philippines. More important to the defeat of Japan was the conquest of Saipan and Tinian islands in the Marianas, which would provide air bases from which long-range bombers could reach Japan. If the broad lines of such a strategy were clear, the precise way the amphibious assaults were to be launched and how _Tennessee_ would conduct the bombardments remained uncertain. It would be a year before gunnery experts worked out all the problems and made pre-assault bombard-

ment almost routine. During that year, many marines would die from mistakes made by men who had not yet learned how to fight a new kind of war.[1]

Before _Tennessee_ could head south for the central Pacific, she had to go north and tie up a "loose end," Kiska Island. Japanese troops had seized Kiska and Attu in the Aleutian Islands chain during June 1942. The United States Navy's routing of the Imperial Japanese Navy at the battle of Midway meant Kiska and Attu were more irritants than threats to American security. Nevertheless, strategists thought it important to take back those islands. The Army Air Corps twice tried to bomb the Japanese off the islands but failed. Navy cruisers shelled the islands, but this proved no more effective than bombing. The army decided an invasion was necessary. While _Tennes-_

see was in the final stage of her rearmament, *Pennsylvania, Idaho,* and *Nevada* were supporting 15,000 American infantrymen as they invaded Attu and defeated the 2,350 Japanese troops and engineers. That campaign took fifteen days. With 10,000 Japanese troops estimated to be on Kiska, the U.S. Army beefed up its invasion force to 34,000 men, and *Tennessee* rushed to add her firepower.[2]

Tennessee was not prepared for the war she was about to enter and there was little time to get prepared. As soon as *Tennessee* left the Puget Sound navy yard in mid-May 1943, Captain Robert Haggart had less than a month to make the 1,500 officers and men crammed aboard work together as a crew; many of these men had little or no battleship experience. As *Tennessee* cruised down the West Coast toward southern California, Haggart put his men through hours of drills. At first nothing worked right. One turret officer recorded in his diary: "A very fouled up comedy of errors in main battery firing: misfires, no buzzer signals, etc. Then we couldn't even track properly." But the constant drilling began to pay off, and by the time *Tennessee* dropped anchor in Long Beach harbor, her crew, though not battle tested, was adequately drilled for the kind of job required of them at Kiska.[3]

That she was headed for Kiska was a military secret, of course, and the men aboard were looking forward to some enjoyable liberty days in Los Angeles as compensation for the long months at Puget Sound and the wearisome drills Haggart and *Tennessee*'s executive officer, Commander S. Y. ("Cy") Cutler, had put them through. But the navy needed *Tennessee* in the Bering Sea and few men got liberty; those who did were given Cinderella liberty and had to be back by midnight. Rather than patronizing the bars, restaurants, and brothels of southern California, the men had to make do with the gedunk (ice cream) stand aboard ship. *Tennessee* stayed in port

just long enough to load foul-weather gear; in less than twenty-four hours, she was off to the war. As the ship steamed north, an aspiring poet on board captured the sentiments of some of the sailors:

> Twas back in the year of 43,
> When the going was rough on the
> *Tennessee*
> The ship was perfect in tip top shape,
> But regulations filled the crew with hate.

> We swab and we sweep
> On this piss poor cruise
> In a checked up suit
> Of undress blues.

> They change the time
> so God Damn fast
> It takes both hands
> To wipe your ass.

> All through the nights
> We dream of delights
> And then we saw Long Beach
> Hove into sight.

> I'll tell you for real
> Twas a happy day
> When the crew watched the anchor
> Slide deep in the Bay.

> Of whiskey and women
> Were all we were sure
> But the skipper and Cy
> Had a far different tour.

> The delight was called gedunk
> Of chocolate and vanilla
> The liberty we got
> Was called Cinderella.

> For Kiska we are bound
> To fight with a runt
> No shacking up duty
> With a beautiful c—t.[4]

There was nothing in the Aleutian islands to make up for the lost liberty at Long Beach. Three months at sea in the northern Pacific tested the patience rather than the fighting skills of the men. During June and July, *Tennessee* spent many long, boring hours patrolling the Bering Sea as the flagship of Task Force Sixteen, commanded by Rear Admiral Howard F. Kingman. Though it was an honor to be the flagship, it did not make the duty enjoyable. The weather was depressing: Damp, cold air cut through clothing, and the sun rarely shone. Men who stood deck watches were rotated every half hour to keep them warm.[5] So far north, the nights were short and did not provide the protective darkness that normally shielded warships from enemy submarines. And the days were long, with the men called to battle stations an hour before dawn — 4:00 in the morning!

Relief from these patrols came in Adak Bay or Dutch Harbor; neither was an improvement over life aboard ship. Adak Bay was nothing more than an anchorage with antisubmarine nets. The men could go ashore and see the wildflowers that covered the island or take a look at the Japanese soldiers held in the prisoner-of-war camp. But Adak offered nothing else. A few hundred miles to the east was Dutch Harbor, a real harbor with tugboats, a small town, a restaurant where meals at inflated prices could be purchased, and even a band that struck up a tune of welcome as *Tennessee* first steamed in. But Dutch Harbor was only slightly better than Adak Bay. For those who liked to fish, and who could get the small amount of fishing gear available, there was excellent trout and salmon fishing. For most of the men, free time meant walking the flower-covered hills, playing cards, or waiting for the occasional USO show to come aboard.

One sailor found an escape from such boredom by going ashore, getting drunk, stealing a navy truck, and running it into a ditch. Captain Haggart sentenced him to five days in solitary confinement on bread and water, a common form of punishment. Haggart punished minor infractions such as failure to clean up personal gear or being out of the proper uniform by extra police duties. But sleeping on watch, being absent over liberty, or showing any form of insolence landed the offender in solitary confinement from three to five and occasionally ten days. Haggart sentenced so many men during the three months in the Aleutian Islands that the cells were in constant use, with men waiting several days to begin their sentences. Solitary confinement on bread and water (usually with a full ration every third day) had been a well-established punishment before the war, and during the war it proved the most efficient punishment Haggart had available to him. To deny a man liberty in Dutch Harbor was hardly a great punishment and to deny him liberty once *Tennessee* returned to California after three months in the Aleutians would have been too severe. To put a man in the brig for twenty days meant that someone else had to pick up his duties. It was better to give an offender a few days in solitary on bread and water to impress upon him that though they were not in combat, they were at war.

On the other hand, Haggart commended men who did their job particularly well by praising them at a meritorious mast. Such was the case for two chief machinist's mates and a fireman second class who were publicly congratulated for their prompt handling of a machinery derangement. Similarly, lookouts and the men who manned *Tennessee*'s motor whaleboat were congratulated for spotting the capsized whaleboat from *Salt Lake City* and rescuing the men from the icy waters of Dutch Harbor.

Rewards and punishments helped keep the men on the straight and narrow while they waited to meet the enemy. In the

Bering Sea, *Tennessee* was on the front line without any American aircraft carriers to shield her from the Japanese navy in the event that the Japanese launched an offensive. Only three months before *Tennessee* had journeyed north, the heavy cruiser *Salt Lake City*, light cruiser *Richmond,* and four destroyers had bumped into a Japanese naval force headed toward Attu. The resulting sea battle was inconclusive, but *Salt Lake City* received the worst of the exchange. If Japanese warships had ventured into the area once, they could do it again, so *Tennessee* and other ships in Task Force Sixteen patrolled the Bering Sea to stop them.[6]

These patrols in the cold and fog were uneventful. There was an occasional suspected submarine contact, and *Tennessee* would rush to get out of the way while the destroyers investigated. But nothing came of these reports, and there was not a trace of Japanese surface ships until the afternoon of Saturday, July 10. *Tennessee* was heading back to her base at Dutch Harbor, cruising at her standard 14 knots with her propellers turning at a comfortable 130 revolutions per minute. Suddenly her radar recorded blips to the west where only Japanese warships could be. Task Force Sixteen turned toward the enemy, and *Tennessee* went to full speed.

With her blisters and added equipment, she had only been able to produce 20 knots at her speed trials in May, one knot less than she had made twenty-two years earlier. Now, with the enemy approaching, the engineering force pushed *Tennessee*'s motors to their maximum 165 revolutions. The captain ordered every unnecessary light turned off so the electricity could be poured into the ship's propulsion motors, and *Tennessee* squeezed out another 10 revolutions and reached 22 knots.

A quarter century earlier, naval architects had designed *Tennessee* to meet the enemy on the high seas and annihilate it.

Now, for the first time, she had a chance to prove herself and pay back Japan for the pain inflicted at Pearl Harbor. But the opportunity vanished at 2:00 A.M., when the radar blips disappeared from the screen. Disbelieving radar operators checked their equipment, and some men aboard ship wondered if the Japanese had perfected a way to mask their ships from radar signals. But *Tennessee*'s spotter aircraft could not find a trace of an enemy, and Task Force Sixteen returned to base concluding that there never had been an enemy, only electronic phantoms that appeared and disappeared without explanation. Two weeks later, radar blips again appeared on the radar screens and once again *Tennessee* gave chase until the images disappeared. These phantom contacts proved very disappointing to the crew, who had to content themselves with the bombardment of Kiska three weeks later.[7]

Tennessee's bombardment of Kiska was puny compared with what she would fire later in the central Pacific battles. Her first bombardment lasted only thirty-five minutes, included only 30 rounds of 14-inch high-capacity shells and 363 rounds of 5-inch antiaircraft shells, and produced no counter fire from the island. Still, to Captain Haggart, it was immensely valuable in "sustaining the enthusiasm and morale of the crew" and was a useful "practice" for a ship whose crew and equipment were new. The Mark 8 radar guided the 14-inch guns flawlessly. Crews on the 14-inch and 5-inch guns worked well. The only error, or casualty, was a broken powder bag on the left gun of turret 3 during the latter part of the "practice." The biggest problem was poor radio communication between the spotter aircraft and the ship. Because the ceiling at Kiska was so low, the ships had to notify the spotting aircraft when a salvo was coming so the plane could drop below the clouds to plot where the shells landed. On one occasion, the plane failed to receive a change of target and "the unexpected passage of a main battery salvo rocked the plane severely and proved disconcerting to the observing spotter."[8]

The weather had deteriorated when *Tennessee* returned to Kiska on August 15 with the full invasion force. Visibility was less than 500 yards and all firing was radar directed. That was not so difficult, since radar could track a prominent point ashore and excellent grid maps allowed accurate calculations for locating any target. Sitting about 12,000 yards offshore, *Tennessee* fired 40 rounds of 14-inch high-capacity shells and 191 rounds of 5-inch antiaircraft shells on what proved to be a deserted island. The Japanese had withdrawn their forces a week earlier under cover of the ubiquitous fog.

The Kiska operation had been deceptively easy. American ships bombarded the island and the Japanese withdrew. *Tennessee*'s gunnery officer, Commander J. E. M. Wood, was not misled. Back in southern California, he took his men through a demanding practice and concluded that there were many obstacles to overcome before *Tennessee* could provide effective fire support. Sudden changes of course and speed made it difficult to track a target ashore by radar; his men needed four minutes of constant speed and direction to effect a track. In addition, the radar operator tracking points ashore on his screen would not be very efficient if he did not have radar charts to study before the battle. Air spots were no more reliable unless the spotter had undergone "considerable drill." In short, *Tennessee*'s sophisticated equipment required experienced men to operate it.[9]

Unfortunately, a fact of life in the wartime navy was that there was neither the time nor the continuity of men aboard ship to establish the proper level of training. When *Tennessee* reached San Francisco at the end of August, 100 seasoned veterans

(men with three months sea duty aboard *Tennessee*) were transferred to other ships and 300 seamen second class reported aboard. Boot camp had introduced the recruits to basic seamanship and naval discipline, but they had to learn their jobs aboard ship. For the gun crews, that meant repeated loading drills. For the men who controlled where to fire, it meant rehearsals until they learned to work their equipment and coordinate their actions. Actual firing practice consisted of two days in southern California and another day in Hawaii. *Tennessee* set off for the central Pacific just before the navy opened a special pre-assault bombardment training site in the Hawaiian islands, so she had to content herself with some practice at Efate Island in the New Hebrides from November 9 to November 11 and some target practice on November 13 as she steamed for Tarawa atoll accompanied by *Maryland* and *Colorado*.[10]

Though a week or so at the Hawaiian training center would have improved the speed and accuracy of *Tennessee*'s gun crews, it would not have solved the ship's basic problem: a bombardment doctrine that had *Tennessee* using the wrong kind of shells, fired from the wrong range, at the wrong rate of fire, and in some cases employing the wrong caliber of gun. What *Tennessee* needed was not more practice but experience against a real enemy.

The doctrine that determined how the ships would fire had been developed over many years. The marines had planned for just such a war since 1921, when *Tennessee* joined the Fleet, and by 1934 they had a "Tentative Manual for Landing Operations." In 1937 battleships began participating in what would become an annual Fleet landing exercise. But the navy's heart was not in amphibious warfare; thus it was not until spring 1941 that the navy established a joint marine-navy training force with only a dozen naval gunnery officers involved.[11]

These studies identified three stages to a bombardment. During the preliminary bombardment, the ships attempted to destroy as many enemy positions and kill as many enemy troops ashore as possible. During the second phase, prelanding gunfire neutralized but did not necessarily destroy the enemy as American troops moved ashore. The idea was for American ships to keep Japanese soldiers from shooting at marines as they set foot ashore. During the final stage, after the landings, troops ashore called upon the navy to blast specific enemy positions blocking the marines' advance.[12]

It seemed reasonable that the longer the bombardment before the invasion, the greater the damage inflicted on the enemy. However, a lengthy pre-assault bombardment would reveal the target to the Japanese navy, which might launch a counterstrike against the American ships massed for the invasion. To prevent that, Admiral Raymond Spruance had a considerable force of six fast battleships, six heavy and five light aircraft carriers, four cruisers, and twenty-one destroyers on the scene. Nevertheless, the naval officers planning the invasion decided that the American airplanes and battleships had so much firepower that two days of their withering bombardment would be enough to destroy most Japanese resistance.[13] After all, Betio Island of the Tarawa atoll was less than a half square mile and the plan called first for Spruance's planes to bomb the defenses and then for *Tennessee*, two other old battleships, two heavy cruisers, three light cruisers, and nine destroyers to blast the island. Five escort carriers and, on the first day, one heavy and one light fleet carrier would provide air support. Surely a flotilla with that much firepower could annihilate Japanese troops crammed into such a small space.

The plan called for aircraft to strike at dawn on the day of the landing, and for the ships to then bombard the island heavily, gradually reducing their fire until it became a slow, constant interdiction. During the last forty-five minutes before the first marines stepped ashore, the ships would fire a massive bombardment and stop five minutes before the scheduled landing so as not to risk hitting their own men. Then planes would strafe the beach to cover the landing marines. That was the plan, but just about everything went wrong.

At 5:07 on the morning of November 20, 1943, *Tennessee* sat 10 miles off Betio Island waiting for the American planes to begin the bombardment. The men on deck watched the cruiser *Santa Fe* exchange shots with a Japanese shore battery that American planes were supposed to have destroyed two days earlier. For an hour, *Tennessee* cruised back and forth in her assigned area, waiting for the American planes. By 6:05 the officers running the bombardment decided not to wait any longer and ordered the ships to commence firing. *Tennessee* fired 9 rounds at 6:11, but just as she established the proper range the American planes arrived and she ceased fire until 6:30, when she began an hour-long bombardment, alternating between salvos from her big 14-inch guns and her 5-inch secondary guns. During this first phase of the assault, *Tennessee* was at medium range, beginning at 17,870 yards (about 10 miles) and working her way to 8,990 yards (about 5 miles) from her target when she ceased fire at 7:30.

At 7:42 *Tennessee* began her covering fire for the assault, hurling 14-inch and 5-inch shells ashore for more than an hour while cruising 5 miles offshore. The marines were supposed to hit the beach at 9:00 A.M. and at 8:54, *Tennessee* ceased fire so as not to have a shell fall among the landing troops. But the landing craft were a half hour behind schedule. The result was that the Japanese defenders on Betio Island had time to regroup themselves and con-front the marines in their most vulnerable state, as they stepped ashore. If the pre-assault bombardment had been as effective as officers aboard *Tennessee* presumed it had been, few Japanese ashore would have been fit to fight. But the nearly 400 tons of explosive shells *Tennessee* had fired into the island did not accomplish their goal.

Almost everyone who witnessed the bombardment shared the belief of one naval observer that "it seemed almost impossible for any human being to be alive in Betio Island. Ton after ton of explosives was rained upon an Island less than 0.4 miles square, and yet, when bombardment was stopped, Japanese manned machine guns and literally annihilated the first two assault waves."[14]

Aboard *Tennessee,* the men on deck watched helplessly as the nightmare ashore unfolded. Survivors from the first wave were pinned down on the beach as the landing craft of the second wave grounded on a reef and the men waded 500 yards ashore in neck-deep water with their rifles held over their heads. "One of the sorriest sights of the war," a marine aboard ship wrote, was to watch these tiny figures struggle toward the beach as the water about them boiled and spouted under the hail of lead. When a bullet found its mark, the marine would disappear beneath the water.[15]

It had been *Tennessee*'s job to knock out those shore installations and she had failed. In something of an understatement, Captain Haggart noted "that the amount of damage done per projectile, falling in assigned target area, was disappointingly small. Greater effectiveness in results obtained are felt to be greatly desired." The problem was not with the gun crews failing to do their job well. Of the 584 rounds of 14-inch shells expended before, during, and after the landings, only 22 misfired, probably because the rammer men on the guns pushed the powder too far into the breech where it failed to ignite. Beyond this error, the gun crews "carried on throughout the operation without personal error or injury" even though the temperatures in the gun compartments reached levels "entirely unfavorable to human efficiency."

Nor is it fair to conclude that *Tennessee*'s fire was worthless. Naval bombardment completely disrupted the Japanese communication system on the island, effectively destroyed fire-control installations (thereby rendering Japanese antiaircraft guns ineffective), eventually silenced the antiaircraft guns, killed several hundred exposed Japanese personnel, and created shock among a large number of other Japanese troops. These "effects made it possible to capture the island, but they did not prevent the enemy from making a determined resistance which cost the assaulting troops a high percentage of casualties." A new doctrine of bombardment had to be developed.

There were two problems that had to be resolved. First, the gunnery officers had to find a way to knock out enemy installations during the preliminary bombardment. Second, they had to figure out how to neutralize the surviving enemy installations and troops at the moment the marines stepped ashore. *Tennessee*'s officers came to some very specific conclusions.

For the preliminary bombardment to be effective, the gunnery officers decided, they would have to use a different kind of shell and fire those shells in a different way. They had used a high-capacity shell designed to detonate as soon as it hit anything. Their explosion produced a huge roar that may have terrified the troops hidden below layers of logs, coral sand, and concrete but left them unhurt. Meanwhile, sand and smoke filled the air, convincing observers aboard ship that their gunfire was effective. The solution was to substitute armor-piercing shells designed to explode only after they had burrowed into their target. These should be fired from a longer distance so

the shells plunged downward. The bombardment should be slow and drawn out, lasting several days. The problem at Betio was that it took less than half an hour of bombardment to so obscure the island with smoke and dust that spotters aboard ship and in the air could not find a target at which to shoot. Radar was no help, since it could not pick up where a shell hit unless it landed at least 50 yards offshore. The solution *Tennessee*'s gunnery staff proposed

was to take several days for the long-range bombardment, allowing time for the smoke to clear between salvos. Then the ships would move closer and fire single-gun salvos at specific targets left standing.

Protecting troops as they landed was another matter. *Tennessee*'s gunnery officers had been thinking about this for some time. After Kiska, they had experimented with fusing a 14-inch shell to explode as it passed over enemy lines. The concussion

and shrapnel from such a large shell would kill or debilitate anyone in a very large area. Unfortunately, the men aboard *Tennessee* never could get the fuses to detonate properly. That was not the problem with the fuses on the 5-inch shells, however. Covering fire for landing troops could be provided by a steady stream of 5-inch shells aimed 50 feet above the beach and fused to explode as they passed over the beach or just beyond. The shards that swept the

PIER
mH18.0-26.3

OBSERVATION TOWER
mH12.1-25.5

RUNWAY CLEARING

OBSERVATION TOWER
mHO6.7-27.7

OBSERVATION TOWER
mHO9.5-11.4

RADIO MASTS
mC97.0-40.5

AGGREGATE PLANT
mC 95.7-41.6

OBSERVATION TOWER

EAST POINT

N.W. POINT

S.W. POINT

SUBJECT BEARING 090°, DISTANCE: 10 MILES

BITITU ISLAND
TARAWA ATOLL

Left: Just 12,000 yards offshore, *Tennessee* had Tarawa well within range of her guns. But at this distance the small, well-fortified, well-camouflaged targets on the island could not be seen, much less knocked out. The result was a great deal of ammunition expended and little damage done.

Above: Poor charts of the islands to be invaded hampered operations. This reconnaissance photograph provided good detailed information on likely targets on Betio Island in the Tarawa atoll. Unfortunately, the island on the chart *Tennessee* gunners were using was rotated 3 degrees clockwise. Consequently, the first few rounds fell short before the men aboard ship discovered the mistake.[16]

ground would pin down the enemy even as the marines landed. The effectiveness of such a plan, however, depended upon the spotters aboard ship seeing where the friendly troops were and that meant bringing the ship close to shore. At Betio, two destroyers had done just that. Entering the lagoon and having a clear view of where the marines were, they had kept up a continuous bombardment of the shore as the landing craft approached the beach.

If the bombardment during phases one and two did not work very well at Tarawa, the supporting fire after the landing provided good results. *Tennessee* fired 116 rounds of 14-inch shells and 522 rounds of 5-inch shells at specific targets the marines wanted destroyed and scored direct hits on gun emplacements, pillboxes, and other fortifications. Though the shore fire-control party was in communication with *Tennessee* and identified the targets the marines wanted destroyed, they could not tell the men aboard ship how accurate their fire was. *Tennessee* still relied on aircraft and shipboard spotters to control the fire. The difficulty of maintaining such accurate gunfire was compounded because the ship moved slowly and had to battle currents. Only a well-trained crew could hold her on a course steady enough for the men in the gun-plot stations to zero in on an enemy target that might be as small as a few yards across.[17]

Once the gunnery officers had sent their findings up the chain of command, there was nothing for them to do but to continue drills while they waited for the new doctrine to be handed down. Life aboard ship returned to a routine that emphasized boredom and fatigue. Though combat at Tarawa had lasted only a few days, it had been preceded by weeks of cruising out and followed by weeks of cruising back. During those weeks, every day was much the same. An hour and a half before dawn, all hands were awakened, and an hour before dawn they went to their battle stations. When Japanese planes did not attack, the men were dismissed from battle stations and ate breakfast. Then there was the routine of repairing machinery, conducting drills, and keeping the ship clean. Every night at sunset the ship was darkened, all watertight hatches and doors were sealed, and the men not on duty could sleep until they repeated the process the next morning.

In these circumstances, the men aboard *Tennessee* felt isolated from the death that accompanied war. Surrounded by massive steel, protected by blisters, and bristling with guns, *Tennessee* oozed power. She was an older battleship and not so fast or so powerful as the battleships that had just been built. But that had its advantages because the navy would not send an old battleship to confront the Japanese fleet. "Old Blisterbutt," as her crew called her,

would seek out tiny Japanese-held atolls in the Pacific and pound them into submission with her big guns. It was a necessary but not a particularly dangerous job. Traveling to Tarawa aboard *Tennessee,* the journalist Robert Sherrod was struck by the way the men felt no more threatened by the Japanese than would "a county clerk in Nebraska."[18] There was no reason for the battle at Tarawa to change that. The marines who died there were killed thousands of yards away from the sailors watching from the security of the ship. Even the violent death of two shipmates on October 26, 1943, came not from the hands of the Japanese but as a result of accident.

Seaman First Class K. V. Munson went to his battle station in turret 2 that morning and like all the other mornings, nothing happened. He settled down for a short nap on the flat steel sheet located in the pit below the breech of the center gun. This was against regulations, of course, but since nothing was going on it seemed to be a good place to catch a nap. Not knowing that Munson was there, someone ordered the gun elevated and the huge breech descended on the hapless sailor, fracturing his skull, crushing his chest, and rupturing most of his internal organs. Without any apparent pain, he lived for fifteen hours, confessed his sins to the Catholic chaplain aboard ship, and died just before midnight.

When *Tennessee* had left San Francisco the preceding September, Munson had missed ship, coming aboard twenty-six days later. On October 13, Captain Haggart sentenced him to two months in the brig and fined him $33 a month for six months. The sentence had not yet been carried out. Perhaps Haggart was waiting until after combat at Tarawa to begin it or perhaps the brig was already filled. Had Munson been in jail rather than in gun turret 2, he would have lived. As it was, his body was sewn into a canvas bag and weighted down with two 5-inch shells. Members of his division,

who served as pallbearers, struggled to lift the body through the hatch to the deck where the crew was gathered to pay their last respects. The band played "Nearer, My God, to Thee," while the flag-draped body was carried across the quarterdeck. The chaplain, wearing a black cassock over his khaki uniform, prayed, marines in khaki uniforms presented arms, and the body was consigned to the sea. The men saluted, the marines fired a volley, the band played "Onward, Christian Soldiers," and the service was over. That afternoon, the chaplain said a mass.

A half hour after Munson was crushed, Lieutenant Harry P. Chapman, Jr., climbed into his spotter aircraft. Someone had failed to attach the plane to the sled on which it would be propelled down the catapult and when the hoist cable was released, the plane began to slide off. A sailor tried to hold it up, but the plane was too heavy. With a look of horror on his face, Chapman began to climb out of the cockpit, realized it was too late, and sat back, prepared to ride the plane down. It slid off the catapult, bounced off the deck and over the side. The spotter aboard the plane bobbed to the surface and was picked up by the destroyer *Hazelwood,* but the lookouts aboard *Hazelwood* could not find Chapman and after giving up the search, the destroyer's guns sank the floating aircraft. That Sunday, a memorial service was held for Chapman.[19]

Except for Munson and Chapman, *Tennessee* did not lose a man between the time she left the West Coast in September 1943 and returned to the West Coast in time for the men to spend Christmas ashore. But so many marines had died at Tarawa that Rear Admiral Robert Conolly and his staff were determined to find a better way to bombard the enemy before the next offensive at Kwajalein atoll in the Marshall Islands. The admiral and his staff devoured the gunnery reports that *Tennessee* and the

In the main battery plot, a gunnery team received information from various sources, analyzed it, and instructed the guns to change their range or direction of fire. In this drawing, cartoonist S. N. ("Woody") Woodall reminds us that each of the 2,000 men aboard *Tennessee* was an individual with his own personality and idiosyncrasies.[20]

other ships at Tarawa had generated and hammered out a new approach toward pre-assault bombardment that mirrored the suggestions put forward by *Tennessee*'s officers after Tarawa. There would be a preliminary bombardment lasting many days and followed by close-range firing on specific targets. Thus during December 1943 and January 1944, American ships and planes bombarded Japanese-held islands in the Marshall chain. On January 29–30, aircraft carriers and fast battleships pounded the Roi and Namur islands of the Kwajalein atoll. Finally, on January 31, *Tennessee* and the rest of the invasion armada arrived.[21] *Tennessee* was the flagship of Task Unit 53.5.1 under Admiral Howard Kingman. This task unit was part of the Northern Support Force (Task Group 53.5) under Rear Admiral Jesse B. Oldendorf, which was part of Task Force Fifty-Three under Conolly. "Close In" Conolly moved his battleships, cruisers, and destroyers until they almost touched the shore. This made for quite a crowd because he had seven old battleships (including *Tennessee*) and eight

heavy and four light cruisers along with a dozen or more destroyers operating in the same waters. On the day of the invasion, he also brought in 12 landing craft equipped as gunboats and 45 LSTs, landing craft large enough to hold tanks.[22]

This was a big operation, and Under Secretary of the Navy James V. Forrestal was aboard *Tennessee* to see what the navy had learned from Tarawa. Forrestal witnessed an almost flawless performance. Skilled spotters in aircraft launched from *Tennessee* along with highly trained radar plotters operating the latest equipment produced very accurate fire from the 14-inch guns. The reliability of these guns was high, with only six misfires in 783 rounds fired during two days of bombardment. More visible evidence of the effectiveness of *Tennessee*'s shooting was the destruction of a blockhouse that was her prime target and the huge explosion after a shell landed in a Japanese ammunition dump. A look at damage ashore after the island was secured convinced Captain Haggart that his ship's fire had been very effective.[23]

Not everything worked perfectly. With so many ships bunched in such a small area around the island, there was serious congestion. *Tennessee* and the cruiser *Mobile* alternated with *Colorado* and *Louisville* in providing constant fire in their assigned area. Occasionally all four ships along with their destroyer screen were crowded into the same area, which made it difficult to maneuver and maintain an accurate track of targets ashore. Also, with battleships as close as 2,000 yards from shore, there was a great danger of ricochets — a shell fired from a ship on one side of the island could skip off the relatively flat terrain and speed toward a friendly ship on the other side of the island. On the second day of bombardment, men poised in *Tennessee*'s high lookout were startled by two large-caliber shells that passed very close to them and tumbled into the sea just 20 yards off *Tennessee*'s starboard bow.[24] No damage was done and these risks were more than offset by the effectiveness of the bombardment; the marines were able to walk across the beach standing up and did not meet resistance

Left: Big guns pounding Kwajalein atoll in February 1944. The exploding shells kicked up so much dust and smoke that the spotters aboard ship had trouble finding a target; the spotters in aircraft were almost as blind.

Above: Occasionally, a large ammunition dump would be hit and the resulting explosion would be satisfying to the gunners, though dangerous to spotter aircraft. This explosion reportedly knocked two spotter aircraft out of the sky.[25]

until 200 yards inshore. In fact, the landing cost the marines so few casualties that the reserve units were not called upon, and Admiral Spruance decided to waste no time in launching a quick strike against the next target in the Marshalls, Eniwetok atoll.

Tennessee had time to do little more than refuel and load more ammunition before she steamed toward Perry Island of Eniwetok atoll and an operation set to start on February 17. Using captured Japanese maps of Eniwetok lagoon, *Tennessee* was able to negotiate the tricky currents and

strong winds within the lagoon, a show of seamanship that earned her and *Pennsylvania* special recognition from their division commander. In fact, the lagoon was so crowded and maneuvering so difficult that *Tennessee* spent much of her time anchored as close as 850 yards from shore, so close that one sailor was shot in the lung by a stray bullet from shore. It was while in this position that *Tennessee* effectively employed 40mm antiaircraft guns during the landing.

In her fire support position at Eniwetok,

Tennessee found herself with a clear field of fire along the enemy lines and parallel to the beachhead. (The technical term is "enfilade fire.") She was so close to the beach that when her 14-inch and 5-inch guns ceased fire, she pinned down Japanese troops along the beach with slow, controlled fire from her 40mm antiaircraft guns. The idea of employing the 40mm guns rather than the 5-inch guns to cover the landing appears to have originated aboard *Tennessee*. Admiral Oldendorf liked the idea and brought it to the attention of his superiors.[26] Eventually it became the standard way of protecting troops at the moment they were most vulnerable.

Following Eniwetok, there was a lull in the fighting. Admiral Nimitz wanted to move against the Marianas where Saipan and Tinian could provide air bases just 1,200 miles from the Japanese home islands and well within range of the new B-29 bomber, the Super Flying Fortress. There were some, most notably General Douglas MacArthur, who objected to this strategy, and it was not until March 1944 that Nimitz was able to overcome this opposition and begin assembling the ships and men for an attack on Saipan. With nowhere else to fight, *Tennessee* could be spared to bombard Kavieng on New Ireland in the Bismarck archipelago where she and several other older battleships were to serve as a diversion to protect the American assault on Emirau Island, 100 miles away. No one told the Japanese gunners on Kavieng that *Tennessee*'s bombardment was only a diversion, and they opened up on the battleship, straddling her with shells on several occasions but not hitting her. *Tennessee* responded with a ten-minute barrage of 14-inch and 5-inch shells, and the Japanese guns went silent.

Kavieng was Captain Haggart's last operation. An officer whose battleship experience was in engineering rather than gunnery, Haggart was well suited to command *Tennessee* during her rearmament. He did well in the various bombardments and received a special commendation for his efforts at Eniwetok; but now he was headed for the naval training center at San Diego. His replacement was Captain Andrew D. Mayer, an ordnance and gunnery specialist who had been gunnery officer aboard *California* from 1935 to 1936.[27]

Captain Mayer took command of a ship whose crew had good reason to believe they had mastered the art of amphibious warfare. At Eniwetok, the 14-inch gun crews had performed almost flawlessly, with no casualties and misfires of less than 1 percent. The aircraft and radar spotters had become so good that the shells landed precisely where they were supposed to with devastating effect. And the gunners aboard *Tennessee* demonstrated the value of 40mm fire from a battleship at the moment of landing. While in Hawaii, *Tennessee* continued to develop her skill at 40mm fire, receiving special training in providing 40mm covering fire for the underwater demolition teams (the frogmen, or UDTs) that removed obstacles to landing craft in the waters close to shore and tested the sand on the beaches just before the invasion.

It was a well-trained, proficient crew that steamed out of Pearl Harbor on May 31, 1944, to attack the Japanese at Saipan. But not everyone in the navy realized how much specialized training was required before a battleship could effectively bombard an island. Rather than have *Tennessee* and the other older battleships conduct a lengthy bombardment, Admiral Spruance ordered his modern, fast battleships to pummel Saipan with their big guns on June 13. But these fast battleships, far superior to *Tennessee* as weapons of naval warfare, stood about 6 miles offshore and blew up buildings that could be seen but had no important tactical value. The smaller, more important targets went unseen and

By the time she got to Eniwetok, *Tennessee* was just a few hundred yards offshore — so close that her new camouflage paint served no purpose. In this position, she was able to maintain continuous 40mm fire on the beach as the marines came ashore.[28]

undestroyed. *Tennessee* and the other older, slower battleships moved in on June 14 and, from the more effective range of 3,000 yards, directed their fire at the strongest Japanese fortifications. But one day of preparatory, close-range bombardment was not enough and on June 15, when the landings were made, most of the Japanese guns and positions remained untouched.[29]

By this stage of the war, the men aboard *Tennessee* were good enough to carry on several different tasks virtually simultaneously. On the day before the landings, they provided long-range covering fire for American minesweepers operating along the west coast of the island. Then *Tennessee* moved close to shore to protect the underwater demolition team heading toward the beach. Just 3,000 yards from shore, men aboard ship could easily see the UDT approaching the reef in four small rubber boats. As the frogmen slipped into the water and swam the rest of the way, *Tennessee* laid down a covering fire from her 40mm guns. At 9:16 A.M., the frogmen radioed back that they could not reconnoiter the area because of heavy machine-gun fire coming from beached Japanese boats, so *Tennessee* turned her 40mm guns on the boats. At 9:38, spotters aboard ship saw the UDT taking heavy fire from mortars and 4-inch guns. *Tennessee* fired her own 5-inch guns at the Japanese 4-inch guns and then laid down a barrage of phosphorous shells ashore to make a smokescreen to cover the withdrawal of the UDT.

This was a particularly hectic time aboard. While the fire-control teams of the 40mm guns and some of the 5-inch batteries concentrated on protecting the UDT, other fire-control teams trained main and secondary batteries on Japanese defenses ashore. The fire-control teams for the remaining secondary and main batteries hunted for concealed Japanese gun emplacements both on Saipan and neighboring Tinian. Heavily camouflaged, the Japa-nese guns were visible only at the instant they fired, when the flash from the muzzle could be spotted. If not destroyed, they could blast landing craft approaching the beach. But these guns were also big enough to bloody a battleship. Since their experience of being straddled by gunfire at Kavieng, the men aboard *Tennessee* were well aware of the importance of spotting and silencing enemy guns before those guns found the range of *Tennessee*. The importance of doing so was also impressed upon the men by a report that *Tennessee*'s sister ship *California* had been hit by shell fire. At 12:38 P.M., two shells landed 50 to 100 feet dead ahead of *Tennessee,* and two minutes later three shells landed 50 to 200 feet off her port side. Frustrated spotters could only report, "Impossible to locate position of batteries firing on ship."

June 15 was D-Day. *Tennessee* provided cover for the advanced transport group as the troops approached their staging areas. Then, at 5:30 A.M., she moved into her fire-support area. At 7:30, as the assault began, she moved just 3,000 yards from shore and delivered very heavy fire from the main, secondary, and 40mm guns until 8:48, when the first wave of marines landed ashore. *Tennessee* then turned her fire further inland. At 9:14, Japanese gunners on Tinian found their range and fired three shells into *Tennessee*. One hit her side, bursting through the blister skin just above the waterline but failed to ignite the fuel oil stored there. A second landed on the deck, smashed through the teak planks, sprayed the deck with fragments that slightly wounded eighteen men, and finally lodged in a potato locker. Two more men were burned by the flash of the exploding shell but were treated and quickly returned to duty. One piece of shrapnel sliced off the fourth toe of a sailor's right foot, and he was transferred to the hospital ship *Solace*.

The third shell did the most damage. Plunging in at a 30-degree angle, the shell penetrated the sternmost 5-inch gun mount on the starboard side. The explosion killed eight men and ignited an oil fire that threatened to travel down to the handling room where gunpowder might be ignited. Gunner's Mate Second Class L. P. Nagel, handling-room captain for gun mount number 7, immediately turned on the sprinkler. Four marines grabbed a firehose and beat back the fire before it could reach perforated powder cases already on the loading tray. As the fire began to subside, Boatswain W. A. Dean grabbed the powder cases and disposed of them. Meanwhile, another shell landed 100 feet off the port beam, and *Tennessee* turned her guns on her tormentors. Seventy-three salvos from her 5-inch guns temporarily silenced the enemy batteries. But at 9:51, a shell landed 100 yards off her starboard beam and then another landed 100 yards off her starboard bow. *Tennessee* responded with forty-eight rounds of fire from her 5-inch guns and declared the enemy batteries silenced at 10:07.

It had been axiomatic in the navy that only a fool sends a ship to fight a fort, but now the rules of warfare had changed. Though *Tennessee* could have dropped 14-inch shells on Saipan and Tinian from a position of relative safety, those shells would not have been effective. To neutralize the enemy, American ships had to get close and risk being hit. Battleships such as *Tennessee* were designed to absorb this kind of punishment. Three shell hits were something she could shake off, and *Tennessee* stayed at her post throughout the day. There was no need to retire to recover her spotter planes because the cruiser *Honolulu,* safely out of range of enemy guns, performed that task. Only after *Tennessee* had retired for the night was there time to consign to the sea the bodies of the eight sailors who had been killed.

The next morning, *Tennessee* was back at her post. About every half hour throughout the day marines ashore called for supporting gunfire that *Tennessee* provided with good results. But at the start of the day, she was a little slow in responding to calls for help. Establishing communications with the shore fire-control party at 8:29, *Tennessee* received her first call for support one minute later. At 8:43, the shore fire-control party radioed "We are under counter-attack, fire immediately." But *Tennessee* did not have a spotter plane in the air, so at 8:44 she maneuvered to launch her planes and at 9:09 commenced firing, dropping twenty rounds on target over the next fifteen minutes. What happened to the marines ashore between 8:43 and 9:09 is not clear.[30]

Up to this point, the Japanese navy had not ventured to challenge the American assaults. But intelligence now reported a Japanese task force headed for the Marianas. Admiral Spruance was not about to send his older battleships to confront the Japanese fleet; his aircraft carriers would take care of that. But in case there was a second, smaller task force sneaking in from the south or on the chance that the main Japanese force might evade the Americans, Spruance ordered his battleships to leave Saipan and head south. There was not a second fleet, however, and the only fighting was at what became known as the "Great Marianas Turkey Shoot," a battle in which carrier-based American aircraft annihilated virtually all the airplanes aboard the Japanese carriers.[31] With the sea around Saipan and Tinian securely in American hands, *Tennessee* returned to Saipan and provided two more days of fire support for the marines ashore. By June 23, the situation on Saipan was secure enough that *Tennessee* could head for the Eniwetok anchorage for reprovisioning and repairs. She still had a hole in her side that needed patching and a 5-inch gun mount that had to be replaced.

Though the battle of the Philippine Sea was a great victory, the failures at Saipan demonstrated that the navy still had much to learn about amphibious warfare. The most important lesson was that it would take a long time to destroy an enemy that was well dug in on a fair-sized island. Thus, while *Tennessee* was being reprovisioned and repaired at Eniwetok, American aircraft and ships bombed and shelled Guam for nearly two weeks before the U.S. invasion. Since *Tennessee* had demonstrated great proficiency at employing 40mm covering fire, she was brought in on July 20 to support the underwater demolition teams in their reconnoitering of the beaches. While providing cover, she also knocked out the visible targets in her assigned fire zone and used her 14-inch and 5-inch guns to rip away all the foliage within 400 yards of the beach. She covered the landing on the following day, and with the marines safely ashore, *Tennessee* and *California* pulled out at 10:22 in the morning and headed for Tinian Island.

The entire Tinian operation went as planned and everything aboard *Tennessee* worked as smoothly as one could have hoped. With well-developed doctrines for covering UDTs and landing forces as well as for providing fire support for the troops ashore, *Tennessee* had become almost perfect in her assigned task. As with Guam, the navy had bombarded Tinian for weeks before the invasion and even shelled at night to kill construction workers who might be trying to rebuild what had been destroyed during the day. *Tennessee* arrived on July 23 and, with *California,* destroyed Tinian Town as part of a bombardment intended to convince the Japanese that the invasion would take place at that spot. *Tennessee* also provided covering fire for the UDT reconnoitering a beach that the Americans did not intend to assault. That this was only a feint did not make any difference to the frogmen who were being shot at, and to protect them *Tennessee* used over 10,000 rounds of 40mm fire, nearly two-thirds more than on Guam. The following morning, *Tennessee* moved to the actual landing area and laid down a massive barrage of 10,877 rounds of 40mm fire while sitting just 2,410 yards offshore. She fired a few 14-inch shells to cover the assault, but her gunnery officers concluded that they were not as effective as the 40mm fire and probably did more harm than good, as ricochets were a serious threat.

The big guns were needed, however, to knock out well-fortified enemy positions. At Tinian there were three well-camouflaged coastal guns dug into the base of a cliff. These guns were believed to have hit *Colorado* twenty-two times on the day of the invasion, killing forty-three officers and men and hospitalizing another ninety-seven. (*Colorado* was in the same position *Tennessee* had been in on the previous day. While *Colorado* suffered, *Tennessee* came through the battle unscathed, further establishing her reputation as a good-fortune ship.) When airplanes failed to silence the guns, *Tennessee* was asked to do the job. It took twenty minutes just to find them, but once they were located, sixty rounds of 14-inch shells knocked out two of them and neutralized the third. So well dug in were these guns that only a direct hit could stop them.

Tennessee gunnery officers also ironed out the wrinkles in communicating with the shore fire-control party. A call for gunfire a week after the invasion required *Tennessee* gunners to drop 5-inch shells close to the marines' front line 6,000 yards from the beach. Able to see the marine positions both from spotter planes and from the ship, gunners aboard *Tennessee* placed their shells close to the American lines with little danger to the marines. One reason for the effectiveness of this fire was a shipboard meeting before the invasion in which the gunnery personnel of *Tennessee* and the shore fire-control party went over every detail of what each needed and expected to receive.[32]

HIT # 1. EXTERIOR VIEW OF MOUNT 7 SHOWING DAMAGED RIGHT GUN PORT.

HIT # 2. EXTERIOR VIEW OF PATCH ON STARBOARD

At Saipan in 1944, three shells (later determined to be 4.5 inches rather than 6 inches) hit *Tennessee* but did relatively little damage.

Below left: One punched a hole in the side blister. The outline of the hole is shown on the patch.

Left: A second penetrated the 5-inch gun mount and killed eight men.

Right: A third crashed through the deck and landed in a potato locker.

Though the overall damage was light, these hits added fear of death to the feelings of boredom, fatigue, and homesickness that most men experienced. An unusually ominous tone crept into the Third Division's gossip section of the ship's newspaper, the *Tennessee Bombarder*, after the shell hits at Saipan: "Did anyone ever stop to think what it would sound like for the Bos'n mate of the watch to pass the word for the first three deck divisions instead of four? If you'll check the position of the hole in the quarterdeck and the many holes in the 'spud locker' you'll know what I mean, we could have been sitting there eating as usual when we took that hit."[33]

HIT # 3.   LOOKING VERTICALLY DOWNWARD ON THE QUARTERDECK FROM THE TOP OF THE VEGETABLE STOWAGE SPACE AT FRAME 98.

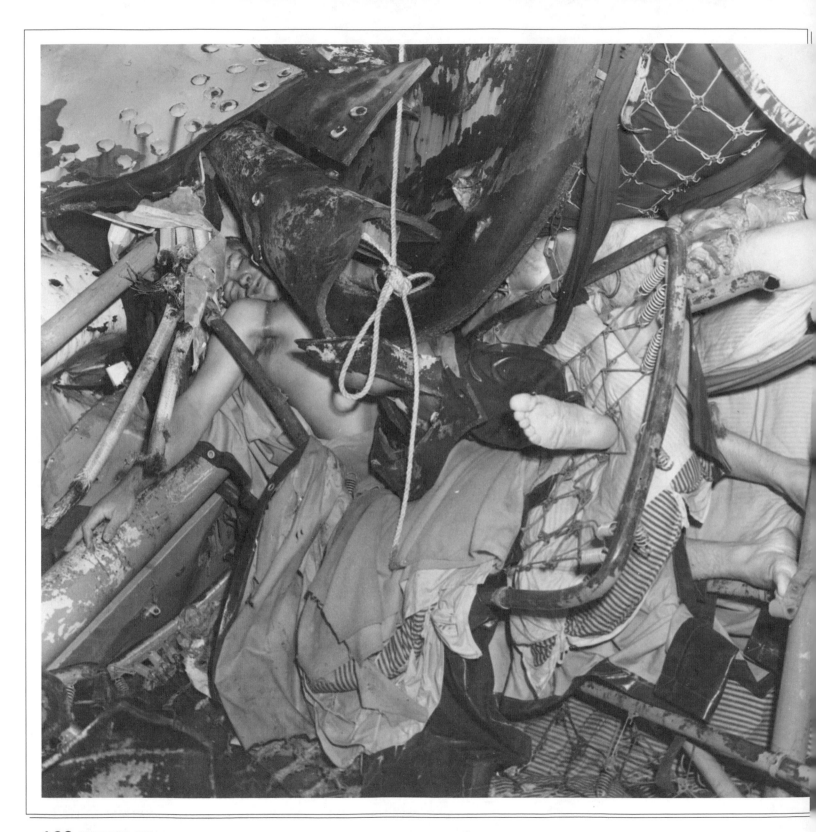

One of the great dangers for ships operating in close quarters was collision. On the night of August 22, 1944, *Tennessee* was in Task Unit 53.5.4 with *California; Pennsylvania* was the guide. The ships were running with lights out but with radar checking the distances between them. A pin sheered off in *Tennessee*'s steering motor and she lost control of her steering at 4:34 in the morning. At 4:36, Captain Andrew D. Mayer took over of the bridge and at 4:37, control was regained using auxiliary steering. Meanwhile, *Tennessee* had swung out of formation but not dangerously so. The steering motor was repaired but reassembled backward, or 180 degrees out of alignment. When power was shifted back to main steering (at 4:46), it overloaded the motor and steering was again lost. Now *Tennessee* was heading dangerously close to *California*. At 8:49, Captain Mayer ordered all his engines to back emergency full and turned on his side-lights to warn *California*. One minute later, *Tennessee*'s starboard bow ripped into the port bow of *California* and the ships were in violent collision through two-thirds of their lengths.

Tennessee hit ahead of the belt armor that protected *California*'s side and ripped into the chief petty officers' quarters thirty seconds before reveille was to be sounded, crushing men as they slept in their bunks. Seven men were killed and one was lost overboard and presumed dead.

Eight more were injured, one seriously. Five bodies in the compartment could not be removed until *California* reached port.

Though *Tennessee* suffered no casualties, she headed back to Hawaii for repairs. *California* was taken to Espíritu Santo Island where a floating dry dock permitted her to be lifted out of the water so repairs could be made. A few weeks earlier, Captain Mayer had received a Bronze Star for his efforts at Saipan. "Skillfully maneuvering his ship into a close-in fire support position alongside a coral reef, Captain Mayer valiantly directed preliminary and assault bombardments against strong Japanese shore installations despite intense enemy counterfire which scored three hits on his ship.... By his superb seamanship, resolute determination and unwavering devotion to duty in the face of grave danger, Captain Mayer upheld the highest traditions of the United States Naval Service." However, six weeks after the collision with *California,* Captain Mayer lost his command and spent the rest of the war in charge of the U.S. naval ordnance plant in Centerline, Michigan. Captain John B. Heffernan, an officer with more destroyer than battleship experience but who was readily available, replaced Mayer. Heffernan had commanded five transports at the Guam assault before becoming chief of staff to the commander, Service Squadron Ten, operating in forward areas. [34]

From forward outboard:

Shows holed blister side plating double[d] frame 118. (This pl[...] been cut away).

A smaller collision than the one with *California* came in Leyte when under the cover of a smokescreen, the auxiliary vessel *War Hawk* plowed into *Tennessee*'s side, peeling back one of her blisters. The damage was not serious, but it did take *Tennessee* out of fire support for the American troops already ashore in the Philippines.[35]

In September, the men of *Tennessee* performed their job again at the island of Angauer in the Palau group, and in October, they covered the landings in Leyte Gulf, the Philippines. Without incident and with great effect, they fired hundreds of 14-inch shells, thousands of 5-inch shells, and tens of thousands of 40mm shells into enemy positions. Fighting ashore remained bitter and the Japanese did not yield easily. For the men aboard ship, however, the task had become almost routine: Steam to the target, spend a week bombarding, then retire for reprovisioning and maintenance.[36] In October 1944, a Japanese fleet interrupted that routine in the middle of the Leyte operation.

It is almost as if having mastered one kind of warfare, *Tennessee* was called to wage an entirely different kind. From January to October 1944, *Tennessee* had fought eight battles against Japanese-held islands and become proficient in doing so. Now she was called on to confront Japanese battleships. In a desperate attempt to stop the American advance after the invasion of the Philippines, the Japanese sent their carriers south from Japan to decoy the American carriers away from Leyte Gulf. At the same time, two other Japanese battleship fleets would come from the west side of the Philippines and move around Leyte Island, one from the north through San Bernardino Strait and one from the south through Surigao Strait. They were supposed to meet at Leyte Gulf and destroy the American ships bunched there. *Tennessee* and five other older battleships along with cruisers, destroyers, and PT boats were ordered to meet the southern force at Surigao Strait. *Tennessee*'s crew first heard what was in store for her on October 24, when the announcement came over the speaker, "Attention all Hands! Attention all Hands! It is expected that a Japanese naval task force will attempt to enter Leyte Gulf tonight. We are making preparations to greet them."[37]

Admiral Oldendorf had deployed his ships well. His battle line steamed slowly back and forth across the east end of Surigao Strait, waiting for the Japanese warships to come within range. Radar contact was made at 43,900 yards, but the American ships held their fire until the Japanese were just over 20,000 yards away to assure the highest percentage of hits. Because his battleships were loaded with more high-capacity shells than armor-piercing ones, Oldendorf was concerned that they lacked sufficient shells to sustain a lengthy battle. *Tennessee* had 396 armor-piercing shells, more than any other battleship present, but those shells could be expended in sixteen minutes of full-salvo rapid fire.

The American battleships needed only thirteen minutes to destroy their enemy. Guided by sophisticated fire-control radar, every one of her sixty-nine shells struck home except for one three-gun salvo that went astray when *Tennessee* suddenly slowed down to avoid colliding with *California*. At 4:26, the target *Tennessee* had been firing upon disappeared from the radar.[38]

After this battle, *Tennessee* went back to the United States for an overhaul. Stopping off in Hawaii, Captain John Heffernan held a press conference at which war correspondents questioned him about the battle. It is easy to see why the American victory at Surigao Strait was so popular at the time and later. It was a decisive victory where warships had stood face to face and fought to the death. It did not matter that the American radar and fire-control systems were so far superior to those on the Japanese battleships that the contest was never in doubt. The Japanese warships came, the Americans fired, the Japanese ships sank. The American victory had been total. But the battle of Surigao Strait was no more important to victory in the Pacific than the now-routine and perhaps somewhat dull

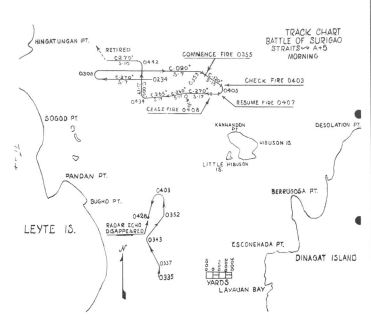

The battle of Surigao Strait was a tactical success for Admiral Jesse B. Oldendorf. By having his battleships steam back and forth across the mouth of the strait, he gave each big gun on the ships a clear shot. The Japanese, on the other hand, could only fire guns in their forward turrets. That was called crossing the enemy's 'T.' *Tennessee* fired her first salvo — three guns from turret 1 — at 3:55 A.M. Fifteen seconds later, turret 2 fired three guns. Within twenty seconds, turret 2 had reloaded, and turrets 1 and 2 fired. One minute and fifteen seconds into the battle, the rear turrets got their chance, firing a 5-gun salvo (the left gun of turret 3 failed to fire). Forty-five seconds later, both aft turrets fired, but two of the six guns misfired. Then at 3:57:45, the forward two turrets fired a six-gun salvo followed by six more salvos every forty-five seconds.

The battle line was then ordered to make a 150-degree turn to the right. *California* misheard the order as 15 degrees. The commander of Battleship Division Two was aboard *Tennessee* and radioed *California* if she had received the turn order. *California* responded yes, thinking the order was 15 degrees. *California* and *Tennessee* were headed for a collision. At 4:04 A.M., *Tennessee* reversed her propellers, and through what navy analysts later called "some clever ship handling," permitted *California* to pass across her bow oblivious to what she had done until the commander of the battle line announced by radio to look out for *California*. At 4:07:50, *Tennessee*'s line of fire was once again available and she fired her final six-gun salvo. The cease-fire order was given at 4:08 A.M. All of *Tennessee*'s salvos were on target except for the one fired just as *Tennessee* maneuvered to avoid hitting *California*. No one knew where that one landed. The photograph shows one of *Tennessee*'s salvos.[39]

One of *Tennessee*'s duties was to take care of her escorts. That meant refueling them as she is doing here for a destroyer and a destroyer escort. Supplying her escorts also meant sending over food, clothing, medical supplies, or anything else that they needed and *Tennessee* could supply.[40]

bombardment of shore installations. Without the extensive firepower that *Tennessee* and the other older battleships provided, the casualties at Kwajalein and Eniwetok would have been so high that strategists might well have shied away from attacks on the more formidable islands of Saipan, Guam, and Tinian.

Lest anyone fail to see this, Admiral Chester Nimitz, commander in chief of the U.S. Pacific Fleet, came aboard *Tennessee* to congratulate the crew on a job well done and to point out to the war correspondents who came aboard with him that his central Pacific strategy had worked brilliantly. One year ago, Nimitz declared, *Tennessee* participated in the "curtain raiser" of the central Pacific campaign by helping to take Tarawa.

Exactly eleven months later, on 19 Oct. 1944 she was 3000 miles further west, at Leyte, in the Philippines.

During the past year our forces in the Central Pacific have attacked and captured, or blockaded and rendered impotent, the Gilberts, Marshalls, Marianas and Palau Islands groups and gained a firm foothold in the Philippine Islands. They have reduced the Imperial Japanese Navy almost to the point of ineffectiveness, and severely damaged Japanese air strength.

In this history-making struggle the *TENNESSEE* has played an important part.[41]

At the end of 1944, the struggle was far from over. The closer to Japan the Americans drew, the tougher Japanese resistance became. Though the men of *Tennessee* would be able to enjoy Thanksgiving and Christmas at home, they would have to return to the Pacific for the final push to victory, and those final battles would be more exhausting and bloodier than anything they had faced earlier.

CHAPTER SEVEN

THE FINAL PUSH TO PEACE

Each succeeding year of the war was harder for *Tennessee* than the one before. In 1942, she never saw the war and divided her time between the Puget Sound Navy Yard and inconsequential patrols in the eastern Pacific. The next year, 1943, brought some combat, though the Kiska and Tarawa operations were not demanding and there was ample opportunity for her to return home and give her men liberty in the States. But when she left California in January 1944, it was ten months before she went home. During those ten months, she steamed 50,000 miles, spent four months in combat, and fired 5,792 rounds of 14-inch shells, 25,855 rounds of 5-inch shells, and 75,213 rounds of 40mm shells. The year 1945 would be still harder because *Tennessee* faced determined Japanese troops at Iwo Jima and Okinawa and confronted the most terrifying weapon of the Pacific war, the kamikaze — Japanese pilots who were prepared to sacrifice their own lives by crashing their planes into American warships. To prepare the ship and her men for what would be the final push to victory in the Pacific, *Tennessee* was sent to the Puget Sound Navy Yard for an overhaul. When she pulled into the harbor just before Thanksgiving, half the crew left for thirty days' leave. Just before Christmas, the rest of the crew got their thirty days' leave.

Death had frequently shown its face to the men aboard *Tennessee* during her four months in combat during 1944. Most of the victims were marines or frogmen. At times, when the wind was right and the ship was close to shore, the men could smell the stench of rotting flesh blowing out to sea. And there were times when the sailors' own vulnerability was apparent, as when *Tennessee* sat waiting for the Japanese at Surigao Strait or after the shells hit her at Saipan. But for the most part, it was not so much fear of dying that wore the men down as it was the long hours, boredom, and homesickness. On a typical bombardment day, all hands were awakened at 4:00 A.M.; they ate breakfast between 4:30 and 5:30 and went to general quarters (battle stations) at 6:00. The rest of the morning, the crew shelled the enemy, a tiresome job that required well-coordinated efforts by the gunnery, engineering, and navigation sections of the ship. With luck, the men would be able to withdraw in the afternoon to eat and repair the damage the big guns had inflicted upon nearby equipment during the bombardment. If *Tennessee* had to stay at her post, the men would be fed sandwiches at their battle stations. Even when the ship was not in actual battle, the men had to go to battle stations an hour before sunrise.

When *Tennessee* was at Pearl Harbor or in an anchorage at an atoll far from the front lines, the men would have some relief from being on constant guard against an enemy attack. But a day at anchor did not mean a day off. Rust and dirt did not vaca-

Most after action reports were brief, two- or three-page documents. But the grueling fighting off Okinawa lasted so long that the 3-inch-thick report needed a special cover. Though *Tennessee's* crew now called their ship the "Big T" rather than the "Rebel Ship," and it had been a quarter century since six hundred Tennesseans had boarded her in spring 1920, the stereotypical view of the sharpshooting, moonshining hillbilly was not lost on this artist.[1]

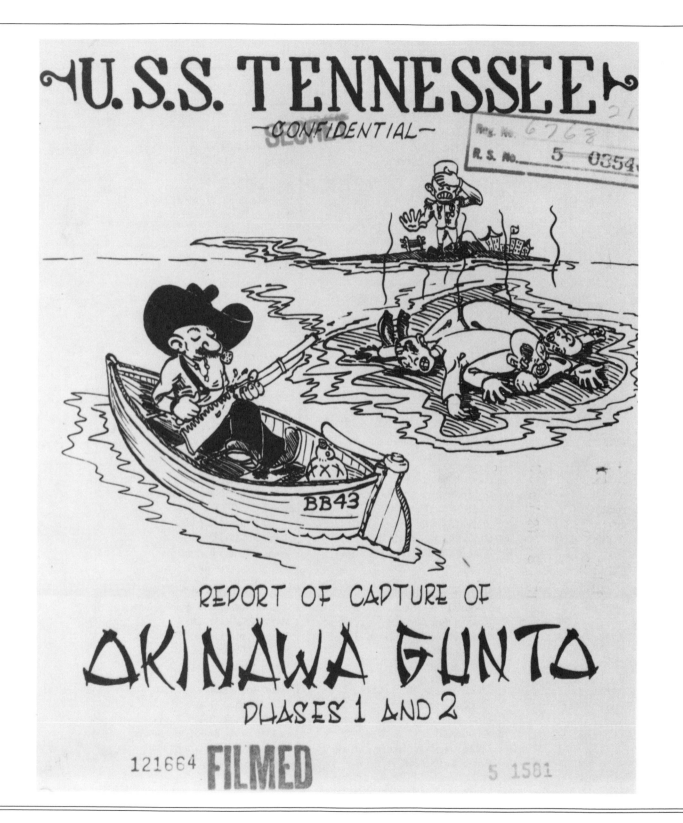

Morning Meal

Stewed Apricots
Hot Cereal, Milk
Scrambled Eggs
Hashed Brown Potatoes
Iced Cinnamon Buns
Bread, Butter, Coffee

Canned Figs, Assorted Cereal, Milk
Grilled Hot Cakes, Table Sirup
Fried Bacon
Iced Jenny Linds
Bread, Butter, Coffee

Canned Prunes
Assorted Cereal, Milk
Boston Baked Beans, Chili Sauce
Hot Corn Bread
Butter
Coffee

Canned Apricots
Hot Cereal, Milk
Grilled Pork Sausage, Milk Gravy
Minced Potatoes
Coffee Cake
Bread, Butter, Coffee

Canned Figs
Assorted Cereal, Milk
Braised Minced Meat on Dry Toast
Cottage Fried Potatoes
Iced Butter Horns
Bread, Butter, Coffee

Canned Prunes
Assorted Cereal, Milk
Baked Pork & Beans, Tomato Catsup
Iced Cinnamon Rolls
Bread, Butter
Coffee

Stewed Apricots
Hot Cereal, Milk
Baked Corn Beef Hash
Hard Boiled Eggs, Chili Sauce
Iced Jenny Linds
Bread, Butter, Coffee

Mid-day Meal

Vegetable Soup, Ckrs.
Chicken Fried Steaks
Mashed Potatoes, Brown Gravy
Braised Green Beans
Cherry Pie
Bread, Butter, Coffee

Tomato Rice Soup, Ckrs.
Roast Loin of Pork, Apple Sauce
Mashed Sweet Potatoes
Bread Dressing, Buttered Kernel
Corn, Peach Cobbler
Bread, Butter, Coffee

Purée of Bean Soup, Ckrs.
Baked Spiced Ham, Pineapple Sauce
Mashed Potatoes
Club Spinach
Spice Cake, Ice Cream
Hot Rolls, Butter, Coffee

Cream of Pea Soup, Ckrs.
Oven Roast of Beef, Natural Gravy
Mashed Potatoes
Peas
Mincemeat Pie, Sliced Cheese
Bread, Butter, Coffee

Corn Chowder, Ckrs.
Grilled Fish Steaks, Tarter Sauce
Potatoes Au Gratin
Chilled Tomatoes
Sliced Pickles, Green Olives
Cottage Pudding, Sauce
Bread, Butter, Coffee

Navy Bean Soup, Ckrs.
Spanish Boiled Beef, Natural Gravy
Mashed Potatoes
Boiled Cabbage, Crackered Corn
Pineapple Cream Pie
Bread, Butter, Coffee

Chicken & Rice Broth, Ckrs.
Chicken Fricassee
Mashed Potatoes, Buttered yams
Hot Biscuits
Chocalate Sheet Cake, Ice Cream
Bread, Butter, Coffee

Evening Meal

Soup, Bread Sticks
Baked Meat Loaf, Onion Gravy
Creamed Sliced Potatoes
Stewed Tomatoes
Iced Cup Cakes
Bread, Jam, Hot Chocolate

Soup, Croutons
Beef a la mode, Brown Gravy
Buttered Peace & Carrots
Roast Potatoes
Tinned Chilled Fruit, Sugar Cookies
Bread, Jam, Tea

Soup, Crackers
Grilled Hamburgers, Tomato Catsup
Country Fried Potatoes, Fried Onions
Buttered Asparagus
Chocolate Pudding
Bread, Jam, Cocoa

Soup, Bread Sticks
Baked Luncheon Meat, Raisin Sauce
Potato Cakes
Candied Carrots, Tinned Chillded
Fruit, Ginger Cookies
Bread, Jam, Tea

Soup, Croutons
Baked Vienna Sausage, Spanish
Sauce
Boiled Pealed Potatoes
Steamed Sauerkraut
Bread & Fruit Pudding
Hot Rolls, Jam, Hot Cocoa

Soup, Crackers
Grilled Ham Steaks, Spice Sauce
Mashed Sweet Potatoes
Boiled Spinach, (Bacon)
Rice and Raisin Custard
Bread, Jam, Hot Tea

Soup, Bread Sticks
Cold Assorted Meats
Chicken Potato Salad
Pickled Beets, Boild Navy Beans
Sliced Tinned Pineapple, Fruit Bars
Bread, Jam, Cocoa

Food was an important way to keep up morale. Special meals were served on holidays, but the day-to-day fare is seen in this menu for the week of July 23–29, 1945. There was a hearty breakfast, a full dinner at midday, and a lighter supper served at night. Perhaps to foster sound sleep, coffee was not served with the evening meal. All items have been retyped as originally spelled.[2]

tion while the men were at battle stations, so cleaning and repairs that were neglected during battle had to be completed. Added to these maintenance duties was the endless task of reprovisioning the ship. All the 14-inch, 5-inch, and 40mm shells that had been fired had to be replaced. Food, clothing, and spare parts had to be brought aboard while the ship was at anchor. This was a job that required all hands to pitch in and help. After Saipan, where *Tennessee* expended 960 rounds of 14-inch shells, 5,167 rounds of 5-inch shells, 14,631 rounds of 40mm shells, it took two days and a night to replenish the ship, and that was fast. "In three and one half years aboard," one crew member wrote in the ship's paper, "I have never seen an 'all Hands' working party like our last one. It was an exhibition to be proud of. With the support of the engineers, a long task was done in record time." Captain Mayer rewarded his men by pushing back reveille after their late-night work session.

Keeping the ship clean and running smoothly was no easy task. With so many men aboard, great attention was paid to details. The daily work sheet, a mimeographed two-page document, told the men when to get up, what drills or duties were in order for that day, and when they should go to bed. It also included reminders from the executive officer of the seemingly trivial things that had to be done if the 2,000 men aboard ship were to live and work together harmoniously:

"Division Officers will take positive steps to see that spit kits throughout the ship are not used for trash."

"If rations are served at battle stations regular galley cups will be issued for coffee at a ratio of approximately 1 cup for each 4 men. These cups are practically impossible to procure in this area and all hands are strongly urged to take all precautions to prevent chipping and insure that all cups are returned to the scullery."

"Division Officers will take steps to see that the men in their divisions wear clean dungarees and under clothing at all times. Dungaree shirts and jumpers with the sleeves cut off will not be permitted at any time."

"All Officers and Men will make every effort to keep the ship as clean as possible during the next few days. When food is served at Battle Stations, Officers and Petty Officers will see that their parts of the ship are policed thoroughly afterwards."

"Remember the traffic rules — up and forward on the starboard side — down and aft on the port side."[3]

With 2,000 or more men crammed into a ship originally designed for 1,200, it would be surprising if men irritated by boredom, danger, and long hours of work did not lash out at each other. One veteran recalled the ship's medical officer commenting after Saipan that the men were so exhausted and overwrought that they could have been confined to sick bay if there had been room. The ship's newspaper, now called the *Tennessee Bombarder,* carried reports of men who had settled their arguments with their fists before once again becoming best of friends.[4] To relieve tensions, a boxing ring might be set up aboard ship and a smoker held while at anchor if there was little danger of attack and all necessary work had been completed. To help boost morale, *Tennessee* received a chief petty officer in charge of athletic recreation in May 1944. The new chief brought aboard Ping-Pong tables, set up punching bags, and organized an interdivisional baseball tournament of 156 games (though the men played only 17 before they left Pearl Harbor at the end of May.) Another outlet for pent-up energy was liberty. Liberty in the central Pacific meant sending the men to a beach on an atoll with a few cans of beer and some food. There they could swim, sunbathe, eat, drink a little, and blow off some steam, usually in the form of a free-for-all

fight between men from different divisions. These battles were not carried back aboard ship, the injuries were superficial, and no charges were leveled against the combatants.

In fact, as the men got closer to the war, the number of infractions aboard ship went down, or at least the number of deck courts-martial and man-days in the brig declined. During 1942, 20 percent of the crew was subjected to a deck or summary court-martial. In the last half of 1943, when *Tennessee* was engaged in the Kiska and Tarawa operations, the court-martial rate fell to 15 percent. During 1944, it fell to less than 5 percent. Man-days in the brig plummeted from a high of 500 per month during the summer of 1942 to 22 per month during the summer of 1944.[5]

Judging from the comments in the ship's newspaper, the hardest thing the men had to cope with was being far from home. A daily mimeographed press summary reported the news from around the world, including sports scores from home. And mail from home came regularly. But mail could also bring a "Dear John" letter to a sailor who was helpless to do anything about it. The navy did not allow a man to leave a war so he could straighten things out with his girl.[6] The best way to get home was to earn a transfer to another post, since transfers usually included enough leave time to visit home. During 1944, over five-hundred men were transferred off *Tennessee,* a bittersweet experience for the men who were going home but who were also leaving behind strong friendships forged in war. The number of transfers declined, however, as *Tennessee* headed for overhaul and a month-long leave for her crew at the end of 1944. Thus it was not only a rested but also an experienced crew that manned *Tennessee* as she steamed out to rejoin the war in January 1945.

When Admiral Nimitz had congratulated the men of *Tennessee* for the wonderful role they had played in the central Pacific campaign, he did not talk about the long-range American bombers preparing to fly against the Japanese home islands from newly constructed airfields on Tinian Island. Nor did he point out that these planes had to avoid the Japanese aircraft based on Iwo Jima, directly on the flight path between Tinian and Japan. Until Iwo Jima was captured, American planes had to fly a lengthy "dogleg" route around the island, consuming fuel and increasing navigational problems. With Iwo Jima in American hands, not only could the planes fly directly, but they would have an emergency landing field halfway between Tinian and Japan and could get American fighter support out of Iwo Jima. If airpower was to bring Japan to its knees, Iwo Jima had to be captured. Thus *Tennessee* would once again have to return to battle.

By the time marines went ashore on Iwo Jima on February 19, 1945, Japan had lost the war. There were still many Japanese, especially in the army, who clung to the belief born of desperation that if they were tenacious in their defense, the Americans would give up the effort. Others, motivated by a grim fatalism, had dedicated their lives to killing as many Americans as possible before they died in battle. But in Tokyo there were some who understood that Japan's only hope was a carrot-and-stick approach. The "stick" would be a stubborn defense that would make the Americans pay dearly for every yard of territory they captured. The "carrot" would be an offer to surrender but only conditionally. The Japanese leaders who pondered surrender had initially hoped to avoid any American occupation of the home islands, but as American victories mounted, they were willing to accept surrender on the condition that the emperor be retained.

To the men aboard *Tennessee,* it made no difference whether Japanese resistance was motivated by an insane belief in ulti-

mate victory, a grim determination to die in combat, or a higher diplomatic plan. At Iwo Jima and Okinawa, the Americans were in for the fight of their lives.

On Iwo Jima, just 650 miles from Japan, General Kuribayashi Tadamichi had placed his 21,000 troops in a maze of underground bunkers, tunnels, and heavily fortified firing positions. He did not expect to hurl the Americans back into the sea, but he did expect to kill enough of them to slow the American march toward the Japanese home islands. For the first time in the central Pacific campaign, the Japanese were able to inflict more casualties on the invaders than they themselves sustained.[7]

Worried by the extent of Kuribayashi's defenses, the marines asked the navy for ten days of deliberate, close-range bombardment. The lesson learned at Saipan and later applied to Guam and Tinian was that only a sustained bombardment could knock out enemy emplacements. But the navy was stretched too thin in the Pacific to provide that kind of bombardment. An aircraft-carrier attack on Japan was being planned and MacArthur needed the navy's help for his operations in the Philippines. The marines got only three days, though the navy promised it would be an intense bombardment.

Tennessee was assigned to blast away the camouflage hiding Japanese installations, destroy the installations, provide covering fire for minesweepers and underwater demolition teams before the invasion, smother the beaches with intense neutralizing fire immediately preceding and during the landings, and use white phosphorous projectiles to lay smoke screens.

At 2:08 on the afternoon of February 16, D-Day minus three, *Tennessee* fired her first shell into Iwo Jima. Slowly and methodically her guns sought out enemy installations until she ceased fire at 5:50 P.M. The 127 rounds of 14-inch high-capacity

The strain of combat made liberty a necessity. Unfortunately, in the middle of the central Pacific, there were not many liberty spots. Unless *Tennessee* could get back to Hawaii, a day of liberty for her men meant a day on a beach such as this one at Majuro atoll. If the setting was not everything that the sailors might desire, it was at least a day off the ship and away from the war. [8]

shells she had fired and the 305 rounds of 5-inch antiaircraft shells expended had ripped into the island with no appreciable effect. The next morning, *Tennessee* closed to within 3,000 yards of the beach to cover the UDTs, and a handful of landing craft that were to launch their rockets against the terraced volcanic ash from as close as a quarter mile of the shore. The Japanese mistook the landing craft for the first wave of an assault and opened fire with their big, hidden guns. As the Japanese gunners pounded the landing craft, *Tennessee* gunners turned their weapons against the now-exposed Japanese batteries. In the middle of this furious firefight, with the 14-inch and 5-inch guns blasting away as fast as they could and the 40mm guns raking the shoreline, a Japanese shell struck *Tennessee*'s 5-inch gun mount number 5. The shell was too small to penetrate the armor, but the shards sprayed the deck, slightly wounding four men and mortally wounding Seaman First Class Leon Andrew Giardini. *Tennessee*'s casualties were insignificant compared with the dead and dying aboard the badly mauled landing craft that came alongside shortly before noon. The pools of blood that sloshed on their decks gave terrifying testimony to how little damage the first day's bombardment had inflicted on the Japanese guns.

For the rest of the day, *Tennessee* and her fellow battleships took careful aim at where they thought the Japanese guns were. Before withdrawing that night, *Tennessee* hurled 249 of her big shells and 1,093 of her 5-inch shells into Iwo Jima. The 5-inch shells were too small to do much damage, so the next day *Tennessee* relied upon her main batteries. This barrage of large-caliber shells stripped away the camouflage and revealed how formidable were the Japanese defenses. The marine commander, looking at what his men were facing, asked for another day of bombardment. But bad weather was coming in, and

At Iwo Jima, landing craft heading to or from the beach came so close to *Tennessee* that her big guns had to hold their fire.[9]

the navy commander refused to delay the landing. So on February 19, the marines went ashore to face an enemy barely scratched by all that *Tennessee* and the other warships and aircraft had done.

In spite of the ineffectiveness of the preliminary bombardment, the landings went virtually unchallenged. Fire from the 40mm and 5-inch guns was so heavy during the landing that the Japanese had to concede the beach to the marines. General Kuribayashi's strategy was to confront the Americans at every point after they had advanced inland where his men would not be so vulnerable to naval gunfire. Marines on the beach would be fired upon by powerful guns burrowed deep within Mount Suribachi where Japanese gunners had a clear field of fire. Further inland, huge mortars lobbed shells onto the beach. These were the guns that *Tennessee* and her fellow warships had been unable to silence, and from a position of relative safety, the men aboard *Tennessee* could see the damage being inflicted on the 30,000 marines who got ashore that day. *Tennessee* had only 266 of her 14-inch shells remaining; she fired all of them as well as an additional 2,299 of her 5-inch shells. Though this gunfire was able to knock out some of the guns located in or near Mount Suribachi, the mortars that continued to rip the beach remained untouched. The commander of one of the navy's fire-support units concluded that "against this well-concealed enemy fire, neither the dive bombers, napalm, marine artillery fire nor ship fire was effective; and the air spotters could not locate it. It was finally reduced by the general weight of the operation overrunning [*sic*] the enemy positions."[10]

Desperate to find these targets, *Tennessee*'s spotter planes flew dangerously low, too low in one case. Men aboard watched as the tail assembly of one plane was shot away by an antiaircraft shell or possibly a friendly shell from an American warship offshore. The plane crashed into the island, killing the pilot and his spotter. These were *Tennessee*'s only casualties on the day of the landing.[11]

Following the landings, *Tennessee* stood by to provide support fire for marine units ashore but had relatively few requests. The marines preferred to use their tanks equipped with flamethrowers and their 105mm and 155mm howitzers. On an average day, howitzers would fire over 5,000 rounds. With that kind of support, the big battleships offshore were not needed except when the marines began a general advance. Then they called upon the navy to lay down a rolling barrage of shells in front and on the flanks of the marines, moving as they moved. Thus on the day after the landings, *Tennessee* dropped in 213 rounds of 5-inch shells, but during the next six days she fired only 22 rounds. When the marines began a major assault on February 27, *Tennessee* increased her fire, expending, over a four-day period, 299 rounds from her main batteries and 1,495 rounds from her secondary batteries. After that, she was called upon only to fire illuminating shells at night. Though the marines continued to dig out Japanese pockets of resistance through March, *Tennessee* took her leave of Iwo Jima on March 7.

From the gunnery perspective, the battle for Iwo Jima was the biggest if not the most intense battle *Tennessee* had ever fought. Over twenty days, she fired into that volcanic island 1,370 main battery shells along with 6,380 rounds from her secondary batteries. (Saipan was more intense, with 967 rounds of 14-inch and 5,314 rounds of 5-inch shells fired in only three days.) But from the human perspective, it is not the number of shells fired but the number of days in combat that is most telling. By this stage of the war, men aboard ship could sleep comfortably as 5-inch or even 14-inch guns were fired — not only had they become used to the sound but they were exhausted.

However, the psychological stress of being in combat day after day with no chance to relax could take its toll. The ten days the men spent at Ulithi following the Iwo Jima campaign were a welcome relief. There were the usual long hours of reprovisioning the ship and the constant repairs to be completed, and the only liberty was on an island filled with sailors. But it was a chance for both the men and the ship to prepare themselves for their next task, the invasion of Okinawa.

The Japanese used the same tactics on Okinawa that they had on Iwo Jima: They yielded the beach to the Americans and then made them pay as the Americans advanced inland. The invasion was set for April 1, 1945, but *Tennessee* was there six days earlier to protect the minesweepers and underwater demolition teams. At 6:36 A.M. on Easter Sunday, *Tennessee* opened fire to cover the invasion. First the 14-inch and 5-inch guns barraged the landing area and then as the troops moved ashore, the 40mm guns strafed the land ahead of the advancing troops. But it was not until April 6 that the Americans reached the well-entrenched Japanese troops and learned what they were in for.

As U.S. troops battled through the hills of Okinawa, *Tennessee* stood offshore for weeks at a time firing her guns, sometimes day and night. Army and marine units ashore valued this support and let *Tennessee* know it:

Cease firing. You have done good work and good shooting. Tennessee is best ship we ever worked with yet. You scored 9 direct hits on pillboxes. It would be a pleasure to work with you again. Thank you for your splendid work.

C.O. Headquarters 6TH MARDIV himself saw the Tennessee fire yesterday and wishes to express his appreciation for the Tennessee's cooperation and deliv-

ery of outstanding support. The main and secondary batteries of the Tennessee broke and drove the enemy back. Her naval gunfire on the almost impossible job did the job. Congratulations to all the men of the Tennessee.[12]

The men did not have any time to bask in such praise; they were too busy trying to keep alive in the midst of furious Japanese suicide air attacks. The first attack came on April 6, just when the troops ashore were encountering Japanese resistance. The last attack came June 22, one day after the island had been secured. Between those dates at least ten mass attacks, ranging from 50 to 300 planes, sought out the ships off Okinawa.

Japanese aircraft attacks were nothing new to *Tennessee*. At Pearl Harbor she had had a taste of what a plane could do to a

battleship. Her rearmament in 1943 had put ninety-nine 5-inch, 40mm, and 20mm guns aboard her, supposedly enough firepower to stop any attacking plane. She did not have a chance to test her air defenses until June 1944, when she fired on several Japanese aircraft and her 40mm guns claimed, with another ship, a share of a kill (called an "assist"). These air attacks did not last long. Typically the plane would be spotted at some distance, tracked by radar and sight, then fired upon for a few seconds before it was hit or flew out of range. At the end of October when six planes came within range, *Tennessee* gunners claimed one kill, one assist, and two damaged.[13]

But on *Tennessee*'s second day off Okinawa, things became hot. At 6:15 in the morning, the first plane came in and was shot down about 5,000 yards from *Tennessee*'s stern. Two minutes later, another

Right: The American landing on Okinawa in April 1944 was unopposed. *Tennessee* sat offshore and bombarded the coast while American troops went ashore in their landing craft.

Above: After the landing on Okinawa, *Tennessee* spent her days and most of her nights providing called fire for the troops ashore.[14]

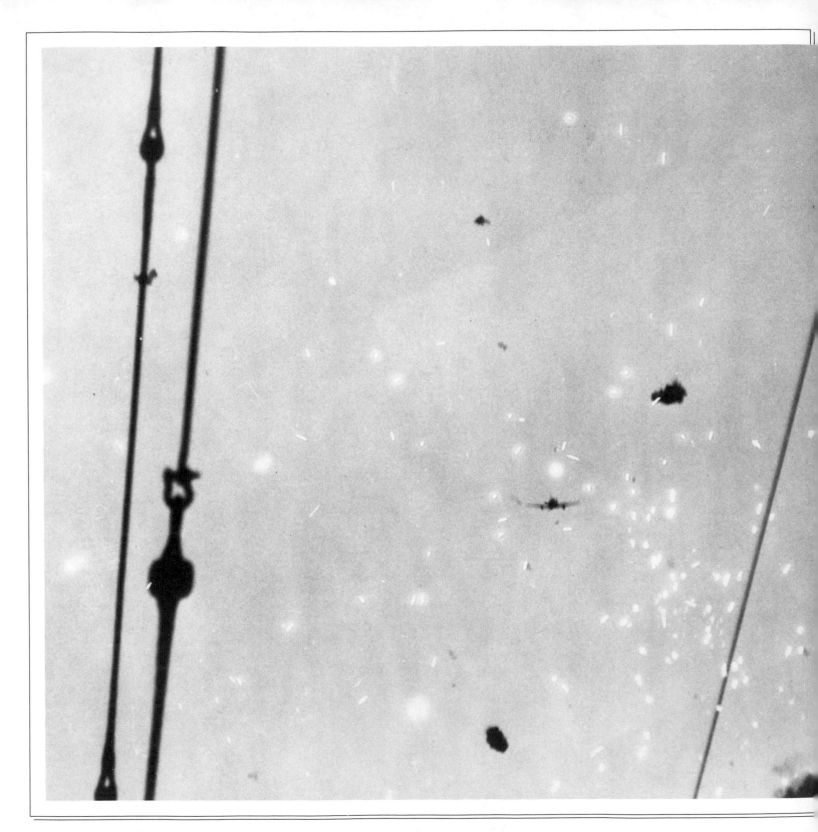

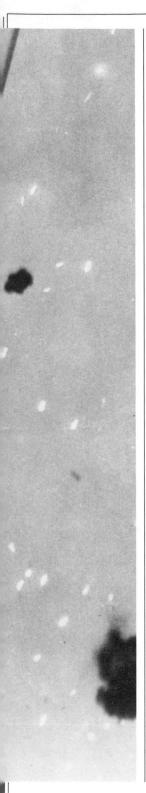

By April 7, 1944, *Tennessee* and the rest of the American ships grouped off Okinawa were facing massive attacks by Japanese suicide pilots.

Right: *Tennessee* helps fill the air with antiaircraft shells to stop the kamikaze pilots.

Left: A view of Japanese planes too often seen aboard ship. This pilot guides his plane at *New Mexico* through a hail of antiaircraft fire.[15]

plane was fired upon as it passed behind *Tennessee*; this one was shot down 5,500 yards off her stern. Five minutes later, a third plane was destroyed when it was still 5 miles away. A fourth plane appeared at 6:30, and *Tennessee*'s 5-inch guns opened fire when it was 5,000 yards away and fired 207 rounds as it circled the ship, crashing 12,000 yards off her bow. These attacks were not suicide missions, nor were the ones that came on April 1 and April 3. The first kamikaze attack came on April 6, when *Tennessee* fought off six attacking planes. On April 7, there was a single plane attack and then nothing for five days.

Sailors had felt safe aboard *Tennessee* as she bombarded islands where the enemy rarely fired back and almost never scored a hit. Now they were running to battle stations almost all the time. Most of the kamikazes never reached *Tennessee* and her fellow battleships shelling the shore. Picket ships far out to sea spotted the raids and radioed their position to American fighters. Many of the untrained kamikaze pilots failed to seek out the bigger ships and crashed into the first warship they encountered. These were often the small destroyers and destroyer escorts serving picket duty. But enough planes got through to make life very dangerous for the fleet off of Okinawa. Fighting an enemy that had to be killed to be stopped was difficult and sometimes killing the pilot was not enough.

On April 12, *Tennessee*'s combat information center made radar contact with approaching enemy planes still 65 miles away. While 10 miles distant, American fighters shot down several of them. Six of the planes got through and headed directly for *Tennessee*. One bomber was shot down when it was still 4,000 yards from the ship. Another plane opted for the destroyer *Zellers*, 2,500 yards from *Tennessee*. But four others flew through the hail of 5-inch and 40mm shells and crashed between 100 and 500 yards from *Tennessee*'s port side. One plane passed directly in front of her and crashed just 75 yards off *Tennessee*'s starboard bow.

There was a seventh attacker. He had broken away from the other six and circled around far ahead of *Tennessee*. Someone should have spotted the plane and turned some of *Tennessee*'s guns on it when it was still several thousand yards away, but the situation was hectic and there was not much time. The entire attack lasted only five minutes and when the seventh attacker turned toward *Tennessee,* still 2,500 yards away, the guns were concentrating on planes just 100 yards away, including the plane that passed directly in front of her bow. The forward guns aboard *Tennessee* opened fire on this last plane at 2,000 yards and had only ten seconds until the plane passed over their gun emplacements. In those ten seconds, 40mm gun number 3 fired 24 rounds and number 5 fired 60 rounds. The 20mm guns fired a total of 410 rounds. J. M. Curnutt, sight setter of 20mm gun number 7, held his weapon on the attacking seventh plane, ignoring the sixth plane even as it passed across *Tennessee*'s bow and directly below the seventh attacker. As a result, Curnutt got off the most shots, seventy-seven.

As the seventh plane reached *Tennessee,* it was smoking badly and one wheel was shot off. The pilot apparently wanted to crash into the bridge where he might kill not only *Tennessee*'s officers but also Rear Admiral Oldendorf, who was using *Tennessee* as his flagship. It is unlikely that this pilot knew Oldendorf was aboard or even which ship he was attacking, but he did know it was a battleship and that the officers were likely to be on the bridge. He came close to hitting his target. By the time he crossed the bow, the pilot had little control over his plane, if indeed he was still alive. His plane slipped slightly to its left and one wing tip ripped an awning off the bridge as

it passed by. It flew under the starboard yardarm, cutting radio antennae and signal halyards. It then crashed into the starboard side, destroying two 40mm gun mounts and two 20mm guns. Just before or upon impact a 550-pound bomb broke loose and penetrated the main deck but did not detonate.

Several men in guns along the starboard side could see the plane coming in and had a second or two to jump for cover. Marine corporal William Henry Putman jumped too far and ended up over the side in the ocean. Down in the boiler room, they got the word by telephone that they were going to be hit. Up on deck, Harry Mehl heard 20mm gun number 7 fire continuously for nearly ten seconds and thought to himself, "That one is getting close." An instant later, there was a huge explosion. Badly burned, Mehl lay on the deck in pain, convinced he was dy-

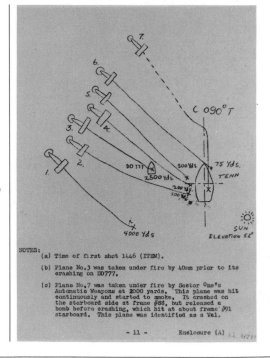

NOTES:

(a) Time of first shot 1446 (ITEM).

(b) Plane No.3 was taken under fire by 40mm prior to its crashing on DD777.

(c) Plane No.7 was taken under fire by Sector One's Automatic Weapons at 2000 yards. This plane was hit continuously and started to smoke. It crashed on the starboard side at frame #82, but released a bomb before crashing, which hit at about frame #91 starboard. This plane was identified as a Val.

-- 11 --   Enclosure (A)

Below left: As this drawing from the after action report shows, seven Japanese planes attacked *Tennessee* on April 12, 1944. Attackers 1 and 3 did not get close — attacker 1 was shot down 4,000 yards from *Tennessee,* and attacker 3 crashed into the destroyer *Zellers.* But attackers 2, 4, 5, and 6 came very close. Plane 6 passed in front of *Tennessee* at the same time that plane 7 was about to crash into *Tennessee's* starboard side.

Left: The navy labeled the large splash a Japanese attacker that had been shot down, possibly attacker 5.

Right: The fire aboard *Tennessee* is burning brightly and the destroyer *Zellers* is in flames in the distance.[16]

ing. As he gasped for breath, his buddies tried to comfort him and stuck cigarettes in his mouth, a nice gesture but the last thing he needed at that time. As fire-fighting crews extinguished the fire and rescue parties began to carry the wounded to sick bay, the chaplain came by. "Say a prayer," he said to Mehl, "and you will be all right." It seemed to Mehl, looking back on this situation decades later, that he recited the wrong prayer for a man who wanted to live, but it was the only one he could think of: "Now I lay me down to sleep, I pray the Lord my soul to keep. If I die before I wake, I pray the Lord my soul to take." Mehl was one of the ninety-nine men aboard who were injured; forty had to be transferred to a hospital ship, and fifty-nine were treated on board. Twenty-two men were killed. Some of the dead were so badly mangled that their remains were literally shoveled

into canvas bags, two 5-inch shells added for weight, and set aside for burial at sea.[17]

Had the bomb exploded, the damage would have been much more severe, but even then it would not have crippled the "Big T," as the men now called her. Battleships were designed to take this kind of punishment, and though several small guns and about 5 percent of the crew had been knocked out, *Tennessee* was still fit to fight. She stayed on her station, and less than an hour later she was firing at another attacking aircraft. This time it took only 20 rounds from her 5-inch guns to shoot down the plane at 8,000 yards. Not until after dark was it safe to call the men to witness the burial service for their shipmates killed nearly five hours earlier. That night, while the men were still on battle stations, there was another enemy air attack. *Tennessee* twisted and turned, changing directions

and speeds to avoid the attacking planes. The next day, *Tennessee* transferred her wounded to the hospital ship *Pinckney* and went back to work. For the next three weeks, she continued to give fire support to the soldiers on Okinawa and to shoot at enemy planes. All together, *Tennessee* stood off Okinawa for thirty-seven days without a break. Fear and fatigue were pushing the men to the limits of their psychological and physical endurance.

Occasionally *Tennessee* would move to a nearby anchorage for reprovisioning under a protective smoke screen. But even then the men were on edge. It was at one such time that Oldendorf, his chief of staff, Commodore George Van Deurs, and a chief quartermaster were standing on the flag bridge looking out into the smoke. They could hear the approach of attacking planes but could not see anything. Van Deurs

Left: What a 40mm gun emplacement normally looks like.

Above right: The destroyed 40mm gun mount number 7. Note the sailors in the lower right corner working on repairs. Marine corporal William Henry Putman was the pointer on 40mm gun mount number 9. One of the other men in the gun saw the plane coming in and yelled for everyone to get down. Putman meant to jump from his seat down behind a splinter shield, but he jumped too far and landed over the side of the ship. When he surfaced, he was surrounded by burning debris from the Japanese plane. "The whole area around me was on fire. Kept my eyes closed and dove under and came up where the water wasn't burning. That was the last thing I saw until I got on this raft. The raft was a long piece of 12 x 12 and I think it might have been a raft from the ship.... Then I saw a parachute was hanging on the raft with a headless body on it (body identified by the destroyer that picked me up as the Jap pilot). That is the only body I saw." Putman returned to the ship on April 15. His friend who had warned him to get down, marine private Roy A. Myers, had been burned on his arms and legs and was transferred in serious condition to the hospital ship *Pinckney*.

Below right: Sailors repairing damage to *Tennessee*. One steel door has been bent and roped shut.[18]

Damage to 40mm quad #7 and splinter shield.

recalled that it was shortly after the kamikaze hit, so "people were a little bit touchy." The three men heard a plane go into a dive and "it sounded like it was coming right for us, and the same idea hit all three of us at the same time — that the other side of the bridge would be an awful good place to be. Nobody said anything but we all started at the same time." There was a narrow opening to slip through, and Oldendorf and the quartermaster got there at the same time and were wedged tight as the plane passed overhead and crashed into the sea. "We got up and dusted ourselves off, looking kind of foolish, and laughed about it."[19]

Tennessee left Okinawa on May 3 and steamed for Ulithi for repairs. The men also got a chance to unwind. On May 19, Admiral Oldendorf handed out sixty-five Purple Hearts, three Gold Stars in lieu of a second Purple Heart, two Bronze Stars (one for an ensign and one for a lieutenant commander), and a Gold Star in lieu of a second Bronze Star for Captain John B. Heffernan. After a month away from battle, *Tennessee* headed back to Okinawa. She arrived on June 10 and continued to shell day and night until June 24.[20] There were still a few kamikazes in the air, but they did not bother *Tennessee* this time and the ship's records show no evidence of her having fired on an enemy plane. For the *Tennessee*, the worst of the war was over.

Tennessee had one final task. She proceeded with other ships in Admiral Oldendorf's command to the China Sea to protect American minesweepers from Japanese air attacks. Ironically, five years earlier, tactical practice had shown that *Tennessee* and the other battleships of the navy were incapable of protecting themselves from a sustained enemy air attack. Now these old battleships had such sophisticated equipment and experienced crews that they were placed where the danger of enemy air attack was the greatest. But then, *Tennessee*'s entire mission during World

War II was one that the battleship sailors between the wars had never envisioned. She would do what conventional wisdom before Pearl Harbor said could not be done: She would fight forts and planes rather than other battleships and she would do all this when she was nearly a quarter century old, ancient by naval warship standards. *Tennessee* did her job so well that she was one of two World War II–era battleships to receive a naval unit citation. The other was the venerable *Pennsylvania.*

It was hard for men who had been through such a long war to get used to peace. On the day Japan surrendered, the daily work sheet aboard *Tennessee* called for all hands to be up at 4:45 in the morning and be ready for an air attack. Two days later, the executive officer reminded the crew that "although President Truman has announced the surrender of Japan, it is necessary for this ship to remain ready to repel all forms of attack. We must be especially prepared to repel an air attack. We want no second Pearl Harbor!" Even when the Japanese were surrendering on the battleship *Missouri,* Admiral Oldendorf had *Tennessee* and his other battleships standing by in case there was a double cross. When these ships ran north to Tokyo at the time of the surrender, they ran with their lights out. But when they returned south after the surrender, they ran with their lights on for the first time since the attack on Pearl Harbor. Gradually the men began to realize that the war was over and that life would get back to normal.[21]

Now there was time for fun and games, as when *Tennessee* invited the men from *New Jersey* for a boxing match in September. Eventually there was liberty in Tokyo. This was a strange experience for many of the men, who just a few weeks earlier had been heroes because they killed "Japs." In the heat of battle, little if any thought was given to the carnage the American war machine was inflicting upon the Japanese

people. (On Okinawa, 70,000 Japanese soldiers died along with 80,000 civilians.) Now the faceless enemy took on personal shapes and the men were exhorted not to treat the Japanese badly. Sixteen thousand miles from home, Bud Galow from Wilkes-Barre, Pennsylvania, and his buddy from Altoona were sitting on a pile of rubble in Tokyo, eating their rations when a young Japanese man struck up a conversation in perfect English. He had been a student at the University of Pennsylvania before the war, had returned to Japan, and was caught there when the war began. The two Americans gave him all the cigarettes they had. It was all part of the remaking of a warrior into a civilian.[22]

Liberty in Tokyo and band concerts aboard ship were pleasant diversions, but what the men really wanted was to go home. That 16,000-mile journey began on October 15. The departure had been delayed by a large typhoon that sank seven ships, damaged beyond repair another nineteen, and inflicted serious structural damage upon thirty-four more. But *Tennessee* was unscathed, and in the company of her sister ship *California,* five destroyers, and a fleet oiler, she started home. The blisters on her side made her too wide to fit through the Panama Canal, so she followed a course laid out by Commodore Van Deurs. He added to the itinerary every city in Asia and Africa he wanted to see. The ships stopped at Singapore, Ceylon, and South Africa. They would even have stopped off at Rio de Janeiro before arriving home at Hampton Roads, Virginia, except that before they began the cruise, serious political difficulties developed in Brazil, and the United States government, trying to avoid even the appearance of interference in Brazil's electoral process, canceled the visit to Rio. Thus *Tennessee* and *California* went directly from South Africa to Philadelphia, where they arrived on December 7, 1945.[23]

The cancellation of the Brazilian visit

* What kinds of ships - destroyers and even smaller types?

U.S.S. TENNESSEE

HAPPY HOUR IN JAPAN

MONDAY OCT 1ST AT 1400

Captain
Harley F. Cope, USN
Commanding

Vice Admiral
J. B. Oldendorf, USN
Commander Battleship Squadron One

Commander
Daniel J. Wagner, USN
Executive Officer

Peace brought a chance to relax and even see some sights. Before leaving for home, there was time for a party in defeated Japan. At first, some of the men who went ashore worried that they would be attacked by Japanese who had not accepted defeat. But there were no incidents. There were, however, few sights for the sailors to enjoy; American bombing had left much of Japan's cities in ashes.[24]

was an indication of how the world was changing. In an era of increasing nationalism, the age of gunboat diplomacy (or battleship diplomacy) had passed. No longer could the United States impose its solution to the political or economic problems of another country simply by flexing some naval muscle. Had the men aboard wanted, they could have seen evidence of

the changing world in the daily press summary published aboard ship. Stories about a revolution in Indonesia, the Soviet-Iranian conflict, starvation in Europe, and the future of U.S.-Soviet relations were scattered among reports about the GI bill, universal military training, mandatory health insurance, and the news that former Chicago Cubs manager Gabby Hartnett was to become the manager of the Buffalo Bisons in the International League.

It is unlikely that the men heading for home gave much thought to the weightier issues. They were looking forward to visiting Singapore, Colombo (Ceylon), and Capetown (South Africa) and those towns were looking forward to having 5,000 sailors with months of pay in their wallets visit them. A huge crowd greeted the ships in Singapore, and news of how much money the Americans were spending prompted prices in Colombo to double and even triple days before the ships arrived there.

That some of the men were looking forward to making good deals in those ports is apparent from the run on cigarettes aboard ship. Just two days into the cruise, a few men began buying large numbers of cigarettes, intending to use them for barter in Singapore or Colombo. In Japan they had been able to buy almost anything with cigarettes. Other men stocked up on cigarettes in the hope of selling the tax-free cigarettes back home. These large purchases started the rumor that there were not going to be enough for the men aboard ship, so the executive officer took direct action. He assured the sailors that there were plenty of cigarettes available. In order to prevent the misuse of those cigarettes, warned the executive officer, men going ashore on liberty would be searched and before landing in the United States, each man's bag would be inspected. Until the hoarding had stopped, the sale of cigarettes would be limited to two packs per person per day.

Life aboard ship was more relaxed than

it had been during the war and perhaps at any time during *Tennessee*'s twenty-five-year history. Relations between officers and men were less formal, and men who wanted to take their bedding on deck to sleep at night could do so. When *Tennessee* crossed the equator, 600 men who had not undergone initiation by King Neptune were submitted to the hazing ritual that had been routine during peacetime. After leaving Capetown, the men aboard celebrated Thanksgiving at sea with a traditional dinner complete with turkey, cranberry sauce, sweet potatoes, giblets gravy, and hot rolls. Perhaps because pumpkin was hard to find in South Africa, the traditional pumpkin pie was replaced by French apple pie and vanilla ice cream. As the men sat down to eat, they were thirty-eight days out of Wakayama, Japan, and fifteen days to Philadelphia.[25]

On the night of December 6, *Tennessee* and *California* arrived at the mouth of the Delaware River and waited for the morning high tide. As *Tennessee* moved up the river, a huge red, white, and blue homeward-bound pennant streamed from her masthead and most of the men aboard were packing to go home. Demobilization was rapid. By the end of the year, 83 percent of the 2,400 officers and men aboard had been transferred off. Those who remained were working to put *Tennessee* into mothballs where she would stay until the navy had need of her again. Some men had a few days to see Philadelphia before their orders came, but others went directly from the ship to the train that would carry them to a mustering-out post.

At Iwo Jima, an officer aboard *Tennessee* had complained to a reporter that people who did not experience this "thing" called war could not understand what it was like. "If you write this thing just the way you see it," he told the reporter, "maybe it might mean something to people back home. They might see what we're going through. They might understand — they never understand back home."[26] It was almost impossible for people who had not experienced combat to understand how it affected men who had lived with it for months or years. And it would prove equally hard for the men who had gone through that hell to talk about it with those who had not. For many men, the biggest battle began when they left *Tennessee* and became civilians.

For *Tennessee*, there was no future. Decommissioned in 1947, she sat in storage during the Korean War. It was clear she was far too old to be of any value to the navy. There were plenty of bigger and faster battleships to satisfy those navy men who thought battleships were necessary to keep the United States strong. So the navy decided to scrap the "Rebel Ship," "Old Blisterbutt," the "Big T." For a while there were those in Tennessee who thought she should be towed up to Memphis and made into a museum. But the Mississippi River, as big as it is, is not big enough to handle a 32,000-ton battleship whose keel would scrape the bottom and whose superstructure would hit bridges. So in 1959, *Tennessee* was sold for scrap.[27] The tea service the people of Tennessee had bought for "their" ship in 1920 was returned to the state. A few souvenirs escaped the scrap yard, but most of *Tennessee* was melted down and remade into steel that would find its way into buildings, bridges, cars, and refrigerators across the United States just as the men who had served on her melted back into civilian life.

In a society that stresses being the best and pays little attention to those who are not ranked number one, it is tempting to try to make *Tennessee* into something more than she was. She was not the biggest, fastest, or most fearsome battleship in the United States Navy. What is important is that for a quarter-century *Tennessee* did what was asked of her and did it very well.

En route home, *Tennessee* and *California* sailors enjoyed liberty in Singapore, Colombo (Ceylon), and Cape Town (South Africa). Here sailors see the sights in Cape Town.[28]

NOTES

Abbreviations

AAR After Action Report, USS *Tennessee* (unless indicated otherwise)

AASP Adolphus A. Staton Papers, Southern Historical Collection, University of North Carolina Library, Chapel Hill, N.C.

AHRP Albert H. Roberts Papers, Tennessee State Library and Archives, Nashville, Tenn.

BATDIVS Battleship Divisions

BATFLT Battle Fleet

BATFOR Battleship Force

BB battleship

BUAERO Bureau of Aeronautics

BUCON Bureau of Construction and Repair

BUENG Bureau of Engineering

BUMED Bureau of Medicine

BUNAV Bureau of Navigation

BUORD Bureau of Ordnance

BUSHIPS Bureau of Ships

CINC commander in chief

CINCATLANT commander in chief, Atlantic Fleet

CINCPAC commander in chief, Pacific Fleet

CINCUS commander in chief, U.S. Fleet

CNO chief of naval operations

CO commanding officer

COM commander

GB General Board

GBH General Board hearings

GBR General Board reports

GBS General Board studies

JB Joint Board

MC Medical Corps

M-964 Microcopy, Fleet Problem series, NA

M-971 Microcopy, annual reports of the Fleet, NA

M-1140 Microcopy, CNO secret and confidential files, NA

NA National Archives, Washington, D.C.

NHC Naval Historical Center, Navy Yard, Washington, D.C.

NRS Navy Receiving Station

NYT *New York Times*

OA Operational Archives

OPNAV Naval Operations

RG Record Group

RG 19 Records of the Bureau of Construction and Repair (navy), NA

RG 24 Records of the Bureau of Navigation and Personnel (navy), NA

RG 38 Records of the Chief of Naval Operations, NA

RG 52 Records of the Bureau of Medicine and Surgery (navy), NA

RG 80 Records of the Secretary of the Navy, NA

RG 90 Records of the Public Health Service, NA

RG 125 Records of the Judge Advocate General (navy), Federal Record Center, Suitland, Md.

RG 313 Records of Naval Operating Forces, U.S. Fleet, Battle Force, Commander, Battleships, NA

RHJP Richard H. Jackson Papers, Hoover Institution, Stanford, Calif.

SECNAV secretary of the navy

SPD Strategic Plans Division

TC *Tennessee* Collection

USNI United States Naval Institute, Annapolis, Md.

USNIP *United States Naval Institute Proceedings*

USNRS U.S. Naval Receiving Station

USNTS U.S. Naval Training Station

WPD War Plans Division, Navy Department

Chapter 1. Men Fight, Not Ships: Creating *Tennessee*

1. Navy's plans for launch: Adm. J. P. McDonald to SECNAV, Apr. 9, 1919, and OPNAV to McDonald, Apr. 16, 1919, files 28547-97 and 28547-98, entry 19, RG 80. The launch: John C. Niedermair interview, pp. 29–31, USNI; *NYT*, Apr. 21, p. 14, Apr. 27, p. 15, Apr. 30, p. 10, and May 1, 1919, p.16. Demobilization: *Nashville Banner,* Nov. 21, 1919, p. 4; Capt. J. K. Taussig, "A Study of Our Navy Personnel Situation," *USNIP* 47 (Aug. 1921): 1153–54. Statistics: *USNIP* 45 (Aug. 1919): 1437–38, and (Dec. 1919): 2083. Demobilization order and Congress: Misc. items, files 1120–1559 and 1120–1770, entry 89, RG 24.

2. Photo: 19-N-12123, NA.

3. Examples of ship recruiting: Frederick S. Harrod, *Manning of the New Navy: The Development of a Modern Naval Enlisted Force, 1899–1940* (Westport, Conn.: Greenwood Press, 1978), pp. 53–54; *Maryville Times,* Dec. 3, 1919, p. 7. Authorization for program: BUNAV telegram 110006, Nov. 6, 1919, as cited in F. H. Poteet to BUNAV, Dec. 22, 1919, file 5525-4627, entry 89, RG 24. Recruiting technique: BUNAV to NRS, Nashville, Nov. 26, 1919, file 9491-18, and W. E. Cheadle to BUNAV, Feb. 3, 1920, file 5525-4812, entry 89, RG 24.

4. Leigh's trip and genesis of whistle-stop campaign: NRS, Nashville, to BUNAV, Dec. 22, 1919, file 9756-264, and Cheadle to BUNAV, Dec. 31, 1919, Feb. 3, 1920, files 5525-4635 and 5525-4812, entry 89, RG 24.

5. Recruiter's message: *Maryville Times,* Dec. 3, 1919, p. 7; *Nashville Tennessean,* Jan. 4, p. 7, Jan. 5, p. 3, Jan. 6, p. 4, Jan. 8, pp. 6–7, Jan. 11, p. 9, Jan. 12, p. 12, Jan. 13, p. 14, Jan. 17, p. 7, Jan. 19, 1920, p. 9; *Memphis Commercial Appeal,* Jan. 26, 1920, p. 12; *Knoxville Journal,* Nov. 26, p. 20, Dec. 3, p. 3, Dec. 7, p. 7, Dec. 10, 1919, p. 16, Jan. 10, p. 5, Jan. 12, 1920, p. 9; *Nashville Banner,* Nov. 21, 1919, pp. 3, 6, Nov. 24, 1919, p. 4; *Chattanooga Daily Times,* Nov. 21, p. 2, Nov. 25, 1919, p. 3, Jan. 14, 1920, p. 2.

6. Robb's fortunes: BUNAV, memo, Feb. 7, 1921, file 26283-3744, entry 19, RG 80; *NYT,* Mar. 8, 1921, p. 7, and Apr. 4, 1921, p. 28. Photo: NH-72008, NHC.

7. Excluding unsavory types: BUNAV circular, Feb. 25, 1920, file 5525-4777-1, entry 89, RG 24.

8. Oscar Holt case: *Chattanooga Times,* Jan. 14, 1920, p. 2; Roberts to Daniels, Jan. 27, 1920, and Daniels to Roberts, Feb. 3, 1920, file 5525-4752, entry 89, RG 24.

9. Keeping a clean ship: *Nashville Banner,* Nov. 21, 1919; *Knoxville Journal-Tribune,* Dec. 10, 1919, p. 16.

10. Tennessee steel: *NYT,* Mar. 26, 1915, p. 1; Mar. 15, 1916, p. 6; Apr. 6, 1916, p. 5. Photo: 181-NYS-4-5, NA.

11. Number of men recruited: BUNAV to NRS, Nashville, Jan. 10, 1920, file 9491-26, entry 89, RG 24. The navy did not keep records on how many men were screened out at the local level. One report for October 1919 shows that of seventy-five applicants in Memphis, only twenty-seven were accepted and sent to Nashville. *Morgan County News,* Nov. 21, 1919, p. 7.

12. Men unfit for service: BUNAV circulars to all NRS, Nov. 11–12, 1919, files 5525-4445 and 5525-4448; C. E. Courtney, inspector of recruiting, eastern division, to all main stations, Dec. 18, 1919, file 5525-4556; BUNAV to Cheadle, Mar. 25, 1920, file 9756-294, entry 89, RG 24. Illiterates and the mentally handicapped: Robert B. Dashiel to Adolphus Staton, Mar. 27, 1920, folder 6, box 1, AASP; Medical Examining Board to COM, USNTS, Great Lakes, Feb. 15, 1920, file 5525-4899, entry 89, RG 24.

13. Blacks excluded: Harrod, *Manning the New Navy,* pp. 59–61. Williams memo to SECNAV, Dec. 15, 1920, file 5525-5806; J. M. Enochs draft letter, Nov. 19, 1921, file 5525-6263, entry 89, RG 24.

14. Workers put on overtime: G. E. Burd, industrial manager, U.S. Navy Yard, N.Y., to SECNAV, Mar. 27 and Apr. 2, 1919, files 28600-470 and 28547-93, entry 19, RG 80. Photo: 181-NYS-4-14, NA.

15. Boot camp experience: Chaplain C. A. Neyman to Roberts, undated, Leigh to Roberts, May 28, 1920, and Staton to Roberts, Feb. 17, 1920, folder 9, box 34, AHRP.

16. Not ready for commissioning: Adm. J. P. McDonald to CNO, Mar. 30, 1920, file 9-BB43, entry 105, RG 19; Leigh to Roberts, Mar. 18, 1920, folder 9, box 34, AHRP. Construction bids and delays: Misc. documents, Nov.–Dec. 1915, file 28547-25, and Roosevelt to BUCON and BUENG, Dec. 28, 1915, file 28547-25, entry 19, RG 80; Daniels to Lemuel

Padgett, Feb. 8, 1916, file 28547-33, entry 19, RG 80; Daniels to Padgett and Benjamin R. Tillman, Aug. 15, 1916, and to Padgett, Feb. 3, 1917, file 28547-37, entry 19, RG 80.

17. Importance of launching as soon as possible: G. E. Burd, industrial manager, U.S. Navy Yard, N.Y., to SECNAV, Mar. 27 and Apr. 2, 1919, files 28600-470 and 28547-93, entry 19, RG 80. Quality of civilian workers: Leigh to Cole, July 2 and 7, 1920, and Leigh to SECNAV, July 8, 1920, files 28547-179 and 28547-184, entry 19, RG 80; George Van Deurs interview, pp. 13, 16, USNI. Too many men arriving in Brooklyn Navy Yard: McDonald to BUNAV, May 15, 1920, file 8955-83, entry 89, RG 24.

18. Photo: 181-NYS-4-15, NA.

19. Commissioning ceremony: *NYT*, June 4, 1920, p. 8. Leaving men in training: Leigh to Roberts, May 17, 1920, folder 9, box 34, AHRP. Work left to be completed: Leigh to Cole, July 2 and 7, 1920, and Leigh to SECNAV, July 8, 1920, files 28547-179 and 28547-184, entry 19, RG 80. Crew slowing down construction: BUCON to CNO, Sept. 27, 1920, file 28547-201, entry 19, RG 80.

20. Conditions aboard: BUCON to CNO, Sept. 27, 1920, file 28547-201, entry 19, RG 80; Leigh to Roberts, Sept. 17, 1920, folder 9, box 34, AHRP. Discipline aboard: Deck logs, June–Sept. 1920, entry 118, RG 24; CINCPAC, annual report, 1921, OA, NHC; Leigh to Roberts, Sept. 17, 1920, folder 9, box 34, AHRP.

21. Getting under way: Leigh to Roberts, June 29 and Sept. 17, 1920, folder 9, box 34, AHRP; Leigh to Cole, Sept. 14, 1920, and Leigh to SECNAV, Oct. 1, 1920, files 28547-211 and 28547-184-1, entry 19, RG 80; Van Deurs interview, pp. 16–17, USNI.

22. Photos courtesy of Ethel Moles, copy in TC, NHC.

23. Turbo-electric power: GBH, Sept. 25, 1928, pp. 276–77, RG 80; R. L. Weber, "The Electric Plant of the Battleship *Tennessee*," *USNIP* 45 (1916): 1397–1408; *NYT*, Oct. 31, 1920, p. 14.

24. Awarding contracts on electric drive: Bureau of Steam Engineering to Navy Department, Apr. 4, 1916, file 28547-30, entry 19, RG 80; *NYT*, Jan. 3, 1919, p. 8.

25. Lack of experience with electric drive: Van Deurs interview, p. 14, USNI. Shortage of trained men: Leigh to BUNAV, July 19, 1920, and Mar. 23, 1921, files 9491-83 and 9491-138, entry 89, RG 24. Engineering casualties: Daniels memo, written after Apr. 21 and before May 9, 1921, file 28547-291, entry 19, RG 80.

26. Turbine casualty: Van Deurs interview, pp. 22–23, USNI; Leigh to BUENG, Oct. 25, 1920, file 26283-

3647, entry 19, RG 80; OPNAV to U.S. Navy Yard, N.Y., Oct. 28, 1920, file 8955-11, entry 115, RG 24.

27. February cruise: Deck log, Feb. 26, 1941, entry 118, RG 24; Staton to Edith Staton, Feb. 28, 1921, AASP.

28. Photo: 19-N-7699, NA.

29. Near collision: Van Deurs interview, pp. 17–19, USNI; deck log, Feb. 26, 1921, entry 118, RG 24; *Tennessee Tar*, Feb. 27, 1921, AASP; Daniels memo, written after Apr. 21 and before May 9, 1921, file 28547-291, entry 19, RG 80. (Van Deurs's recollection of the event has the wrong date, admiral, and liner but is otherwise consistent with the written record.) Stopping test: *NYT*, May 22, 1921, p. 2.

30. Leigh decides to continue cruise: Leigh to CNO, Mar. 2, 1921, file 28547-264, entry 19, RG 80. Trip to Guantánamo: *Tennessee Tar*, Feb. 28–Mar. 7, 1921, AASP; Staton to Edith Staton, Mar. 7, 1921, AASP.

31. Electric-motor fire and repair: Van Deurs interview, pp. 26–29, USNI; transcript of phone conversation, Leigh and CNO, Mar. 22, 1921, file 28547-281, entry 19, RG 80; Lieutenant T. A. Solberg, "Rewinding a Main Drive Motor on a Dreadnought," *USNIP* 48 (Sept. 1922): 1529–38.

32. Photo: 19-A-22B-138, NA.

33. Debate over gun size: *NYT*, Mar. 21, 1915, pp. 11, 13. Importance of reducing flight time: J. V. Chase, "Accuracy of Fire at Long Ranges," *USNIP* 46 (Aug. 1920): 1175–78. Guns on U.S. and foreign ships: "Professional Notes," *USNIP* 47 (Dec. 1921): 1968–69; GBS, May 25, 1915, May 31, Oct. 3, and Oct. 17, 1916, file 420-6, RG 80, NA.

34. Debate on volume of fire: GBH, Apr. 6, 1938, p. 9, RG 80.

35. Gun trials: Chief, BUCON to industrial manager, U.S. Navy Yard, N.Y., May 24, 1921, and acting industrial manager, U.S. Navy Yard, N.Y., to chief, BUCON, June 23, 1921, file 57-BB43, entry 105, RG 19; Board of Inspection and Survey to CNO, June 21, 1921, file 28547-310, entry 19, RG 80.

36. Rebuilding motor: Daniels memo, Mar. 15, 1921, file 28547-291, entry 19, RG 80; Solberg, "Rewinding a Main Drive Motor," pp. 1529–38.

Chapter 2. Up to the Challenge

1. Appropriations: Paolo Coletta, "Josephus Daniels," in *American Secretaries of the Navy* (Annapolis Md.: Naval Institute Press, 1980), 2:527–28.

2. Photo: 80-G-466532, NA.

3. Navy officers' worldview: BUNAV, Bulletin no. 3, June 21, 1922, file 507-3-23, entry 17, RG 38; memo, "Military Characteristics of New Construction," Sept. 26, 1921, box 1, RHJP; Capt. R. R. Belknap,

"The Blue-Orange Situation, Blue," Nov. 5, 1921, and Capt. Frank Schofield speech to newspaper owners and editors, Feb. 1924, lectures and speeches series, SPD, OPNAV, OA, NHC; GBH, Mar. 6, 1922, pp. 70, 72, 75, 78, and Oct. 26, 1923, pp. 492–95, RG 80, NA; final report of the Special Board, Jan. 17, 1925, pp. 4–7, GBH, RG 80; Rear Adm. W. L. Rodgers, "Military Preparedness Necessary to the Economic and Social Welfare of the United States," *USNIP* 51 (Oct. 1925): 1848–49.

4. Navy's view of Japan: Akira Iriye, *After Imperialism: The Search for a New Order in the Far East, 1921–1931* (Cambridge, Mass.: Harvard University Press, 1965); Michael Barnhart, *Japan Prepares for Total War: The Search for Economic Security, 1919–1941* (Syracuse, N.Y.: Syracuse University Press, 1987). Stereotypical views of Japan: William Howard Gardiner, vice president of the Navy League of the United States, GBH, Oct. 26, 1923, pp. 492–95, RG 80; strategic and tactical situation, joint Army-Navy Problem 1, 1926, Naval War College Operations Problems, series 2, box 14, SPD, RG 80, NA.

5. War Plan Orange: William Reynolds Braisted, *The United States Navy in the Pacific, 1909–1922* (Austin: University of Texas Press, 1971), 472–73.

6. Photo: 19-LC-22M-1, NA.

7. Visual spotting: Naval War College, "Construction of Fire Effect Tables," Mar. 1922, file 156-29, roll 42, M-1140.

8. Plunging fire: Thomas Hone and Norman Friedman, "Innovation and Administration in the Navy Department: The Case of the *Nevada* Design," *Military Affairs* 45 (Apr. 1981): 57–62.

9. Double hull construction: Daniels to Lemuel Padgett and Benjamin R. Tillman, Aug. 15, 1916, file 28547-37, entry 19, RG 80.

10. Photo: 181-NYS-4-10, NA.

11. Torpedo tubes: BUORD to CNO, "Torpedo Tubes on Capital Ships," Aug. 9, 1921, series 2-2, William Veazie Pratt Papers, OA, NHC; GBH, Apr. 4, Apr. 19, 1922, pp. 388, 835, July 14, 1924, pp. 311–17, Nov. 8, 1924, p. 391, Feb. 5, 1925, pp. 1–15, Feb. 8, 1928, pp. 18–32, Sept. 25, 1928, p. 269, and Jan. 17, 1929, p. 4, RG 80, NA; Fleet correspondence, June 1–July 31, 1926, file A5-1 Sur. Ves. 1926–27, entry 179, RG 38; COM, BATDIVS, BATFLT, annual report, 1926, p. 54, 1927, p. 10, and CINCBATFLT, annual report supplemental, 1926, p. 21, roll 5, M-971; COM, BATDIVS, BATFLT, annual report, 1934, p. 11, roll 9, M-971; GBR, Feb. 14, 1928, Oct. 18, 1933, OA, NHC; GBS, Apr. 5, 1929, file 420-11, RG 80, NA; Capt. Milton Davis to COMBATFOR, June 4, 1934, file BB43/L9, entry 115, RG 19.

12. *Tennessee-Mutsu* vulnerability: "Construction of Fire Effect Tables," Naval War College report, Mar. 1922, file 156-29, roll 42, M-1140; annex 2 of "Blue Estimate and Preliminary Discussion," Fleet Problem 2, M-964.

13. Shell hits at Pearl Harbor: See pp. 83–84 below.

14. New battleship design: GBS, Jan. 26, 1917, file 420-6, RG 80, NA; Capt. E. J. King, "Some Ideas about the Effects of Increasing the Size of Battleships," *USNIP* 45 (Mar. 1919): 387–406.

15. Seven ships scrapped: *Washington* (BB47, 75.9 percent complete), *South Dakota* (BB49, 38.5 percent complete), *Indiana* (BB50, 34.7 percent complete), *Montana* (BB51, 27.6 percent complete), *North Carolina* (BB52, 36.7 percent complete), *Iowa* (BB53, 11.0 percent complete), *Massachusetts* (BB54, 11.0 percent complete) (*The Battleship in the United States Navy* [Washington, D.C.: Naval History Division, 1970], pp. 48–49).

16. Effect of Five Power Treaty: Thomas Buckley, *The United States and the Washington Conference, 1921–1922* (Knoxville: University of Tennessee Press, 1970); GBH, special hearing on aviation, 1924, p. 577, RG 80, NA. Fleet Problem objectives: A brief summary is at the beginning of M-964, which contains all the Fleet Problems.

17. Role of aircraft in Fleet: CINCUS, annual report, 1925, p. 25, roll 5, M-971; summary, Feb. 1923, pp. 3, 75, 97, 140, Fleet Problem 1, M-964; CO, *Tennessee*, to CINCBATFLT, Feb. 26, 1923; chief umpire's report, Jan. 25, 1924, Fleet Problem 3, p. 4, M-964; COM, Aircraft Squadron, to CINCUS, Feb. 15, 1924, Fleet Problem 4, M-964.

18. Airplane versus battleship debate: GBH, Mar. 10, pp. 229–33, Mar. 18, pp. 299, 314, 317, Apr. 17, p. 647, May 6, p. 864, May 12, pp. 928–29, and May 13, 1919, pp. 947–50, RG 80, NA; Michael Sherry, *Rise of American Airpower: The Creation of Armageddon* (New Haven, Conn.: Yale University Press, 1987), ch. 2; Lt. Com. Guysbert B. Broom and William Oliver Stevens, "The Fate of the Dreadnought," *USNIP* 47 (Feb. 1921): 157–67; Rear Adm. Bradley A. Fiske, "The Warfare of the Future," *USNIP* 47 (Feb. 1921): 191–200.

19. Mitchell and bombing test: *NYT*, May 29, p. 6, Aug. 29, 1920, p. 6, Jan. 26, p. 4, Jan. 29, p. 1, Jan. 31, p. 8, and Feb. 10, 1921, p. 1. Navy's position: GB to SECNAV, Feb. 2, 1921, file 420–6, serial 1056, GBS, RG 80, NA (also in file 237-3, roll 117, M-1140); *NYT*, Feb. 7, p. 1, and Mar. 1, 1921, p. 17. Navy officers believe battleships invulnerable: GBH, Feb. 9, pp. 34–43, and Feb. 16, 1921, p. 71, RG 80, NA; CINCPAC to CNO, Mar. 7, 1921, file 111-57, roll 22, M-1140;

Capt. William D. Leahy testimony before House Naval Affairs Committee, *NYT*, Jan. 30, 1921, p. 1.

20. Navy's original plan: CNO circular, Sept. 17, 1920, director, gunnery exercises, to CNO, Jan. 17, 1921, file 395(11), entry 178, RG 38. Navy bows to public pressure: SECNAV memos to CINCATLANT, Jan. 17, Feb. 24, 1921, file 395(11), entry 178, RG 38. Officers posturing: *NYT*, Feb. 7, p. 1, and Mar. 13, 1921, p. 16.

21. *New York Times* editorial: *NYT*, Feb. 9, 1921, p. 8. Navy limits army tests: William Mitchell to CINCATLANT, May 17, 1921, file 395 (11), entry 178, RG 38.

22. Leahy manages the news: Leahy memo, June 17, 1921, file 395 (11), entry 178, RG 38; *NYT*, June 22, 1921, p. 1; Joint Army-Navy Board memo, Feb. 28, 1921, J.B. No. 349, serial 128, file 111:67, roll 23, M-1140.

23. Planes miss target: *NYT*, June 22, p. 1, June 30, p. 1, and July 1, 1921, p. 1.

24. Mining effect of bombs: Leahy to CNO, Aug. 3, 1921, file 395 (11), entry 178, RG 38. Misrepresentation of sinking in press and newsreels: Capt. W. S. Pye, "Aircraft in the National Defense from the Naval Point of View," undated, SPD, OPNAV, lectures and speeches file, GB file 420-11, RG 80, NA. Press reaction: *USNIP* 47 (Sept. 1921): 1451–61.

25. Board's conclusions on tests: "Report of the Joint Army and Navy Board on Bombing and Ordnance Tests," *USNIP* 47 (Oct. 1921): 1641; summary of Fleet Problem No. 1, Feb. 1923, p. 75, M-964.

26. Sims on aircraft carriers: *NYT*, July 15, 1923, 7-3, 13. Eberle inquiry: GBH, "Result of Development of Aviation on the Development of the Navy," Jan. 17, 1925, RG 80, NA.

27. Photo: 80-G-455916, NA.

28. Decision not to modernize: *NYT*, Apr. 5, 1934, p. 7.

29. *Mutsu* modernized: Anthony J. Watts and Brian G. Gordon, *The Imperial Japanese Navy* (Garden City, N.Y.: Doubleday, 1971), pp. 56–61.

30. Redefining *Tennessee's* useful life: Navy Department, *Ships Data: U.S. Naval Vessels* (Washington, D.C.: GPO, July 1, 1935, and January 1, 1938), p. 15 in each edition.

31. Navy views threat of aircraft: GBH, Mar. 23, 1927, pp. 60, 63–64, and Sept. 25, 1928, p. 273, RG 80, NA; COM, Carrier Division 1, to COM, Battleships, BATFOR, Mar. 9, 1940, file 15-2(1), RG 313.

32. Photo: 19-A-22B-133, NA.

33. Antiaircraft guns on ships: GBH, Oct. 9, 1922, p. 639, RG 80, NA; CINCBATFLT to CNO, Oct. 30, 1926, BUORD to CNO, Jan. 24, 1927, CINCUS to CNO, Feb. 21, 1927, GB to SECNAV, Mar. 30, 1927, and CNO to CINCBATFLT, Mar. 30, 1927, file 162-41:1, roll 45, M-

1140; GBH, Mar. 23, 1927, pp. 60, 63–64, and Sept. 25, 1928, pp. 269-74, RG 80, NA.

34. CNO response to *Ostfriesland* sinking: CNO to BUORD, Aug. 13, 1921, and CNO to CINCPAC, Sept. 9, 1921, file 156-11:1, roll 24, M-1140. New targets developed: GBH, special board, final report, p. 19, RG 80, NA. Ineffective antiaircraft fire and *Tennessee's* success: CINCBATFLT, annual report, 1925, p. 30, roll 5, M-971; *NYT*, Mar. 26, p. 4, and Mar. 29, 1925, p. 2; CNO to Fleet, Apr. 30, 1925, file 535 (212), entry 178, RG 38.

35. NcNamee warning: Rear Adm. Luke McNamee to CNO, Jan. 24, 1929, as printed in GBH, Feb. 6, 1929, pp. 7–9, RG 80, NA.

36. Night antiaircraft exercise: *Tennessee's* and other battleships' reports to COM, Battleships, Mar. 2, 1935, file A5-5/Bomb Exercises, RG 313.

37. Ineffective antiaircraft fire in 1940: W. R. Sexton to CNO, June 12, 1940, in GBS, Aug. 13, 1940, file 420-11, RG 80, NA.

38. Carrier becomes primary target: GBH, June 26, 1922, pp. 321–23, 540, and June 10, 1931, pp. 274–76, RG 80, NA.

Chapter 3. Battle Efficiency

1. Photo: NH84665, NHC.

2. Speed in firing guns: Gerald Hanggi and L. S. Sabin interviews, TC, NHC.

3. Description of explosion: *NYT*, June 14, 1924, p. 1. A dozen years later: Hanggi interview, TC, NHC.

4. *Naval Ordnance: A Textbook Prepared for the Use of the Midshipmen of the United States Naval Academy* (Annapolis, Md.: U.S. Naval Institute, 1939), ch. 9, plate 10.

5. Causes of *Mississippi* explosion: *NYT*, June 14, p. 1, June 15, p. 1, and June 17, 1924, p. 9; "*Mississippi*," *USNIP* 49 (Aug.–Sept. 1924): 1377, 1575; "The Battleship *Mississippi* Disaster," *Scientific American* 131 (Sept. 1924): 176.

6. Gun accidentally fires: *NYT*, June 15, 1924, p. 1.

7. Novatny's meritorious mast: Sabin interview, TC, NHC.

8. Powder bags breaking: COM, Battleships, BATFOR, Mar. 28, 1939, file A5-1, Day Battle, RG 313.

9. Scuttle casualty: File 14550, vol. 677, Dec. 20, 1926, entry 30, RG 125. Photo: 19-A-22B-74, NA.

10. Turnover rate: *Tennessee* muster rolls, quarterly reports, entry 134, RG 24; CINCBATFLT, annual report, 1924, p. 13, roll 4, M-971.

11. Sabin's experience: Sabin interview, TC, NHC.

12. Retaining experienced ensigns: CINCPAC, annual report, 1923, p. 13, roll 3, M-971; COMBATFOR, annual report, 1933, p. 19, roll 9, M-971; Pettengill to

BUNAV, Nov. 30, 1928, and BUNAV to *Tennessee*, Dec. 17, 1928, file BB43/P16-1(36), entry 90, RG 24.

13. Cluttered schedules: COMBATFOR, annual report, 1932, p. 11, roll 9, M-971.

14. Cash bonus: CNO to CINCPAC, Oct. 26, 1921, CNO to gunnery officer, *New Mexico*, Nov. 12, 1940, file 440 (48), entry 178, RG 38. Firing on wrong target: CO, *Nevada*, to CNO, Mar. 23, 1934, file Af-1(11), RG 313.

15. Variation in gun accuracy: Chief observer to COM, Battleships, Aug. 30, 1940, file A5-1(9), RG 313.

16. Photos: NHF122, p. 15, NHC (left); courtesy of Vice Adm. L. S. Sabin, USN (Ret.), TC, NHC (above).

17. 1938 short-range competition: *Tennessee Tar*, Aug. 20, Aug. 27, 1938, TC, NHC.

18. Indirect fire: CINCBATFLT, annual report, 1925, p. 34, and 1926, p. 38, roll 5, M-971; CINCBATFLT, annual report, 1927, p. 30, roll 6, M-971; M. M. Taylor memo, circa Jan. 1927, file A5-1 Sur. Ves. 1926–27, entry 179, RG 38; CNO memo, Sept. 1927, file A5-1(2), entry 179, RG 38; CNO memos, Dec. 6–13, 1927, file Af-1/FS Gun Ex. 1928–29, entry 179, RG 38; *Tennessee Tar*, June 1920, TC, NHC.

19. Decision to put planes on battleships: GB to SECNAV, June 23, 1919, file 111-1, roll 19, M-1140; GBH, in 1917: Aug. 20, pp. 14–21, Sept. 6, p. 118; in 1918: June 18, pp. 765–76, Sept. 4, pp. 985–86, Sept. 23, pp. 1079–88, Dec. 5, pp. 1307–8; in 1919: Mar. 5, pp. 159–62, Mar. 8, p. 196, Mar. 18, pp. 192–94, May 6, p. 858, Apr. 2, p. 475, Apr. 4, p. 528, May 6, p. 860, Apr. 17, p. 647, May 2, p. 833; in 1921: Apr. 27, pp. 119ff.; in 1922: Mar. 3, p. 28, Mar. 11, p. 321, Mar. 27, p. 322, Apr. 5, pp. 298–315, Nov. 7, pp. 761–80, Dec. 5, pp. 851–52, RG 80, NA; WPD chief to CNO, Mar. 27, 1922, and GB to SECNAV, Apr. 27, 1922, GB No. 449, file 111-87, RG 80, NA; SECNAV to chief, BUAERO, Nov. 23, 1922, file 111-78:2, roll 24, M-1140.

20. Photo: NH 80549, NHC.

21. Photo: 80-G-1009392, NA.

22. Spotter aircraft problems: CINCUS to Board on Observation of Gunfire by Aircraft, Aug. 19, 1924, Board on Observation of Gunfire by Aircraft to CINCUS, Nov. 26, 1924, and CINCBATFLT to CINCUS, Dec. 9, 1924, file 111-60:2, roll 23, M-1140.

23. Spotting improves: CINCBATFLT, annual report, 1925, pp. 30–31, roll 5, M-971.

24. Launching and recovering aircraft: Harold Pullen and Hanggi interviews, TC, NHC; CO, *West Virginia*, to COM, Battleships, BATFOR, Mar. 2, 1936, file A5-5, RG 313; CINCBATDIVS, annual report, 1927, p. 14, roll 6, M-971.

25. Catapults and planes placed aboard:

CINCBATFLT, annual report, 1924, p. 57, and CINCBATDIVS, annual report, 1924, pp. 6–7, roll 4, M-971; CINCUS, annual report, 1925, pp. 25, 39, roll 5, M-971; CINCUS to Board on Observation of Gunfire by Aircraft, Aug. 19, 1924, file 111-60:2, roll 23, M-1140.

26. Association of aviators and gunnery officers: CINCUS to Board on Observation of Gunfire by Aircraft, Aug. 19, 1924, file 111-60:2, roll 23, M-1140.

27. Trunnion malfunction: CINCUS, annual report, 1926, p. 47, 1927, pp. 29–30, and 1929, p. 43, rolls 5, 6, and 7, M-971; CINCBATDIVS, annual report, 1927, pp. 14, 37–38, 1930, p. 129, and 1934, p. 10, rolls 6, 8, and 9, M-971; BUORD to CNO, Sept. 21, 1933, file FF1/A9(11), follows CINCUS, annual report, 1933, roll 9, M-971.

28. Fuel consumption: Engineering Efficiency Score, Dec. 1935, file A5-7(1), RG 313.

29. Record of Inquiry, June 17, 1937, file BB43/A17-24, RG 80; file 19290, vol. 968, June 17, 1937, entry 30, RG 125. Stapler's career can be traced in the annual editions of U.S. Bureau of Navigation, *Navy Directory* (Washington, D.C.: GPO, 1937–1941). Photo: 80-G-1021368, NA.

30. Water conservation: *Tennessee Tar*, Feb. 28, 1921, AASP. Off-the-record oil: Arthur L. Specht, Harold Pullen, and Sabin interviews, TC, NHC; Lt. Comdr. R. R. Smith, "Engineering Economy on Battleships," *USNIP* 50 (Jan. 1924): 18–27. Most economical speed: CO, *California*, to COMBATFOR, Dec. 23, 1935, file A5-7(3), RG 313.

31. Change in speed competition: Sabin interview, TC, NHC.

32. Electric motor room casualty: Board of Investigation, report, April 16, 1923, file 26283-4878:1, entry 19, RG 80. Photos courtesy of Vice Adm. L. S. Sabin, USN (Ret.), TC, NHC (left); 19-A-22B-68, NA (right).

33. Engineering casualties: Misc. reports in file A5-7(5), RG 313.

34. "E" awards: GBH, May 23, 1923, pp. 210ff, RG 80; engineering "E" award list, CO memo, June 10, 1941, ship's file Af-7(4), TC, NHC.

35. Installing 5-inch guns and phones: Files BB43/L-94(M), BB43/L-95(280183), and BB43/S74(5) (M), entry 22, RG 80; file BB43, entry 115, RG 19.

Chapter 4: Life aboard a Peacetime Battleship

1. Photo: NH 80553, NHC.

2. Clothing allowed aboard: Ridley McLean, *The Bluejackets' Manual: United States Navy*, 10th ed. (Annapolis, Md.: U.S. Naval Institute, 1940), pp. 6, 13–14, 239, 243–44.

3. Bunks and hammocks: Board of Inspection to chief,

BUCON, May 6, 1921, file 57-BB43-3, entry 105, RG 19; CINCBATFLT, annual report, 1925, p. 81, roll 5, M-971; COMBATDIVS to CINCBATFLT, Nov. 29, 1924, file 8956-101, entry 89, RG 24; GBH, Oct. 14, 1926, pp. 442–444, RG 80; Richard Fife, J. C. Bradford, Kenley Burchfield, Gerald Hanggi, and James Beddingfield interviews, TC, NHC.

4. Ventilation: COM, Battleships, BATFOR, to Battleships, BATFOR, May 15, 1935, file FF2-1, entry 179, RG 38; BUMED to BUCON, Feb. 16, 1928, file BB43/S38, entry 15, RG 52; misc. items, file BB43/S38-1, entry 115, RG 19; sanitary report, 1927, file BB43/A9-4(3), entry 38, RG 52.

5. Photo: NH 82909, NHC.

6. Bathing: COM, Battleships, BATFOR, to Battleships, BATFOR, May 15, 1935, file FF2-1, entry 179, RG 38; *Tennessee Tar,* July 15, Dec. 9, 1939, TC, NHC; *Tennessee Tar,* Feb. 28, 1921, AASP; deck log, Apr. 22, 1921, entry 118, RG 24; Jess Deacan and Fife interviews, TC, NHC.

7. Heads: Hanggi and Arthur L. Specht interviews, TC, NHC; CINCUS, annual report, 1928, p. 77, roll 7, M-971; COM, Battleships, BATFOR, to Battleships, BATFOR, May 15, 1935, file FF2-1, entry 179, RG 38; chief, BUMED, to BUSHIPS, Mar. 18, 1941, file BB43/S36-1, entry 15, RG 52.

8. Food for enlisted men: Deck logs, various dates, entry 118, RG 24; Burchfield, Fife, Bradford, Beddingfield, Hanggi, and Deacan interviews, TC, NHC; COMBATDIVS, annual report, 1925, p. 18, and CINCUS, annual report, 1926, p. 68, roll 5, M-971; CINCBATFLT, annual report, 1929, p. 147, roll 7, M-971; COMBATFOR, annual report, 1931, p. 53, roll 8, M-971.

9. Board of Inspection, March 29–30, 1923, file 28547-351, entry 19, RG80 (left). Photos: TC, NHC.

10. Battle of the dishwasher: CINCBATFLT, annual report, 1925, p. 99, 1926, p. 114, and 1927, p. 53, roll 5, M-971; BUCON correspondence, file BB43/S34, entry 115, RG 19.

11. Shipboard routine: McLean, *Bluejackets' Manual,* ch. 25.

12. Photo: TC, NHC.

13. Religious services: *Tennessee Tar,* misc. issues, TC, NHC; file "Christian Flag," entry 377, RG 24; CINCBATFLT, annual report, 1930, p. 172, roll 8, M-971; COMBATFOR, annual report, 1933, p. 57, roll 9, M-971. New York religious service: File "Fleet Services 1934," entry 377, RG 24.

14. Photo: 19-A-22B-34, NA.

15. Library: *Tennessee Tar,* Apr. 2, July 23, 1938, July 1, 1939, TC, NHC; *Tennessee Tar,* Mar. 9, 1921, AASP; BUNAV to BUCON, Aug. 29, 1919, file 2835-3904,

entry 89, RG 24; C. R. Train to R. N. Dunbar, Mar. 6, 1924, file 55415-3733, entry 89, RG 24; CINCBATFLT, annual report, p. 142, in CINCUS, annual report, 1929, roll 7, M-971; misc. items, file BB43, entry 90, RG 24.

16. Photo: 19-A-22B-32, NA.

17. Dances: *Tennessee Tar,* Aug. 10, 1925, Sept. 7, 1935, Nov. 12, 1938, June 10, July 1, and July 8, 1939, TC, NHC; CINCPAC, annual report, 1923, p. 20, roll 3, M-971. Smokers: *Tennessee Tar,* Aug. 24, Sept. 7, 1935, May 9, May 30, 1936, and Oct. 7, 1939, TC, NHC. Films: *Tennessee Tar,* Aug. 24, 1935, and Mar. 25, 1939, CINCBATFLT, annual report, 1924, p. 81, roll 4, M-971. Ship's service fund: *Tennessee Tar,* Oct. 17, 1936, and Nov. 5, 1937, TC, NHC.

18. Photos courtesy of Henry D. Meyer, TC, NHC.

19. Athletic competition: COM, Battleships, BATFOR, to Battleships, BATFOR, Mar. 6, 1934, file P10-1, RG 313.

20. Iron man award: *Tennessee Tar,* July 11, 1934, and July 27, 1935, TC, NHC.

21. Crew participation in athletics: COM, Battleships, BATFOR, to Battleships, BATFOR, Mar. 6, 1934, file P10-1, RG 313.

22. Exhorting men to win: *Tennessee Tar,* July 11, 1934, TC, NHC.

23. Restrictions imposed on athletics: "Battle Force Athletic Rules 1934," file FF2-1 for 1935, entry 179, RG 38.

24. Football banished and restored: COM, Battleships, BATFOR, to BATFOR, May 24, June 17, 1936, and Mar. 16, 1937, responses dated Mar. 22–Apr. 7, and COM, Battleships, BATFOR, to Battleships, BATFOR, May 19, 1937, file P10-1(1), RG 313.

25. Measuring morale: R. H. Jackson to CINCUS, undated, file P18/1 (5809), box 2, RHJP; file P18-1/FF2(6), folder P18-1/1-10, box 971, entry 90, RG 24.

26. Desertion rate: Files 57375-15, 36, 117, 136, 147, 215, 231, 297, and 308, entry 89, RG 24.

27. Photo courtesy of Andrew D. Cooper, TC, NHC.

28. Lampshire and Bradford interviews, TC, NHC. Photo: NHF-122, p. 14, NHC.

29. Diebel case: Record of proceedings of a board of investigation, June 15, 1921, file 26250-2823, entry 19, RG 80.

30. Recruiting statistics: Extracted from Secretary of the Navy, *Annual Report of the Secretary of the Navy* (Washington, D.C.: GPO, 1931–1941).

31. Number of blacks aboard: *Tennessee* muster rolls, entry 118, RG 24; H. L. Lampshire interview, TC, NHC; *Tennessee Tar,* Mar. 18, 1921, AASP.

32. Racial segregation of crew: Bradford interview,

TC, NHC; *Tennessee Tar,* Dec. 14, 1935, May 15, 1937, Mar. 11, Apr. 15, June 3, and July 22, 1939, TC, NHC.

33. Racism aboard ship: Frederick S. Harrod, *Manning the New Navy: The Development of a Modern Naval Enlisted Force, 1899–1940* (Westport, Conn.: Greenwood Press, 1978), pp. 59–61; *Tennessee* muster rolls, entry 134, RG 24; *Tennessee Tar,* Nov. 5, 1938, TC, NHC, for item cited; other examples: *Tennessee Tar,* Sept. 7, Nov. 9, 1935, Apr. 8, 15, 22, and May 13, 1939, TC, NHC; chaplain's editorial: *Tennessee Tar,* July 23, 1937, TC, NHC; Lampshire, Bradford, and Hanggi interviews, TC, NHC.

34. Courts-martial: *Tennessee* muster rolls, quarterly reports, entry 134, RG 24; schedule of punishments for 1923, file 28547-347, entry 19, RG 80; schedule of punishments for 1937, file P13-1, RG 313; GBH, Oct. 17, 1923, pp. 446–49, RG 80, NA. Courts-martial held and punishments awarded are published in the deck logs, entry 118, RG 24.

35. Captain's punishment: Deck logs, May–Dec. 1927, entry 118, RG 24.

36. Flag biographies, OA, NHC. Photo: NH 80559, NHC.

37. Penalties for AOL: COM, Battleships, BATFOR, to Battleships, BATFOR, Oct. 26, 1937, file P13-1, RG 313.

38. Advancement in rating: Deacan, Specht, Bradford, Hanggi, Fife, and Harold Pullen interviews, TC, NHC; *Tennessee Tar,* Nov. 10, 1934, and Feb. 12, 1938, TC, NHC.

39. Married sailors: *Tennessee Tar,* May 15, 1937, Apr. 2, Apr. 23, 1938, TC, NHC.

40. Coop case: File 18026, vol. 863, Jan. 10, 1933, entry 90, RG 24. Printer's case: BUNAV circular letter, July 10, 1933, file P2-4(15), entry 90, RG 24. Madsen case: File 18419, vol. 891, Aug. 17, 1934, entry 90, RG 24. Barker case: File 18577, vol. 904, Jan. 4, 1935, entry 90, RG 24. Clark case: File 18896, vol. 932, Apr. 1, 1936, entry 30, RG 125.

41. Motor vehicle deaths: *Tennessee Tar,* Dec. 8, 1934, May 14, 1938, May 21, 1938, and Nov. 11, 1939, TC, NHC.

42. Nonlethal accidents: File 14550, vol. 677, Dec. 20, 1926, and file 15425, vol. 732, Aug. 23, 1928, entry 30, RG 125; asst. SECNAV to CNO, Feb. 1, 1930, file P2-4(1), entry 90, RG 24; misc. items, file P3-1, RG 313; Hanggi interview, TC, NHC. Shell explosions: File 15037, vol. 704, Oct. 18, 1927, and file 15852, vol. 763, Dec. 5, 1928, entry 30, RG 125.

43. Excessive heat: Staton to Edith Staton, AASP; CO, *Tennessee,* to COMBATFOR, Apr. 28, 1934, folder P3-1, general administrative file, COM, Battleships,

BATFOR, RG 313.

44. Unattributed press clipping citing an article in the *Honolulu Star Bulletin.* Photo courtesy of Jess Deacan, TC, NHC.

45. Illness: 1927 sanitary report, file BB43/A9-4 (3), entry 38, RG 52.

46. Efforts to control VD: Chief Pharmacist J. Levansaler to George H. Brady, BUNAV, July 13, 1920, Levansaler to Charles Hines, Mar. 30, 1921, file 19119-21, entry 415, RG 24; "Measures for the Prevention and Control of Venereal Diseases," General Order 530, Apr. 1920, file 26181-100, entry 19, RG 80; bulletin 105, Apr. 15, 1921, bulletin 109, Aug. 15, 1921, and bulletin 112, Nov. 15, 1921, files 26181-127:1 and 26181-127:2, entry 19, RG 80; CINCUS, annual report, 1923, p. 40, roll 4, M-971; CINCBATFLT, annual report, 1930, p. 178, roll 8, M-971; Harrod, *Manning the New Navy,* p. 135; CINCPAC, annual report, 1922, p. 21, and 1923, pp. 19, 40, roll 4, M-971.

47. VD among public: Allan M. Brandt, *No Magic Bullet: A Social History of Venereal Disease in the United States since 1880* (New York: Oxford University Press, 1985), pp. 123–29. Navy yields to pressure: Brandt, *No Magic Bullet,* pp. 122–29; "Measures for the Prevention and Control of Venereal Diseases," General Order 530, Apr. 1920, file 26181-100, entry 19, RG 80.

48. VD board report: Aug. 7, 1925, file 26181-163:1, entry 19, RG 80, published in *United States Naval Bulletin* 23 (Dec. 1925): 535 (hereafter cited as VD Board Report with page number of *Naval Bulletin*).

49. Navy resumes issuance of prophylactic kits: General Orders 69 and 69 (modified), Aug. 7, 1925, and Feb. 24, 1926, file 26181-163:1, entry 19, RG 80; COMBATFOR to chief, BUMED, Oct. 24, 1934, file A2-9/P3-1(034-26), entry 15, RG 52.

50. VD diversion program: VD Board Report, pp. 537–38.

51. Bremerton dances: CINCBATFLT, annual report, 1926, supplement, p. 124, roll 5, M-971. Concealing VD: Capt. Douglas G. Sutton (MC) to Capt. M. E. Higgins (MC), Feb. 22, 1937, file P3-1/A9-10, entry 15, RG 52.

52. Punishment: General Order 69 (modified), Feb. 26, 1926, file 26181-163:1, entry 19, RG 80. Rates of infection: Fleet rates are usually reported in the annual reports of the surgeon general of the U.S. Navy, CINCUS, and COMBATFOR. See especially CINCUS, annual report, 1940, p. 35, roll 10, M-971. Reports for *Tennessee* are more sporadic, but see above and medical bulletin of Feb. 18, 1936, in general administrative file, COM, Battleships, BATFOR, file P6-1, filed in folder P3-1/P3-2, RG 313.

53. Refusal to sell condoms aboard: Lt. (j.g.) J. A.

Millspaugh (MC), "The Prophylaxis of Venereal Disease," *U.S. Naval Medical Bulletin* 34 (Jan. 1936): 34.

54. Failure to punish offenders: Statistics compiled from *Tennessee* quarterly reports, entry 134, RG 24.

55. Photo: 80-G-1009395, NA.

56. Dealing with VD problem in 1934: COMBATFOR, annual report, 1934, pp. 47–48, roll 9, M-971; COMBATFOR to chief, BUMED, Oct. 24, 1934, file A2-9/P3-1(034-26), entry 15, RG 52.

57. Dealing with VD problem in 1935: CINCUS, annual report, 1936, pp. 53–55, roll 10, M-971. Hot showers: Millspaugh, "Prophylaxis of Venereal Disease," p. 32. Holding officers responsible: Kent C. Melhorn, Fleet medical officer, to Rossiter, Nov. 20, 1935, and O. J. Mink to Melhorn, Nov. 27, 1935, file P3-1/P3-2 (113), entry 15, RG 52.

58. Parran's campaign: Brandt, *No Magic Bullet*, ch. 5. Impact on navy: Medical officer correspondence, file 0425/Diseases, general classified records, group 6, entry 10, RG 90. Decline of VD in 1930s: SECNAV to all ships and stations, July 19, 1940, file P3-1, RG 313.

59. VD rate during 1940–41: File P3-1, RG 313; CINCPAC, annual report, 1941, roll 10, M-971.

Chapter 5. From Peace to War

1. Photo: NH 50931, NHC.

2. U.S. and Japanese naval power: Stephen E. Pelz, *Race to Pearl Harbor: The Failure of the Second London Naval Conference and the Onset of World War II* (Cambridge, Mass.: Harvard University Press, 1974), passim.

3. *Panay* incident: Jonathan G. Utley, *Going to War with Japan, 1937–1941* (Knoxville: University of Tennessee Press, 1985), pp. 3–31.

4. Navy routine during Sino-Japanese War: Felix L. Johnson interview, USNI.

5. Roosevelt orders Fleet back to Pacific: Utley, *Going to War*, pp. 58–59.

6. Men and current events: J. C. Bradford interview, TC, NHC.

7. *Tennessee Tar*, May 6, 1939, TC, NHC. Photo: 80-G-414594, NA.

8. Photo: 80-G-41099, NA.

9. Visit to New York: *Tennessee Tar*, Apr. 1, 1939–May 20, 1939, TC, NHC.

10. Transfer of Fleet to Pearl Harbor: U.S., Congress, Joint Committee on the Investigation of the Pearl Harbor Attack, *Hearings* (Washington, D.C.: GPO, 1946), Sumner Welles testimony, part 2, pp. 463, 546.

11. Richardson-Roosevelt disagreement over Fleet location: James O. Richardson, with George C. Dyer, *On the Treadmill to Pearl Harbor: The Memoirs of Admiral James O. Richardson* (Washington, D.C.: Naval History Division, Navy Department, 1973), pp. 324–29.

12. *Tennessee's* overhaul at Bremerton: Deck logs, Apr.–Aug. 1940, entry 118, RG 24.

13. Recreation facilities in Hawaii: CINCPAC, annual report, 1941, roll 3, M-971; *Tennessee Tar*, misc. issues, fall 1940, TC, NHC. Trips back to California: Deck logs, Jan.–June 1941, entry 118, RG 24; *Tennessee Tar*, Oct. 26, 1940, TC, NHC.

14. Dances in Hawaii: *Tennessee Tar*, Oct. 26, 1940, TC, NHC.

15. Slide toward war: Utley, *Going to War*, pp. 83–89.

16. Stark's war plan: Utley, *Going to War*, pp. 110–16.

17. New men aboard ship: *Tennessee* muster rolls, quarterly reports, entries 134 and 135, RG 24.

18. Promotions: Gerald Hanggi, Bradford, Richard Fife, and James Beddingfield interviews, TC, NHC; *Tennessee Tar*, Mar. 22, 1941, TC, NHC.

19. Fleet prepares for war: COM, Battleships, BATFOR, to CNO, July 10, 1941, file A5-7/Confidential, box 51, RG 313.

20. Photo: 80-G-32689, NA.

21. Diplomatic confrontation: Utley, *Going to War*, pp. 151–75; Michael Barnhart, *Japan Prepares for Total War: The Search for Economic Security, 1919–1941* (Ithaca, N.Y.: Cornell University Press, 1987), pp. 162–262; Herbert Feis, *The Road to Pearl Harbor: The Coming of the War between the United States and Japan* (Princeton, N.J.: Princeton University Press, 1950), pp. 227ff.

22. Pearl Harbor considered safe: Gordon Prang, *At Dawn We Slept: The Untold Story of Pearl Harbor* (New York: McGraw-Hill, 1981), passim.

23. Diplomacy ends: Prang, *At Dawn We Slept*, pp. 353ff.

24. *Tennessee* during Pearl Harbor attack: Deck logs, entry 118, RG 24; AAR, Dec. 11, 1941, serial 0157, and AAR, Feb. 11, 1942, serial 020, OA, NHC; 1st Sgt. Roger M. Emmons (MC), "Pearl Harbor," TC, NHC; Beddingfield, Bradford, Fife, and Edgar James interviews, TC, NHC.

25. Photos: 80-G-32611, NA (left); *Tennessee* AAR, Dec. 11, 1941, serial 0157, OA, NHC (right).

26. "*Tennessee*," in James L. Mooney, ed., *Dictionary of American Naval Fighting Ships*, 8 vols. (Washington, D.C.: Naval History Center, Navy Department, 1981), 7:89. Photos: 80-G-387573, NA (right). 19-N-28387, NA (below).

27. Post–Pearl Harbor attack activities: *Tennessee* war diary, OA, NHC (hereafter cited as "war diary");

deck logs, Dec. 1941–Apr. 1943, entry 118, RG 24.

28. Photos: 80-CF-2054-2 (top left); 80-G-6146 (bottom left); 19-N-45068, NA (right).

29. Photo: 119-N-54769, NA.

Chapter 6. Learning How to Fight a New Kind of War: From Kiska to Surigao Strait

1. Pacific strategy: Ronald Spector, *Eagle against the Sun: The American War with Japan* (New York: Free Press, 1985), pp. 220–26, 252–56.

2. Aleutian campaign before *Tennessee* arrived: Stetson Conn et al., *Guarding the United States and Its Outposts*, vol. 2 of *Western Hemisphere: United States Army in World War II* (Washington, D.C.: Office of the Chief of Military History, 1964), pp. 260–98.

3. Comedy of errors: Robert C. Baumrucker diary, May 25, 1943, OA, NHC.

4. Sailor's poem: TC, NHC.

5. Poor weather in Bering Sea: Jess Deacan interview, TC, NHC.

6. Liberty and discipline in Aleutians: Baumrucker diary, OA, NHC; deck logs, July–Sept. 1943, entry 118, RG 24.

7. Phantom Japanese fleet: Deck logs, July 10, 1943, and July 11, 1943, entry 118, RG 24.

8. Preliminary Kiska operation: AAR, serial 002, Aug. 7, 1943, OA, NHC.

9. Kiska bombardment: AAR, serial 004, Aug. 23, 1943, OA, NHC; Conn et al., *Guarding the United States*, 2:295–98. Wood's report: Comdr. J. E. M. Wood, "Shore Bombardment Practice Report," Oct. 9, 1943, file A5-1 (15), RG 313.

10. Bombardment practice: War diary, Oct.–Nov. 1943, OA, NHC.

11. Prewar amphibious assault planning: Jeter A. Isely and Philip A. Crowl, *The U.S. Marines and Amphibious War: Its Theory and Its Practice in the Pacific* (Princeton, N.J.: Princeton University Press, 1951), pp. 25–70, 168; Robert D. Heinl, Jr., "Naval Gunfire Training in the Pacific," *Marine Corps Gazette* 32 (June 1948): 11.

12. Stages of bombardment: Robert D. Heinl, Jr., "Naval Gunfire: Scourge of the Beaches," *USNIP* 41 (Nov. 1945): 1309–13.

13. Tarawa pre-assault plans: Isely and Crowl, *Marines and Amphibious War*, pp. 214–29; Henry I. Shaw et al., *Central Pacific Drive*, vol. 3 of *History of U.S. Marine Corps Operations in World War II* (Washington, D.C.: GPO, 1966), pp. 53–55; AAR, Betio Island, Dec. 10, 1943, serial 0010, and AAR, Betio Island, Dec. 18, 1943, serial 0011, OA, NHC.

14. Tarawa pre-assault bombardment: AAR, Betio

Island, serial 0010, Dec. 10, 1943, OA, NHC.

15. Eyewitness accounts of landing: MSgt. Roger M. Emmons, "Tarawa Bombardment," *Marine Corps Gazette* 32 (Mar. 1948), 45–46.

16. Photos: NH 89330 (left) and NH 89329 (above), NHC.

17. Assessment of bombardment: AAR, serial 0010, Dec. 10, 1943, OA, NHC; battle experience, bulletin no. 15, Gilbert Islands, pp. 67/24–25, OA, NHC; Shaw, *Central Pacific Drive*, p. 111; COM, Fifth Amphibious Force, "Report on Galvanic Operation," serial 00300, OA, NHC.

18. Routine at sea: Daily work sheets, Jan. 31, Feb. 17, Mar. 20, and Mar. 23, 1944, TC, NHC. Death as distant: Robert Sherrod, *Tarawa: The Story of a Battle* (New York: Duell, Sloan, and Pearce, 1944), p. 6.

19. Munson and Chapman deaths: Deck logs, Oct. 13, 26, and 27, 1943, entry 118, RG 24; Baumrucker diary, Oct. 26, Oct. 27, 1943, TC, NHC; war diary, Oct. 26, 1943, OA, NHC; Sherrod, *Tarawa*, p. 8; Rocky Williams interview, TC, NHC.

20. Photo: NH 89327, NHC.

21. Conolly reviews tactics: Isely and Crowl, *U.S. Marines*, pp. 251, 256. Preliminary bombardment of Marshall Islands: Shaw et al., *Central Pacific Drive*, pp. 136–37; I. E. McMillan, "Naval Gunfire at Roi-Namur," *Marine Corps Gazette* 32 (July 1948): 51.

22. Crowded waters: Isely and Crowl, *U.S. Marines*, p. 256.

23. Effectiveness of bombardment: Comments by Comdr. J. E. M. Wood, gunnery officer, AAR, Feb. 10, 1944, serial 003, OA, NHC.

24. Ricochets: AAR, Feb. 10, 1944, serial 003, OA, NHC; battle experience, bulletin no. 17, Marshall Islands, pp. 70–116 and 70–149, OA, NHC. Few casualties at Kwajalein: Isely and Crowl, *U.S. Marines*, pp. 277–78, 291. Close to shore: AAR, Feb. 28, 1944, serial 005, OA, NHC.

25. Photos: NH 89331 (left) and NH 89333 (above), NHC.

26. Use of 40mm guns: AAR, Feb. 28, 1944, serial 005, with endorsement by Oldendorf, Mar. 15, 1944; AAR, COM, Battleship Division Two, to COM, Task Unit 51.17.2, Feb. 28, 1944, serial 0012, OA, NHC.

27. Kavieng operation: AAR, Mar. 24, 1944, serial 025, OA, NHC. Change of command: War diary, Feb. 22–May 31, 1944; flag biographies of Haggart and Mayer, OA, NHC.

28. Photo: 80-G-233224, NA.

29. Preliminary bombardment of Saipan: Isely and Crowl, *U.S. Marines*, pp. 329–31.

30. *Tennessee* at Saipan: AAR, June 30, 1944, serial

064, OA, NHC.

31. Battle of Philippine Sea: AAR, Aug. 14, 1944, serial 079, OA, NHC.

32. Guam and Tinian operation: AAR, Aug. 14, 1944, serial 079, OA, NHC. Samuel Eliot Morison, *New Guinea and the Marianas*, vol. 8 of *History of United States Naval Operations in World War II* (Boston: Little, Brown & Co., 1962), pp. 359–62.

33. Photos: *Tennessee* AAR, serial 064, June 30, 1944, OA, NHC. *Tennessee Bombarder*, July 2, 1944, p. 4.

34. Tennessee War Diary, entries for August 23–28, 1944, OA, NHC; report of COM, Cruiser Division Four, serial 00108, Aug. 26, 1944, including report of *Tennessee* to Admiral Oldendorf with Oldendorf's endorsements, OA, NHC; report of *California*, serial 0018, Aug. 23, 1944, OA, NHC. Flag biography of Mayer, OA, NHC. Photos: 80-G-374136 (left), 80-G-314177 (top right), and 80-G-314165 (bottom right), NA.

35. Photo: *Tennessee* AAR, serial 0019, Oct. 23, 1944, OA, NHC.

36. Angauer operation: AAR, Sept. 28, 1941, serial 0100, OA, NHC. Leyte operation: AAR, Oct. 31, 1944, Serial 0110, OA, NHC.

37. "Preparations to greet them": *U.S.S. Tennessee: December 7, 1941–December 7, 1945* (Philadelphia: privately published, 1946), p. 64.

38. Battle of Surigao Strait: AAR, Oct. 31, 1944, serial 0108, OA, NHC; "The Battle for Leyte Gulf, Strategical and Tactical Analysis," vol. 5, Naval War College study, 1958, pp. 480–86. OA, NHC.

39. Map and data on battle: *Tennessee* AAR, serial 0108, Oct. 31, 1944, OA, NHC. Photo: 80-G-331390, NA.

40. Photo: 80-G-374343, NA.

41. Nimitz speech: "Memorandum for the Crew," Dec. 7, 1944, citing press reports; *Tennessee Bombarder*, Nov. 18, 1945, TC, NHC.

Chapter 7. The Final Push to Peace

1. Photo: *Tennessee* AAR, serial 0120, May 13, 1945, OA, NHC.

2. Photo: Mimeo sheet, *Tennessee* ship records, TC, NHC.

3. Work routine and regulations: Daily work sheets, Jan. 31, Feb. 17, Mar. 20, and Mar. 23, 1944, TC, NHC; *Tennessee Bombarder*, July 2, 1944, p. 6, TC, NHC.

4. Fist fights: Page 3 of a fragment from *Tennessee Bombarder*, undated but probably June 1944, after *Tennessee* had spent 45 days at Pearl Harbor, TC, NHC.

5. Athletics: *Tennessee Bombarder*, May 28, 1944, pp. 3, 11, TC, NHC. Liberty: Bud Galow, Rocky Williams, and James N. Dyer interviews, TC, NHC. Discipline: *Tennessee* muster rolls, quarterly reports, entry 134, RG 24.

6. Homesickness: *Tennessee Bombarder*, misc. entries, 1944, TC, NHC.

7. Iwo Jima campaign: Ronald Spector, *Eagle against the Sun: The American War with Japan* (New York: Free Press, 1985), pp. 494–503; Samuel Eliot Morison, *Victory in the Pacific*, vol. 14 of *History of United States Naval Operations in World War II* (Boston: Little, Brown & Co., 1964), pp. 3–66; Jeter A. Isely and Philip A. Crowl, *The U.S. Marines and Amphibious War: Its Theory and Its Practice in the Pacific* (Princeton, N.J.: Princeton University Press, 1951), pp. 432–530; AAR, Mar. 12, 1945, serial 026, OA, NHC; war diary, Feb. 16–Mar. 7, 1945, OA, NHC.

8. Photo: 80-G-231069, NA.

9. Photo: 80-G-310301, NA.

10. Inability to locate mortars: Isely and Crowl, *U.S. Marines*, p. 506.

11. Loss of spotter plane: War diary, Feb. 19, 1945, OA, NHC.

12. Good shooting at Okinawa: AAR, July 3, 1945, serial 0160, OA, NHC.

13. Air attacks during 1944: AAR, June 26, 1944, no serial, and Nov. 1, 1944, serial 0115, OA, NHC.

14. Photos: 80-G-309925 (right) and 80-G-314670 (above), NA.

15. Photos: 80-G-328845 (right) and 80-G-326638 (left), NA.

16. Drawing: *Tennessee* AAR, serial 0121, May 16, 1945, OA, NHC. Photos: 80-G-328599 (left) and 80-G-328600 (right), NA.

17. Kamikaze attacks: AAR, May 16, 1945, serial 0121, OA, NHC; deck logs, April 1945, entry 118, RG 24; Williams, Dyer, Galow, and Mehl interviews, TC, NHC.

18. *Tennessee* AAR, serial 0121, May 16, 1945, OA, NHC. Photos: 80-G-374258, NA (left); *Tennessee* AAR, serial 005, Apr. 16, 1945, OA, NHC (top right); *Tennessee* AAR, serial 0120, May 13, 1945, OA, NHC (below right).

19. Van Deurs story: Van Deurs interview, USNI, p. 529.

20. Awards issued: Deck logs, May 1945, entry 118, RG 24.

21. Transition from war to peace: Daily work sheet, Aug. 12, 1945; executive officer's memo, Aug. 15, 1945, TC, NHC; Van Deurs interview, p. 560, USNI.

22. Liberty in Tokyo: Galow and John Ulku interviews, printed programs for New Jersey Smoker and Happy Hour in Japan, TC, NHC.

23. Planning cruise home: Van Deurs interview, pp. 563–64, USNI; Frank D. McCann, Jr., *The Brazilian-American Alliance, 1937–1945* (Princeton, N.J.: Princeton University Press, 1973), pp. 478–79.

24. Photo: TC, NHC.

25. Homeward cruise: *Tennessee Typhoon*, Oct. 17, 18, 21, and 31, Nov. 4, 5, 6, 16, and 22, 1945, TC, NHC.

26. Arriving in Philadelphia: *NYT*, Dec. 8, 1945, 1-5. Mustering out shipmates: *Tennessee* muster rolls, entry 135, RG 24. "They never understand": John P. Marquand, "Iwo Jima before H-Hour," *Harper's Magazine* 190 (May 1945): 493.

27. Scrapping of *Tennessee*: *Nashville Banner*, Feb. 26, p. 24, Mar. 4, p. 11, and Mar. 20, 1959, p. 10.

28. Photo: 80-G-374334, NA.

Oral History Interviews and Correspondence, TC, NHC

Adamson, Frank "Champ"
Baumrucker, Robert O.
Beddingfield, James
Borris, John
Bradford, J. C.
Burchfield, Kenley
Chubb, Phillip D.
Cooper, Andrew B.
Deacan, Jess
DuBeau, Robert J.
Dyer, James N.
Fife, Richard
Galow, Bud
Hanggi, Gerald
Holland, Roy
James, Edgar
Lampshire, H. L.
McPherson, Gordon
Mehl, Harry
Meyer, Henry D.
Mitchell, Paul N.
Peterson, Merlin Ray
Powell, Vernon L.
Pullen, Harold
Sabin, L. S.
Sherfey, Sam
Specht, Arthur L.
Tomlin, H. R. "Pinky"
Ulku, John C.
Williams, Rocky

AN ESSAY ON SOURCES

There is an almost endless supply of books about battleships, especially battleships in the twentieth century, books that are abundant with photographs and line drawings. There are several fine works dealing with the role of the navy in American foreign policy and aspects of the social history of the United States Navy. The *United States Naval Institute Proceedings* contains dozens, perhaps hundreds, of useful articles pertinent to navy developments affecting battleships during the 1920s and 1930s and occasionally an article on *Tennessee.* Complete citations for these books and articles are in the notes, and readers interested in reading further in one aspect or another of the ship's history should consult the notes in the appropriate chapters of this work. An excellent bibliography of works on battleships and *Tennessee* is Myron J. Smith, Jr., *Battleships and Battle-Cruisers, 1884–1984: A Bibliography and Chronology* (New York: Garland Publishing, 1985).

One book that deals specifically with *Tennessee* is the "cruise book" for World War II, *U.S.S. Tennessee: December 7, 1941–December 7, 1945 (*Philadelphia: privately published, 1946). Much like a college or high school yearbook, *U.S.S. Tennessee* relates stories, includes pictures of the crew, and generally summarizes the ship's adventures during World War II. There is a copy in the New York Public Library.

There is not enough information in the secondary sources to begin to construct an accurate history of *Tennessee.* The important sources for researching the history of this ship are the records the navy maintained and housed in the National Archives, Washington, D.C. (Though the National Archives is building a new repository in Maryland, Navy Department records are likely to remain in the Archives building in Washington.) Most important among those records is the ship's deck log (RG 24, entry 118.) The deck log provides a day-by-day account of the ship's movements and activities. Every court-martial and punishment is listed. Often it itemizes what food was brought aboard. Accidents and injuries are listed as well as the ship's location, other ships present, and the men who reported aboard or transferred off. Though tedious to review, the deck logs provide a detailed picture of the ship.

A great deal of personnel information not included in the deck logs is in the muster rolls (RG 24, entry 134, for material up to June 30, 1939, and entry 135, for material after September 1, 1939). Not only do the muster rolls provide a list of every man who served aboard *Tennessee,* but they quantify a vast amount of data on such things as men on the sick list, rating changes, absences over liberty, desertions, reenlistments, and many other categories valuable in trying to create a picture of life aboard ship.

A major source for life in the Fleet and aboard *Tennessee* during the 1920s and 1930s is the Records of Naval Operating Forces, United States Fleet, Battle Force, Commander, Battleships (RG 313.) There is a file on *Tennessee* under her hull number, BB43, in this and most other collections. But the bulk of the material is arranged according to the navy filing manual, which has a special file classification for almost every subject; general information as well as information specific to *Tennessee* can be found in those files. Records for World War II are in the Federal Record Center, Suitland, Maryland. The Navy Department's perspective on a variety of issues is revealed in the records of the General Board (RG 80), which consist of the very useful hearings, occasionally useful studies, and comparatively useless reports. The hearings have also been microfilmed and are available from Scholarly Resources of Wilmington, Delaware.

Fishing for information in general navy files can also be rewarding. In almost any file, there is a little information that pertains to *Tennessee* or at least an issue that affected *Tennessee*. See especially the general correspondence of the Bureau of Navigation and Personnel (RG 24, entry 89, for the years up to 1925, and entry 90, for the years since 1925). Records of the Bureau of Construction and Repair (RG 19, entries 105 and 115) not only deal with ship construction and repair but also contain the material inspection reports for *Tennessee*. Within the material inspection reports is a wealth of detail on what the ship looked like, what was wearing out, and how clean she was. I found it valuable in constructing a social history of the peacetime warship. One of the larger files that can be useful is Records of the Secretary of the Navy (RG 80, entry 19).

Prewar records examined but that produced only small amounts of information pertinent to *Tennessee* are the Records of the Chief of Naval Operations (RG 38, entries 177, 178, 179, 180, and 181), Records of the Bureau of Medicine and Surgery (RG 52, entries 15, 38, and 39), and Records of the Bureau of Ordnance (RG 74, entry 26).

The National Archives has microfilmed several manuscript collections, including the valuable Annual Reports of Fleets and Task Forces, 1920–1941. (Microfilm copy M-971, rolls 1–10, are applicable.) Chief of Naval Operations, Secret file, 1919–1927, is less useful (microfilm copy M-1140, 117 rolls with an index in M-1092). The annual Fleet Problems conducted from 1923 until the start of World War II are a useful source of what the navy was planning (microfilm copy M-964).

Photographs of *Tennessee* are in the Still Picture Branch, especially RG 19 and RG 80, of the National Archives. Motion pictures are in the Motion Picture, Sound, and Video Branch and focus on the period of *Tennessee*'s commissioning and sea trials.

The Naval Historical Center (NHC), Building 57, U.S. Navy Yard, Washington, D.C., is the other major source of unpublished information. Though most of its records deal with the wartime period, the Operational Archives of the NHC houses the papers of the naval operations section of the Strategic Plans Division. The lectures and speeches in Series I and the material on war plans in Series II are most useful.

The bulk of the Operational Archives holdings deal with World War II, including the war diary and after action reports for *Tennessee*. An after action report might be as small as one page summarizing a brief encounter with a Japanese plane or dozens of pages detailing operations against a Japanese-held island. The war diary is a detailed summary of where the ship went and what she did during the war. Both sources are essential for telling her story.

The third major source of material is the *Tennessee* Collection, housed in the NHC. This is material that has been generously donated by veterans of *Tennessee*. It includes several hundred copies of the ship's newspaper, memorabilia from the ship, and oral history interviews (audiocassettes as well as written notes from brief interviews). The Navy Department did not bother to save this kind of information, and it is my hope that people who have additional materials in their possession will contribute them to this collection for use by historians of the twenty-first century.

INDEX